PUBLICATIONS

OF THE

NAVY RECORDS SOCIETY

Vol. 155

ANGLO-AMERICAN NAVAL RELATIONS, 1919–1939

The NAVY RECORDS SOCIETY was established in 1893 for the purpose of printing unpublished manuscripts and rare works of naval interest. The Society is open to all who are interested in naval history, and any person wishing to become a member should apply to the Hon. Secretary, Pangbourne College, Pangbourne, Berks., R98 8LA. The annual subscription is £30, which entitles the member to receive one free copy of each work issued by the Society in that year, and to buy earlier issues at much reduced prices.

SUBSCRIPTIONS and orders for back volumes should be sent to the Membership Secretary, 8 Hawthorn Way, Lindford, Hants GU35 0RB.

THE COUNCIL OF THE NAVY RECORDS SOCIETY wish it to be clearly understood that they are not answerable for any opinions and observations which may appear in the Society's publications. For these the editors of the several works are entirely responsible.

The principal architects of the inter-war navies of, respectively, Britain and the USA.

Admiral of the Fleet Lord Chatfield. Courtesy of the Imperial War Museum.

Admiral William Veazie Pratt, US Navy. Photograph from the William V. Pratt Papers, Naval Historical Collection, Naval War College, Newport, RI, USA.

ANGLO-AMERICAN NAVAL RELATIONS, 1919–1939

Edited by

MICHAEL SIMPSON
M.A., M.Litt., F.R.Hist.S., Reader (ret.) in
History, Swansea University

PUBLISHED BY ASHGATE
FOR THE NAVY RECORDS SOCIETY
2010

Published by
Ashgate Publishing Limited
Wey Court East
Union Road
Farnham
Surrey GU9 7PT
England

Ashgate Publishing Company
Suite 420
101 Cherry Street
Burlington, VT 05401–4405
USA

Ashgate website: http://www.ashgate.com

British Library Cataloguing in Publication Data

Anglo-American naval relations, 1919–1939. – (Navy Records Society publications)
1. Naval history, Modern – 20th century. 2. Great Britain – History, Naval – 20th century. 3. United States – History, Naval – 20th century. 4. Great Britain – Military relations – United States – History – 20th century. 5. United States – Military relations – Great Britain – History – 20th century.
I. Series II. Simpson, Michael (Michael A.)
359'.03'09042–dc22

Library of Congress Cataloging-in-Publication Data

Anglo-American naval relations, 1919–1939 / edited by Michael Simpson.
p. cm. – (Navy Records Society publications)
Includes index.
ISBN 978–1–4094–0093–6 (hardcover : alk. paper)
1. United States – Military relations – Great Britain – Sources. 2. Great Britain – Military relations – United States – Sources. 3. United States. Navy – History – 20th century – Sources. 4. Great Britain. Royal Navy – History – 20th century – Sources.
I. Simpson, Michael (Michael A.)
E746.A546 2009
355'.0310973041–dc22 2009035082

ISBN 9781409400936

Printed on acid-free paper

Typeset in Times by Manton Typesetters, Louth, Lincolnshire, UK.

Mixed Sources
Product group from well-managed forests and other controlled sources
www.fsc.org Cert no. SGS-COC-2482
© 1996 Forest Stewardship Council
FSC

Printed and bound in Great Britain by
TJ International Ltd, Padstow, Cornwall

In memoriam

Captain Stephen Wentworth Roskill, CBE, DSC, MA, DLitt, FBA, FRHistS, RN.
1903–1982
Naval officer, author and scholar.
Official Naval Historian of the Second World War.
Life Fellow of Churchill College, Cambridge,
and founder of the Churchill Archives Centre.
Editor of one of these volumes, Councillor, Vice-President and Life Vice-President of the Navy Records Society.
Inspiring and encouraging mentor.

CONTENTS

LIST OF ILLUSTRATIONS

PREFACE

This is the second volume of a projected set of five. The first volume, *Anglo-American Naval Relations, 1917–1919*, was published in 1991; since then, other studies have supervened. It is now intended to complete the series, down to 1945. The scheme is for Mr Robin Brodhurst, author of a biography of Admiral of the Fleet Sir Dudley Pound, to edit the two volumes corresponding to Pound's time as First Sea Lord – June 1939 to October 1943. It is intended that I should edit the volume for 1943 to 1945.

The years between 1919 and 1939 were dominated by a series of naval arms limitation and disarmament conferences and the first four Parts of this volume acknowledge this. Part V, 'The Sailors Meet', deals with the encounters of serving officers and men of the two navies and their observations on each other's navy. Finally, Part VI, 'Edging towards an Alliance', details the hesitant and limited steps towards co-operation between 1937 and 1939 when a second world war looked increasingly likely.

The materials used for the Royal Navy have been drawn from the Admiralty papers at The National Archives, Kew, London; the National Maritime Museum, Greenwich, London; and the Churchill Archives Centre, Churchill College, Cambridge. For the United States Navy, I have drawn on The National Archives, Washington, DC; the Operational Archives, Naval Historical Center, Washington Navy Yard; The Manuscripts Division of The Library of Congress, Washington; and the Franklin D. Roosevelt Presidential Library, Hyde Park, New York. I have avoided using diplomatic or political documents where possible; many of the documents on foreign policy have been published in the series *Documents on British Foreign Policy* (London: HMSO, various) and *Foreign Relations of the United States* (Washington, DC: Government Printing Office, various).

Punctuation marks have been inserted on occasion to clarify passages or to mark omissions. At times, numbered paragraphs in official communications have been omitted, resulting in breaks in their sequence. Missing words are indicated thus: [——]. If there is some doubt about a word it is expressed thus: [? word]. Place names are contemporaneous.

Places and dates of origin, where known or where appropriate, are placed at the head of documents. All Admiralty communications originated from London. Details of ships and aircraft have been obtained from a variety of sources, such as *Conway's All the World's Ships, 1922–1946* and *Jane's Fighting Ships* for various years; dates given are for the first flight of an aircraft and for completion in the case of ships. Career notes have been compiled from the *Navy List* for the Royal Navy; for the United States Navy, recourse has been had to the American equivalent and the co-operation of the Navy Department Library. Service and civilian details have been obtained from the *New Dictionary of National Biography*, the *American National Biography* and *Who Was Who.*

ACKNOWLEDGEMENTS

I am grateful to the Navy Records Society, its Publications Committee and its General Editor, Dr Roger Morriss, for their encouragement to return to the theme of Anglo-American naval relations and for their assistance in the production of this volume. I would like to thank also Mrs Annette Gould for her assistance. I owe particular thanks to former colleagues in the Department of History of the University of Wales Swansea, especially Professor Muriel Chamberlain, and to former doctoral students Dr James Levy and Dr Simon Rofe. I am, once again, indebted to Ashgate Publishing and its former Senior Editor, Ellen Keeling, and her successor, Celia Barlow. For hospitality, I have to thank Mr Aleister Smith in Ealing and my former college in Cambridge, Fitzwilliam. The Scouloudi Foundation and the British Academy have underwritten the financial costs and I am most grateful to them.

Many of the papers have come from The National Archives in Kew, from which I have received admirable service; Crown Copyright material has been reproduced by kind permission of Her Majesty's Stationery Office. I am indebted to the staff of the Churchill Archives Centre, Churchill College, Cambridge, for much cheerful assistance. The National Maritime Museum at Greenwich has helped my research with its customary cordiality and efficiency. In the United States, I have been assisted most capably by the National Archives in Washington, DC, and College Park, Maryland, notably by Susan Elter. The Operational Archives, Naval Historical Center and Navy Department Library, all at the Washington Navy Yard, have been of particular help. I am grateful, too, to the staff of the Manuscripts Division of The Library of Congress. I owe an especial debt to the staff of the Franklin D. Roosevelt Presidential Library at Hyde Park, New York, notably to Robert Parks. Evelyn Cherpak, archivist at the Naval War College, Newport, RI, deserves my especial thanks, as do Professor Paul Kennedy and Professor Paul Halpern. Many other friends have assisted me with insights and information. Most of all, as always, I owe the greatest of all debts and thanks to my wife Sue, who has had to put up with more than forty years of research and writing – and still does so with cheerfulness, patience and love.

GLOSSARY OF ABBREVIATIONS

AA	Anti-Aircraft
Actg	Acting
ACNS	Assistant Chief of Naval Staff
Adm	Admiral
Admy	Admiralty
Amb	Ambassador
AMC	Armed Merchant Cruiser
ANCXF	Allied Naval Commander, Expeditionary Force
AoF	Admiral of the Fleet
A/S	Anti/Submarine
Asst	Assistant
ASW	Anti-Submarine Warfare
Atl F	Atlantic Fleet
AWI	America and West Indies Station
BAD	British Admiralty Delegation
BatDiv	Battleship Division [US]
BCF	Battle Cruiser Fleet
Bd	Board
BS	Battle Squadron
BU	broken up
Bu	Bureau [US]
C	Central
CA	Cruiser Attack [US]
Cab	Cabinet
Calif	California
CAS	Chief of the Air Staff
Capt	Captain
CC	Constructor Corps [US]
Cdr	Commander
Cdre	Commodore
Cdt	Commandant [of a US Navy Yard]
CEx	Chancellor of the Exchequer
Chllr	Chancellor
Chf	Chief

Chm	Chairman
CID	Committee of Imperial Defence
CIGS	Chief of the Imperial General Staff
CinC	Commander-in-Chief
CL	Cruiser Light [US]
Cmdg	Commanding
Cmdt	Commandant
CNO	Chief of Naval Operations [US]
CNS	Chief of the Naval Staff
Cntrlr	Controller
CO	Commanding Officer
Col	Colonel
Con	Conservative
Conf	Conference
Conn	Connecticut
COS	Chiefs of Staff
CoS	Chief of Staff
CruDiv	Cruiser Division [US]
CS	Cruiser Squadron
CSO	Chief Staff Officer
Cttee	Committee
DC	District of Colombia
DCNO	Deputy Chief of Naval Operations [US]
DCNS	Deputy Chief of Naval Staff
DD	Destroyer [US]
Delegn	Delegation
Dem	Democrat [US]
Dep	Deputy
Dept	Department
DF	Destroyer Flotilla
Dir	Director
DNE	Director of Naval Engineering
DNI	Director of Naval Intelligence
DNO	Director of Naval Ordnance
DP	Director of Plans
DSD	Director of Signal Division
DTSD	Director of Training and Staff Duties
E	east
ed	editor
ent	entered
esp	especially
Eur	Europe

F	Fleet
FAA	Fleet Air Arm
FAdm	Fleet Admiral [US]
FCapt	Flag Captain
Fcs	Forces
FDR	Franklin D. Roosevelt
FE	Far East
FGO	Fleet Gunnery Officer
FL	First Lord of the Admiralty
Fla	Florida
FM	Field Marshal
FO	Flag Officer
For O	Foreign Office
FOIC	Flag Officer In Charge
FS	Foreign Secretary
FSL	First Sea Lord
FY	Fiscal Year [US]
Ga	Georgia
Gen	General
Gen Bd	General Board [US]
GF	Grand Fleet
Govr	Governor
Govt	Government
HC	Heavy Cruiser
H Cmnr	High Commissioner
HF/DF	High Frequency/Direction Finding
HM	His Majesty ['s]
HMAS	His Majesty's Australian Ship
HMCS	His Majesty's Canadian Ship
HMG	His Majesty's Government
HMNZS	His Majesty's New Zealand Ship
HMS	His Majesty's Ship
Home F	Home Fleet
HR	House of Representatives [US]
HS	Home Secretary
i/c	in charge
IDC	Imperial Defence College
IE	Immediate Effectives
Imp	Imperial
in	inch
Ind	Indiana
Inspr	Inspector

instr	instructor
IR	Immediate Reserve
JCS	Joint Chiefs of Staff [US; Australian]
k	knots
Lab	Labour
LC	Light Cruiser
Ld	Lord
Ldr	Leader
Lib	Liberal
LN	League of Nations
LPC	Lord President of the Council
LPS	Lord Privy Seal
Lt	Lieutenant
Lt-Cdr	Lieutenant-Commander
Maj Gen	Major General
Mass	Massachusetts
Me	Maine
Med F	Mediterranean Fleet
Md	Maryland
mgr	manager
M, Min	Ministry
Minr	Minister
MO	Missouri
MP	Member of Parliament
Mr	Master
N	Navy
N	north
NA	Naval Attaché
Natnl	National
NAWI	North America and West Indies Station
ND	Navy Department [US]
N Dist	Navy District [US]
NH	New Hampshire
NJ	New Jersey
NRS	Navy Records Society
NS	Naval Secretary
NSC	Naval Staff College
NWC	Naval War College
NY	Navy Yard [US]
NY	New York
NZ	New Zealand
ONI	Office of Naval Intelligence [US]

ONO	Office of Naval Operations [US]
Ore	Oregon
PM	Prime Minister
Pa	Pennsylvania
Pac F	Pacific Fleet
Parl Sec	Parliamentary Secretary
Pay Mr Gen	Paymaster General
PCZ	Panama Canal Zone [US]
Pmnt Sec	Permanent Secretary
Post Mr Gen	Postmaster General
Pres	President
RA, RAdm	Rear Admiral
RAF	Royal Air Force
RAN	Royal Australian Navy
RCN	Royal Canadian Navy
Reprv	Representative [US]
Repub	Republican [US]
ret	retired
RFC	Royal Flying Corps
RI	Rhode Island
RM	Royal Marines
RN	Royal Navy
RNC	[Britannia] Royal Naval College
S	south
S Af	South Africa
SC	South Carolina
SD	State Department [US]
Sec	Secretary
Sec N	Secretary of the Navy [US]
Sen	Senate, Senator [US]
sig	signal
SL	Sea Lord
SMP	Senior Member Present [US – General Board]
solr	solicitor
SNO	Senior Naval Officer
spist	specialist
Sqdn	Squadron
SSt	Secretary of State
t	[displacement] tonnage
Tenn	Tennessee
TF	Task Force [US]
trng	training

tt	torpedo tubes
UK	United Kingdom
US, USA	United States of America
USMC	United States Marine Corps
USNA	United States Naval Academy [Annapolis]
U Sec	Under Secretary
VA, VAdm	Vice Admiral
Va	Virginia
Visct	Viscount
V Pres	Vice President [US]
W	west
W Af	West Africa
W Apps	Western Approaches
War Cab	War Cabinet
Wash	Washington [state]
W Frt	Western Front
WO	War Office
WPD	War Plans Division [US]
WW I	World War I
WW II	World War II

A BRIEF BIBLIOGRAPHY

Lord Chatfield, *The Autobiography of Admiral of the Fleet Lord Chatfield*, volume I, *The Navy and Defence* (London, 1942); volume II, *It Might Happen Again* (London, 1947).

A. Dobson, *Anglo-American Relations in the Twentieth Century* (London and New York, 1995).

C. Hall, *Britain, America and Arms Control, 1921–1937* (London, 1987).

J. P. Levy, *Appeasement and Rearmament: Britain, 1936–1939* (Lanham, Md., 2006).

R. W. Love, Jr. (ed.), *The Chiefs of Naval Operations* (Annapolis, Md., 1980).

M. H. Murfett (ed.), *The First Sea Lords: from Fisher to Mountbatten* (Westport, Conn., and London, 1995).

P. P. O'Brien, *British and American Naval Power: Politics and Policy, 1900–1936* (Westport, Conn., and London, 1998).

B. Ranft, ed., *The Beatty Papers*, Volume II, *1916–27* (NRS, Aldershot, 1993).

D. Reynolds, *The Creation of the Anglo-American Alliance, 1937–1941: A Study in Competitive Co-operation* (London, 1981).

S. W. Roskill, *Sea Power between the Wars*, volume I, *The Period of Anglo-American Antagonism, 1919–1929* (London, 1968); volume II, *The Period of Reluctant Rearmament, 1930–1939* (London, 1976).

M. A. Simpson (ed.), *Anglo-American Naval Relations, 1917–1919* (NRS, Aldershot, 1991).

PART I

THE WASHINGTON CONFERENCE
1919–1923

On 21 November 1918, the American Admiral William S. Sims stood on the quarterdeck of the dreadnought USS *New York*, flagship of an American force under Rear Admiral Hugh Rodman, US Navy, which had constituted the 6th Battle Squadron of the Grand Fleet.[1] From that viewpoint Sims watched the German High Seas Fleet steam to Scapa Flow to surrender to Admiral Sir David Beatty and his Grand Fleet.[2] This suggests an intimacy in Anglo-American naval relations, forged by wartime collaboration since April 1917, and in truth there was a sense of warmth between the two English-speaking navies from which Britain's other allies were excluded, less by deliberate policy than by cultural difference.[3]

Sims' account of the wartime relationship, however, reveals an Anglophilia not shared by other American officers, who were highly critical of the Royal Navy's lack of a formal Admiralty staff and its supposed inability to conduct offensive operations against the Imperial German Navy. To a certain extent, these criticisms were valid, though Americans lacked an appreciation of the realities of the situation and approached maritime warfare with a rather inflexible doctrine.[4] There were, however, deeper and darker issues separating the two navies. The rise and rise of the United States Navy in the wartime years had a double impetus – that nation's burgeoning economic strength, greatly accelerated by wartime trade with, and financing of, Britain and her allies, which led

[1]William S. Sims, US Navy (1858–1936): USNA 1880; gunnery expert; naval aide to Pres Theodore Roosevelt 1907–09; NWC 1912–13; Capt 1913; Destroyer Force, then *Nevada* 1913–16; RA & Pres., NWC, Feb 1917; VA & Cdr, US N Forces in Eur Waters, Mar 1917–Mar 1919; Pres., NWC 1919; ret 1922. W. S. Sims, *Victory at Sea* (Garden City, NY, 1920).

New York: battleship, 1914, 27,000t, 21k, 10×14in.

Hugh Rodman, US Navy (1859–1940): Capt, Gen Bd; RA 1917; Bat Div 9, Atl F 1917; cdr, 6th BS, GF, Dec 1917–19; CinC, Pac F 1919.

[2]David Beatty (1871–1936): ent RN 1884; Nile, China, 1898–1900; Capt 1900; RA 1910; NS to FL (Churchill) 1912–13; cmd BCF 1913–16; VA 1915; CinC, GF 1916–19; Adm 1919; AoF & FSL 1919–27; Earl 1919. S. W. Roskill, *Admiral of the Fleet Earl Beatty: the Last Naval Hero* (London, 1980).

[3]M. A. Simpson (ed.), *Anglo-American Naval Relations, 1917–1919* (Aldershot: Scolar Press for NRS, 1991), *passim.*

[4]Simpson, pp. 26, 57, 59–64.

to a soaring national pride and expanded moral, strategic and commercial horizons; and the call of the normally pacific President Woodrow Wilson, angered by British blockade policy and determined to curb it (and regain the domestic political initiative), for the US Navy to be 'incomparably the greatest in the world'.[1] Will and means were thus united in 1916 and a programme launched that would enable the US Navy to match the Royal Navy in strength by 1919.

American performance was disappointing in terms of wartime construction but, from 1919 to 1922, a vast fleet of dreadnoughts, carriers, destroyers, submarines, submarine chasers and other auxiliaries was turned out. Moreover, America's hitherto minuscule mercantile marine was considerably enhanced, a powerful post-war challenge to the Red Ensign's global dominance. The First Lord during the latter part of the war, Sir Eric Geddes, had immediate and substantial American naval and mercantile aid in mind but, in the longer term, sought to deflect America from her twin purposes of building a navy to contest the Royal Navy's historic supremacy and a merchant marine to challenge the Merchant Navy's monopoly of the world's carrying trade.[2] His efforts were stymied by the sudden collapse of the Central Powers in the autumn of 1918, culminating in the Armistice with Germany on 11 November.

The behind-the-sea-wall battle over maritime supremacy now shifted to the peace negotiations in Paris (December 1918–July 1919). There were differences over the proposed handling of the interned German fleet – the Americans counselling moderation (essentially to ensure that the Royal Navy remained facing Europe), the British arguing for emasculation – but the conflict over 'freedom of the seas', the second of Wilson's Fourteen Points, produced a battle between the President, who wanted untrammelled passage of the sea lanes in wartime, and the British Prime Minister, David Lloyd George, who held to Britain's traditional wartime policy of blockade.[3] This was resolved only by Lloyd George's assent to a nascent League of Nations (Wilson's proposal to resolve international problems peaceably) and the President's decision not to press the matter of free seas, as the League was expected to obviate such issues. Even if this

[1]Woodrow Wilson, address at St Louis, Mo, 3 Feb 1916, in A. S. Link et al., *The Papers of Woodrow Wilson*, vol. 36 (Princeton, NJ, from 1979), pp. 119–20. Thomas Woodrow Wilson (1856–1924): Pres., Princeton U., 1902–10; Govr., NJ, 1911–12; Pres., 1913–21.

[2]Eric Geddes (1875–1937): mgr, timber co., India; NE Rly, 1906; Dep Gen Mgr 1914; Dep Dir Gen, Min of Supply 1915; Dep Gen Transportation, & later Inspr-Gen, BEF 1915–17; Controller of Navy May 1917; FL 20 July 1917–11 Dec 1918; Minr of Transport 1919–22; Chm, Cab economies cttee ['Geddes axe'], Feb 1922 Con MP, Cambridge, 1917–22; Chm, Imp Airways, Dunlop Rubber.

[3]David Lloyd George (1863–1945): solr; Lib MP Caernarvon Boroughs 1890–1945; CEx 1908–15; Minr of Munitions 1915–16; SSt for War 1916; PM 1916–22; Earl 1945.

conflict was neutered, however, the underlying threat to British naval hegemony persisted; indeed, Josephus Daniels, a hitherto pacific Secretary of the Navy, announced a 'repeat' 1916 programme just after the war ended.[1] This was not parity; it was a naked bid for supremacy. It was intended to force the American people into a League of Nations, thus avoiding the additional naval expenditure, and it was designed to cow the dithering Europeans into signing up to Wilson's League. When Lloyd George blustered, Wilson's confidant, Colonel Edward M. House, told him bluntly, 'We had more money, we had more men, our national resources were greater.'[2] It was true. The sailors, however, still cleared for action, resulting in the 'Naval Battle of Paris' in March 1919.[3] Most British statesmen had no wish to compete with the United States in a shipbuilding war they knew they could not win. Wilson, for his part, was anxious to secure British membership of the League. Statesmanlike common sense prevailed; House and Lord Robert Cecil engineered a tacit acceptance of parity and a British promise to join the League in return for a (vague) American undertaking to drop much of the 1916 programme and all of that of 1919.[4] This bridge between the two sides persisted from April 1919 until the autumn of 1921, when widespread desire for a more permanent global naval settlement heralded the Washington Conference of November 1921 to February 1922.

The British approached the Washington Conference with furrowed brows. Beatty, now First Sea Lord, a man who could take on the 'frocks' (the politicians), was resigned to no more than parity with the US Navy but worried that suspension of battleship construction would cause atrophy in the relevant shipbuilding and armour plate facilities. In any case, he faced the comparative obsolescence of the Royal Navy's dreadnought strength because of America's more modern construction and, in a tight financial situation, knew he would not get the money for new ships to match it [1, 2, 13]. An American memorandum confirmed Beatty's likely scenario [3]. The First Lord, Walter Long, put a stark alternative to the War Cabinet: either persuade the Americans to abandon most of their 1916 programme, or be prepared to equal it, despite the great

[1]Josephus Daniels (1862–1948): newspaper edr & owner, NC; Dem poln; Sec Navy 1913–21; Amb to Mexico 1933–42; author of several books on period.

[2]Edward M. House (1858–1938): well-to-do Texan, 'Col', Dem poln; intimate assoc. of W. Wilson, 1913–19; dip missions to Eur; member, US delegn, Paris Peace Conf, 1918–19.

[3]'Naval Battle of Paris': Simpson, p. 490.

[4]Lord Robert Cecil (1864–1958): U Sec, FO; Minr of Blockade & (later) Econ Warfare 1916–18; LPS 1923; Visct Chelwood 1923; Chllr Duchy of Lancaster 1924–7; keen advocate of League; resigned over Geneva Conf.

House-Cecil Notes: Simpson, pp. 491–2.

Ironically, America did not join the League, her own creation.

cost, a choice reiterated by Beatty [4, 5].[1] Unlike the pre-1914 naval race with Germany, this incipient contest had no menace behind it, for since 1895 successive British governments had ruled out a war with the United States – partly because of cultural ties with the republic but also because Britain's Western Hemisphere possessions (Canada, Bermuda and the Caribbean islands) would be vulnerable in a war; appeasement was therefore the order of the day [6]. Compromise, however, appeared to be far from the American mind, as Daniels reiterated Wilson's policy of having a Navy 'incomparably the most adequate in the world', a sentiment reinforced by the US Navy's own think-tank, the General Board [10, 12]. The British could only sit tight and wait to see if the Americans meant what they said, or if they decided to join the League of Nations, in which case they would not need a Navy as large as envisaged [11, 14]. Initial indications from the incoming Republican administration of Warren Harding were that it was as fervently nationalist as its Democratic predecessor [16].[2]

While the British reconciled themselves to future parity with the Americans, other problems arose [17]. The economic crisis affecting post-war Britain threatened the continued existence of a small light cruiser squadron in Latin American waters. This was regarded as essential by both the Foreign Office and the Admiralty, as a means of maintaining British influence, particularly in 'showing the flag' for purposes of fostering goodwill and trade; the Cabinet was assured that if Britain withdrew its physical presence, the United States would usurp its historic role [15]. Even more serious was the future of the Anglo-Japanese Alliance, signed in 1902 and renewed in 1912. This had been fundamental in British strategy until the end of the Great War, for it acknowledged tacitly that, if Britain faced a major seaborne threat in home waters, it no longer had the strength to defend its empire east of Suez. The burgeoning power of Japan adopted this role, enjoying the prestige of association with Britannia. The alliance was due for renewal in 1921 [7–9, 18, 19]. There now being no potential enemy in Europe, or anywhere in the world, the rationale for the alliance was at least debatable. Certain dominions, notably Canada and South Africa, opposed its extension, though Australia and New Zealand still felt it gave them security. Not only Canadian sentiment but also that of many influential Britons argued that its only future aim was to compel Britain to side with Japan in a war with the United States. This was unthinkable, especially after the warmth of the

[1]Walter Long (1854–1924): Con MP 1882–1921; Pres., Local Govt Bd 1915–16; Col Sec 1916–19; FL 16 Jan 1919–Feb 1921; Visct 1921.

[2]Warren G. Harding: small town newspaper ed; Repub; Govr., Ohio 1911; Sen, 1913–20; Pres., 1921–3; d. of cerebral haemorrhage 2 Aug 1923.

wartime relationship, and there was also a clear racial choice in favour of the 'Anglo-Saxon cousins'. Japan, moreover, had provided less assistance than had been hoped for during the late war and had exploited the European powers' absorption in the struggle on home ground by extending her power in Asia, notably in a China riven by internal strife. It was not in Britain's interest – morally, strategically or commercially – to underwrite Japan's imperialist ambitions in China and the Pacific. The Americans, having precipitated two dangerous clashes with the Japanese before 1914, felt increasingly that a future incident would lead to war between them and were thus determined to end the alliance.[1] Britain was therefore faced with a stark choice in this matter: either Japan or the United States.

While the British were debating what to do over naval construction and the Anglo-Japanese alliance, toying with summoning an international conference to deal permanently with these and other questions, the new American Secretary of State, Charles Evans Hughes, seized the initiative. Hughes was determined to broker a settlement on naval armaments, the Pacific, and America's 'ward of court', China, seeing them as intimately related. He was impelled also to call a limitation conference by Senator Borah's resolution tacked on to the Naval Appropriations bill for 1921. The United States may have sought also to gain the moral high ground which its prolonged, acrimonious and ultimately fruitless debate over the League of Nations had ceded.[2] Both the Lloyd George and Harding administrations were forced to consider a permanent solution to the naval race then developing between them because many of their political supporters, the press and the public were calling for a 'peace dividend' of lower taxes, and 'open diplomacy' leading to a new international 'era of good feelings'. Peace organisations in both countries (but especially in the USA) were important lobby groups for disarmament of all kinds throughout this period; farmers, labour, churches, academics and women's groups were actively in support of limitation.

The conference assembled in Washington on 12 November 1921. The head of the British delegation was the seasoned statesman and former First

[1]From 1905, there were diplomatic agreements between US and Japan alternating with crises precipitated by local racist action of San Francisco School Board (1906), and California Land Tenure Act (1913).

[2]Charles Evans Hughes (1862–1948): progressive Repub, lawyer; Govr, NY; Assoc Justice, Supreme Court, 1910–16; Repub Pres candidate, 1916; Sec of State, 1921–25; Chief Justice, 1930–41.

William E. Borah (1865–1940): progressive Repub; Sen, Idaho, 1903–40; like many progressives, also 'isolationist' in foreign policy.

Resolution requested Pres. call conf of US, UK & Japan to reduce building programmes over next 5 years (sec. 9, Naval Appropriations Act, 12 July 1921).

Lord, A. J. Balfour, no stranger to negotiating with the Americans and a shrewd, calm and genial diplomat.[1] The able and energetic Cabinet secretary, Maurice Hankey, was made secretary of the conference but reported on its progress to the Prime Minister.[2] Beatty attended for a time but soon returned to London to try to influence Lloyd George and other 'frocks'. For the Americans, Hughes held the reins and steered the conference. Japan, France and Italy, the other sizeable naval powers, were represented. It was a conference dominated by politicians; 'the views of the governments,' said Lord Curzon, Britain's Foreign Secretary, 'should prevail'.[3] The most prominent naval officers, reduced to an advisory though still influential role, were Captain William Veazie Pratt, US Navy, and Rear Admiral Sir Ernle Chatfield, RN, both rising stars and exceptionally capable men, able to get on with (and thus influence) politicians.[4]

Hughes's opening remarks have gone down in history, justly, for they were breathtakingly bold and, as they were intended, swayed the other delegates and set the tone for the conference. Hughes was said to have sunk more battleships than all the admirals in history. He proposed a cessation of battleship and battlecruiser building and the scrapping of older dreadnoughts, resulting in a ratio of 5:5:3:1.75:1.75 for, respectively, Britain, America, Japan, France and Italy [20]. By doing so he effectively terminated America's 1916 programme, to Britain's immense relief [21, 22, 30]. 'We accepted his [Hughes's] proposal because we wanted limitation of armament and it does not jeopardise our security', Hankey reported to the Prime Minister [29]. Britain had got an end to the massive American building programme at the expense of her own historic supremacy but since Paris in 1919 she had decided to accept equality at sea [2, 3, 5, 17, 30, 31], a position on which the Americans also were determined [10, 12].

[1]Arthur J. Balfour (1848–1930): Con MP; Chf Sec, Ireland 1887–91; PM 1902–05; lost party leadership 1911; FL 1915–16; FS 1916–19; LPC 1919–22, 1925–29; Earl 1922; scholar.

[2]Maurice Hankey (1877–1963): Col, RM; Sec, CID 1912–38, & War Cab 1916–19, & Cab 1919–38; Baron 1938; Minr w/o Portfolio 1939–40; Chllr, Duchy of Lancaster 1940–1; Paymr-Gen 1941–2.

[3]George N. Curzon (1859–1925): Viceroy of India 1898–1905; Earl 1911; LPS 1915–16; LPC 1916–19; FS 1919–24; Marquis 1921; LPC1924–5. Curzon to Balfour, 9 Dec 1921, R. Butler et al. (eds) *Documents on British Foreign Policy* [henceforth *DBFP*], series I, vol. 14 (London, 1966), p. 545.

[4]William Veazie Pratt, US Navy (1869–1957): USNA 1889; NWC 1912–13; Capt & DCNO, 1917; *New York* 1919; Destroyer Force, Pac F; Gen Bd; RA; battleship div; Pres., NWC; cdr, battleships, Pac F; Adm & CinC, US Fleet 1929; CNO 1930–3. Ernle Chatfield (1873–1967): ent RN 1886; Flag Capt to Beatty, *Lion*, Jutland 1916; RA & 4SL 1919; 3SL & Controller 1925; VA 1926; Atl F 1929; Adm & Med F 1930; AoF & FSL 1933–8; Baron 1938; Minr for Co-ord Defence 1939–40.

The central proposition had been accepted readily enough but the Americans proposed, rather casually, a ten-year holiday in capital ship construction; Lloyd George, who feared the conference would fail, hurried to accept this, too, backed by Churchill but despite repeated Admiralty objections [19, 22, 24–6, 28, 39].[1] As Curzon told Balfour, 'in [the] view of the Board [of Trade] the long run economic advantages of a naval holiday scheme more than outweighed any immediate dislocation'.[2] Politics, rather than statesmanship, ruled. Beatty, however, was adamant that such a long holiday would produce two major problems. In the first place, lack of dreadnought orders would cause the slipways and armour firms to go out of business and, secondly, the resumption of building in 1931 would require 14 dreadnoughts to be commenced at once, to replace obsolete ships. There was a certain amount of horse trading to sort out the details. The USA was allowed to complete two battleships, Britain to build what became the *Nelson* and *Rodney*, and Japan to keep the new *Mutsu*.[3] On Chatfield's advice, Balfour accepted a 35,000-ton limit on capital ships. A generous settlement was allowed on aircraft carriers, a new form of vessel, mainly because the Americans wished to convert two projected battle cruisers to carriers.[4] Britain hoped to secure the abolition of the submarine, its recent scourge, but none of the other powers was supportive. The furthest they would go was to sign the 'Root Resolutions', imposing cruiser-style warfare on undersea craft; the British thought, rightly, that they would prove ineffective in wartime [34, 35].[5] Britain did, however, avoid the limitation of the number of cruisers, a substantial force of which she required for trade protection.

Although the two English-speaking powers had settled on parity, Japan's hope for similar status was stymied, though she secured local supremacy in the Far East, reinforced by a clause prohibiting further fortifications in the Pacific. The five major powers and China, plus three others, signed a Nine Power Treaty vaguely promising China a brighter

[1]Winston L. S. Churchill (1874–1965): Subaltern, India & Sudan, 1890s; war correspondent, Cuba & Boer War 1898–1900; MP (Con, Lib, Con) 1900–65; Pres., Bd of Tr, Home Sec & FL 1908–15; col, W Frt 1915–16; Minr Muns 1917–19; Sec War & Air 1919–21; Chllr Ex 1924–9; pol wilderness 1930s; FL 3 Sept 1939–10 May 1940; PM 1940–5; Ldr of Opposn 1945–51; PM 1951–5; knighted 1955.

[2]Curzon to Balfour, 18 Nov 1921, *DBFP*, series I, vol. 14, p. 485.

[3]US battleships: *Colorado*, *West Virginia*: 1921, 32600t, 21k, 8×16in, 18×5in.

British: *Nelson*, *Rodney*: 1927, 33000t, 23k, 9×16in, 12×6in, 6×4.7in.

Japanese: *Mutsu*: 1920, 33800t, 25k, 8×16in, 18×5.5in, 8×5in; sunk 1943, internal explosion.

[4]*Saratoga*, *Lexington* (sunk 1942): 1927, 35,000t, 33.25k, 8×8in, 12×5in, 63–90 aircraft.

[5]Elihu Root: NY lawyer; cons Repub; Sec War 1901–05; SSt 1905–09; Senr 1909–16; member of US Delegn.

and more stable future, though none of them was willing to give up its 'imperial' position there. The Anglo-Japanese alliance came to an end, replaced by a Four Power Treaty between the main Pacific landholders – Japan, Britain, the USA and France. It hardly sufficed as an adequate replacement, however, as the Soviet Union was excluded and the four countries agreed merely to converse if trouble arose; the American Senate would not sanction anything more meaningful.[1] The Four and Nine Power Treaties – 'without which no limitation of armaments could prove satisfactory or durable', remarked Balfour – were thus vital to the signing, on 8 February 1922, of the Five Power Treaty [8, 9, 18, 31, 32, 36].[2]

The naval treaty's reception by politicians, the press and public opinion everywhere was generally favourable. Disarmament satisfied the universal demands of the times – for peace, liberal democracy, and economic recovery. Naval officers everywhere were nevertheless highly critical of it [22, 25–8]. '[I]t was an article of faith among American naval officers that the Washington Conference was an unmitigated disaster for the US Navy and contrary to the national interest,' wrote Nathan Miller, though Pratt, who loaded Hughes's dramatic salvo, pointed out that the US Navy was at last able to embark on a balanced construction policy and enjoy better relations with the Royal Navy [38].[3] Perceived inferiority in range and armour of many American dreadnoughts could be corrected under the treaty [37]. Japan was offended by the demise of the alliance with Britain and was left with 'a fig leaf'.[4] As Alan Dobson has said, 'there was no avoiding the conclusion that Japan was being isolated by the two great Anglo-Saxon powers' [36].[5] Britain, said Chatfield, stood to offend either America or Japan but calculated that, in the long term, America would be more useful to her. Hankey observed, 'We were faced with violent antipathy between the Japanese and the Yankees' [31, 32].[6] Britain, however, got most of what she wanted; as Chatfield recalled, 'The Navy felt we might have done worse.'[7] Her main complaints were that the

[1]Four Power Treaty: Senate Reservation: 'The US understands that in the statement in the preamble or in the terms of this treaty there is no commitment to armed force, no alliance, no obligation to join in any defence.'

[2]Balfour to Lloyd George, 6 Feb 1922, *DBFP*, series I, vol. 14, p. 643.

[3]N. Miller, 'The American Navy, 1922–1945', in K. Neilson and E. J. Errington, eds., *Navies and Global Defense: Theories and Strategy* (Westport, Conn., 1995), p. 139.

[4]R. W. Love, Jr, *History of the US Navy, I (1775–1941)* (Harrisburg, Pa, 1991), p. 553.

[5]A. P. Dobson, *Anglo-American Relations in the Twentieth Century* (London, 1995), p. 50.

[6]Chatfield to V Adm Sir Roger Keyes, 28 Oct 1921, in P. G. Halpern (ed.), *The Keyes Papers, II (1919–38)* (London: Allen & Unwin for NRS, 1980), pp. 56–7.

[7]Lord Chatfield, *The Navy and Defence* (London, 1942), p. 197.

E. Goldstein, 'The Evolution of British Diplomatic Strategy for the Washington Conference', in *Diplomacy and Statecraft*, Washington Conference issue, 1993, p. 30.

10-year holiday was ill-thought out, precluding a staged replacement programme, reducing shipbuilding and armour plate capacity, and playing a tonnage rather than a numbers game [24, 39]. Though parity had been conceded swiftly, the British impression was that it was 'a concession [to the US] to which their needs do not really entitle them' [19].

The Washington Naval Treaty was a political and diplomatic settlement from which most naval opinion was excluded [33]. 'What was significant at the time,' wrote Paul Kennedy, '… was the dominance of the political over the military arm of government.'[1] It was not, however, a disaster for any of the navies concerned, for their governments proved slow and reluctant to build up to the limits allowed. It had nevertheless hardly regulated lighter craft and that loophole encouraged a race in cruisers, which occasioned a second conference in Geneva in 1927.

[1]P. M. Kennedy, *Strategy and Diplomacy, 1870–1945* (London, 1983), p. 169.

1. *Memorandum by First Lord*[1]

25 March 1919

Future Naval Programme

12. The pressure of the financial situation will be very great indeed, and I think the universal opinion will be that, for at all events a year – possibly even longer – every effort should be made to avoid expenditure in connection with shipbuilding. In other words, I believe that it will be held very generally that we ought in present circumstances to run such risk as there may be in relying on older ships, rather than at a moment when money is very, very scarce, to embark upon fresh expenditure which could not be really wisely controlled owing to the fact that so little is known of the future naval armaments of the world.

13. I call attention to a letter which I have seen in the *Irish Times*, written by Mr Morton Frewen, who has a very accurate knowledge of American affairs and is following them very closely.[2] If his views are correct, it is quite clear that the threatened competition in merchant shipbuilding is not within the range of practical politics; it is a legitimate inference that the agitation for a large Navy will die down, and in these circumstances it is difficult to see with whom we shall have to compete, or how we can justify asking for more men and ships than we can show to be absolutely necessary for the ordinary protection of the Empire.

2. *Memorandum for the Board of Admiralty*[3]

17 July 1919

Naval Policy

The USA will have – not at some future date, but now – fully manned and in instant readiness – 18 Dreadnought battleships and 11 pre-Dreadnought battleships.

[1]Walter Long.
[2]Morton Frewen (1853–1924): MP 1910–11; journalist.
[3]Probably by Beatty.

The Admiralty propose to have fully manned and in instant readiness – 21 Dreadnought battleships and battlecruisers (plus *New Zealand* with Admiral Jellicoe and *Australia* in Australian waters).[1]

The Chancellor of the Exchequer has suggested that this might be reduced to – 15 Dreadnought battleships and battlecruisers (plus *New Zealand* and *Australia*).[2]

The effect would be that the British Navy would be in a position of actual inferiority in respect of Dreadnoughts, without taking account of 11 USA pre-Dreadnought battleships.[3]

The acceptance of this position would, I suggest, be regarded generally as the handing over of sea-supremacy by the British Empire to the USA.

The Admiralty consider that a war with the USA is improbable, but they consider that they would be failing in their duty if they did not recommend a policy of keeping the British Navy, upon which the Empire depends, at a strength at least equal to that of the US Navy.

...

The object of the USA in projecting this big fleet is not clear; it may be that it is only intended as a weapon to be used to obtain a general reduction of Armaments by the League of Nations. The Admiralty are themselves considering proposals for presentation to the League which will effect large reductions if they are agreed upon by the Nations.

3. *Memorandum by First Lord for the War Cabinet*

12 August 1919

Post-War Naval Policy

Before the Board of Admiralty can draw up a definite programme for 1920–21, there are certain questions which they would desire to have answered by the Government, as these questions involve the consideration

[1]*New Zealand*: battlecruiser, 1911, 18,500t, 25k, 8×12in, 10×4in; BU 1922.

Australia: battlecruiser, 1911, 18,000t, 25k, 8×12in, 14×4in; sunk as target 1924.

AoF Earl Jellicoe of Scapa (1859–1935): ent RN 1872; RA 1907; Cntrllr & 3SL 1908; VA & CinC, Atl F 1910; 2SL 1912; Actg Adm & CinC GF Aug 1914–Nov 1916; FSL Dec 1916–Dec 1917; reported on Imp defence 1919; Gov-Gen NZ 1920–4; Visct 1917; Earl 1925. A. T. Paterson (ed.), *The Jellicoe Papers*, 2 vols. (London: NRS, 1966 and 1968).

[2]Sir Robert Horne (1871–1940): Con MP, Glasgow; KC; Admy, 1917–18; M Lab 1919–20; Pres, Bd of Trade 1920–1; CEx 1921–2; Visct 1937.

[3]As WW I showed, these were unable to stand in line of battle and were relegated to escorting troop convoys; all were disposed of 1921–2.

of the general policy of the Government, especially in regard to foreign relations.

1. What is to be the policy of the Government as regards the supremacy of the seas –

(a) Over the USA?

(b) Over any probable combination?

We have held the supremacy of the sea for some 300 years, and hitherto the dispute has been as to how many and what Powers were to be regarded as our potential enemies, over whom we ought to have supremacy.

There has never been any dispute as to the fact that no one Power could be permitted to pass us in naval strength.

As things stand now, the Power which caused us the greatest anxiety – Germany – has, for the time being at all events, disappeared. France and Italy are our Allies, and are exhausted by the war. In the opinion of the Board of Admiralty, the only Navy for which we need have regard, and in respect of which we desire a decision of the Government, is the Navy of the USA.

The facts in regard to the Naval strength of Japan are given in Appendix II [not reproduced], but it is considered that Japan may be put aside for the present, whether as an individual opponent or as a partner in any probable combination against us.

As regards the US, the situation is difficult. I give in Appendix I the figures which I have already circulated to the Cabinet with my Memorandum on the Estimates, but corrected up-to-date. It will be seen that if the USA carry out their programme of 1916, abandoning altogether their additional new programme, we shall have a very narrow margin in 1923–24, and some of their ships will outclass ours in fighting power.

It will be seen also that the new USA Fleet Organisation provides for 18 Dreadnought battleships and 11 pre-Dreadnought battleships being kept fully manned and in instant readiness, as compared with the Admiralty proposal to keep 21 Dreadnought battleships and battlecruisers fully manned and in instant readiness.

It will also be seen that the USA Navy personnel for 1920 is to be 170,000 men.

It seems unlikely that the traditional policy of the USA should so alter that they should become an aggressive power, but yet it is obvious that if they continue to maintain a Naval Force of this size, a very moderate reduction in the Admiralty proposals in regard to Capital Ships would place this Country in a position of manifest inferiority.

It is unnecessary for me to remind the Cabinet of the strength of feeling in this country and throughout the Empire in favour of the maintenance of our sea supremacy.

The facts and figures are of course known to everybody who is interested in naval questions; and I think it must be recognised that the Government must now definitely decide whether they are prepared to maintain the supremacy which we have held for so long.

2. The second question (which has a very close relation to the first) is: Are we to deal finally with the question of the strength of our Naval forces independently of the provisions of the Covenant of the League of Nations or not?

It will be recollected that Article 8 of the Covenant states that the Members of the League recognise that the maintenance of peace requires the reduction of national armaments to the lowest point consistent with national safety. It then provides that the Council of the League, 'taking account of the geographical situation and circumstances of each State shall formulate plans for such reduction for the consideration and action of the several Governments,' and that 'such plans shall be subject to reconsideration and reservation at least every 10 years'. It further provides that 'after these plans have been adopted by the several Governments, the limits of armaments therein fixed shall not be exceeded without the concurrence of the Council'.

Unless we are to throw away the principle of the mutual reduction of armaments, I suggest that we should not take any serious action independent of the procedure under the Covenant …. It might be advisable to sound [out] the USA beforehand as to whether they will take joint initial action with us in putting forward such proposals through the Council of the League. We shall then know whether the object of the USA in projecting this big Fleet (as some people think) [is] merely to have a powerful weapon with which to obtain a general reduction of Armaments, or whether it is really their intention to force us to the alternatives of either competing with or accepting numerical inferiority to them.

3. There is a third question on which we seek information. In pre-war days … we largely abandoned the policy which had been previously pursued of 'showing the flag' in foreign and other waters. The information which reaches the Board of Admiralty from many quarters convinces us that the time has come when it is necessary that the White Ensign should be seen in all these places. This does not necessarily mean a large number of expensive ships, but it does mean a sufficient number of light cruisers to enable us to show the flag in these waters. Only recently we have had evidence of the effects produced by the appearance of our ships in South American waters; and the Board of Admiralty ask the Cabinet whether they are in future to pursue the policy known as 'showing the flag'. This, again, is a subject upon which very strong feeling exists in this country

and in the Empire. There is every indication that the USA and Japan are both well aware of the advantages which flow from the presence of their ships in foreign waters, and that they are doing all that they can to push their trade and their general interests, by sending their ships to stations where prior to 1904 we had the monopoly.[1]

4. A further question is: What should be the period of time during which we may reckon on immunity from war with a great Power or combination of small Powers giving an equivalent enemy force and therefore a reduction in our naval preponderance[?]

It has been suggested that it should be for a period of either five or 10 years. On the one hand, we know accurately what the position [relative] to the US Navy and the Japanese Navy will be at end of five years, whereas, unless the League of Nations operates, it is impossible to say what they will be at the end of ten. On the other hand, if we could fix upon the longer period, it would undoubtedly enable us to make more effective reductions than at present. The view of the Admiralty is, however, that as our actual information only covers the shorter period, the question whether the longer period can safely be adopted must depend upon whether the Covenant of the League of Nations, which names 10 years, as the extreme period at which revisions of Naval and Military strength shall take place, makes an auspicious beginning.[2]

Appendix I

The United States Navy

The following statement shows the position of our own and the US Navies now and in 1923–24 in respect of Capital Ships of *Dreadnought* Type:[3]

1919	Great Britain	USA
Dreadnought Battleships	33	18
Battle Cruisers	9	0
1923–24		
Dreadnought Battleships	33	29
Battle Cruisers	10	6

[1] In 1904–05, the FSL, AoF Sir John Fisher, withdrew or scrapped ships on distant stations, concentrating on home waters.

[2] 10 Year Rule: established by Lloyd George, 1919; renewed in 1925–8, when it became a rolling commitment, ended only in 1932.

[3] *Dreadnought*: battleship, 1906, 17,000t, 21k, 10×12in. First 'all big gun ship', gave type generic name; BU 1923.

Numbers of Capital Ships to be maintained in commission with full crews by the two Navies.

...

The new USA Fleet Organisation is to consist of two main Fleets of practically equal strength – the Atlantic and Pacific – with a small Asiatic Fleet and still smaller Auxiliary Squadrons in various locations. The Atlantic and Pacific Fleets are to consist of four divisions of Battleships, two divisions of Cruisers, 18 divisions of Destroyers, three divisions of Submarines, and two divisions of Minelayers, together with repair ships and other Auxiliaries.

The USA, therefore, intend to keep in full commission:

Battleships (Dreadnought)	18
Battleships (pre-Dreadnought)	11

The Admiralty propose to keep in full commission:

Battleships and Battle Cruisers (Dreadnought)	21

(in addition to the *New Zealand* on special service with Lord Jellicoe, and the *Australia* in Australasian Waters).

US Naval Personnel

(according to last hearing before Congress, 21 June [1919])

Total personnel at present	241,000
Total personnel (1920)	171,000

(This reduction in personnel is on account of the fact that the US Naval transportation service will have completed the repatriation of American troops in Europe by the end of this year).

USA Capital Ships under construction (Dreadnoughts)

	Laid Down	Authorised but not Laid Down
Battleships	5	6
Battle Cruisers	0	6

Mr Daniels has recommended to Congress that only the ships of the 1916 programme and before should be proceeded with, and it is more than probable that Congress will accept this recommendation.[1]

Under the terms of the reorganisation of the US Navy announced during the last fortnight, it appears that the full number – 29 battleships (15 in Atlantic, and 14 in Pacific) – will when completed be kept in full commission.

[1]Josephus Daniels, Sec N.

4. *Lieut. H. H. Frost, US Navy, to Admiral William S. Benson, US Navy*[1]

3 September 1919

...

Comparison of the British and US Navies

Great Britain		*United States*
	I. Modern Ships Completed	
33	Battleships	15
9	Battle Cruisers	0
2	Cruisers	0
69	Light Cruisers	3
28	Flotilla Leaders	0
327	Destroyers	185
156	Submarines	68
6	Aircraft Carriers	0
	II. Modern Ships Building	
0	Battleships	6
1	Battle Cruisers	0
9	Light Cruisers	8
2	Flotilla Leaders	0
7	Destroyers	132
15	Submarines	88
2	Aircraft Carriers	0
	III. Obsolete Ships	
28	Old Battleships	23
27	Old Cruisers	15
21	Old Light Cruisers	15
152	Old Destroyers	41
34	Old Submarines	23

[1]Lt H. H. Frost, US Navy: member of plans secn, CNO office.

RAdm William Shepherd Benson, US Navy (1855–1932): USNA 1877; Capt 1909; *Utah* 1911–13; Cmdt, Philadelphia NY & 4th N Dist 1913–15; first CNO 1915–19; Chm, US Shipping Bd 1920–8.

5. *Memorandum by First Lord for War Cabinet*

24 October 1919

Naval Policy and Expenditure

...

3. The revised Post-War Fleet shown as an appendix [not reproduced] to this Memorandum constitutes in the opinion of the Admiralty the minimum naval force on which it is open to them, subject to the grave conditions stated later, to base their calculations. This Force provides for the number of Capital Ships (a) in commission and (b) in reserve being:

(a) In Commission: 16 Battleships, 4 Battle Cruisers
(b) In Reserve: 13 Battleships, 3 Battle Cruisers,
as compared with which the other great Navy of the world (the US) comprises:
18 Dreadnought Battleships [and] 11 pre-Dreadnought Battleships in full commission.

4. The personnel required for this British Force in order to man the ships in commission and to provide two-fifths crews on mobilisation for the ships in reserve, with a margin sufficient to work the Fleet under peace conditions, is approximately 126,000 officers and men. The US naval personnel voted is 171,000 officers and men for the first six months of 1920.

...

8. If the Fleet be reduced to this extent, it must be clearly understood that Great Britain will no longer be supreme upon the sea. We shall be supreme in European Waters, but as regards the seas as a whole the supremacy will be shared with the US. Our immediate position with the US will be one approximately of equality, but will rapidly become one of marked inferiority, if we undertake no new construction and the USA continue their 1916 Programme, which consists of capital ships more powerful than any British ship with the exception of the *Hood*.[1] By the end of the year 1923 we shall have passed to the position of being the second Naval Power unless either:

(a) The US can be induced by diplomatic means (whether by use of the machinery provided by Article 8 of the Covenant of the League of Nations or otherwise) to abandon or modify the 1916 Programme; or,

[1] *Hood*: battlecruiser, 1920, 42,000t, 31k, 8×15in, 12×5.5in, 8×4in; sunk by *Bismarck*, 24 May 1941.

(b) The [British] decision to start no programme of new construction is reconsidered, in the light of the US's action, in 12 months from now.

9. Already the mere rumour of the passing of our sea supremacy has called forth emphatic protests from other parts of the Empire, and it will undoubtedly have important effects on our prestige and our diplomatic and commercial interests.

10. It has been suggested [that] it was well understood before the war that the US did not enter into our comparisons of naval strength. This is not strictly accurate. All that was ever said by any Government was that in applying the 'Two-Power Standard' the US, owing to their distance from Europe, should not be counted as one of the two principal Powers against whose possible *combination* we were providing. The arguments used had reference to the difficulties of effective co-operation between an American and a European Power, though no doubt the fact that up to that time the US had faithfully followed the tradition of the Monroe Doctrine in having no European interests was not without its influence.[1] Even this view, however, was hotly contested and would certainly be contested again.

11. But now it is not a question of our naval strength *vis-à-vis* an hypothetical combination of two Powers, but in comparison with the US Navy alone, at a time when the War has had the result of making the US for the first time a factor in European politics. From their own pronouncements we know that the USA have grasped the truth that for the Navy to be an effective weapon it should be at least equal in strength to the possible antagonist, and everything goes to prove that the present intention is to maintain their Navy at a strength at least equal to our own. Such a state of affairs might possibly have been viewed with complacency at the end of the war had the US been in the same position as it was at the commencement. But this is not so. The US are building up a Mercantile Marine with the idea of competing with Great Britain in the world carrying trade. They propose to protect that trade with a strong Navy, and the fact cannot be ignored that conflicts of interest may arise with the US in the same way as with other Powers in our history.

12. It is not suggested that this involves war between the US and the British Empire. Having acquired by peaceful means the supremacy of the sea, their subsequent victories are probably destined to be commercial

[1]Monroe Doctrine, 1823, in which Pres James Monroe declared that existing Eur colonies in W Hemisphere could remain but not be increased, nor could Eur nations interfere with independent Latin American states. In return, the US forswore intervention in Eur affairs. Over the next century the US used it as an excuse to intervene in many parts of C & S America, esp after Roosevelt Corollary, 1904–5.

and diplomatic, but the effect of these upon our trade and Empire may be no less serious on this account.

13. The Board of Admiralty would be failing in their duty if they did not thus point out clearly what is involved in the decisions which the Cabinet now have to make.

14. The Board believe it to be unquestionable that Great Britain owes her leading position among the Nations to her long-maintained pre-eminence upon the sea. They believe that this pre-eminence cannot be relinquished without her ability to hold her position being profoundly affected, with all that that position involves in respect of prestige, authority, and commercial advantage. …

6. *Admiralty Memorandum for the CID*

October 1919

Imperial Naval Defence

Part III: Selection and Maintenance of Naval Bases.

War against the USA

17. The chances of such a war are remote, being so opposed to the fundamental interests of both parties, that the wisdom of constructing bases merely with that end in view is open to doubt. At the same time, it is well to consider the question before any new works are undertaken.

Situation in the Atlantic

18. Imperial naval policy would primarily be directed towards securing as complete a control of the Atlantic as possible, and the position of the bases required for attaining that object would partly depend on the attitude of the USA to Canada. If it were merely a question of protecting British trade in the Atlantic and interrupting the enemy's communications, existing bases in Home Waters and the Mediterranean would suffice for the main fleet.

19. If on the other hand, Canada were attacked by the USA, and an endeavour were made to send her military assistance, the Empire would be committed to an unlimited land war against the USA, with all the advantages of time, distance and supply on the side of the USA. In that case, a fleet superior in fighting power to that of the USA would have to be concentrated in Canadian waters, and the ability of the Empire to support Canada in a land campaign, therefore, depends on the existence of a first class war anchorage in Canadian waters. Halifax is vulnerable

to attack from the land side, and the possibility of obtaining a large ice-free anchorage elsewhere should be investigated by the Canadian authorities.

20. But whatever form a war with the USA might take, Bermuda would be favourably situated as a base for anti-submarine operations. Also, if used as an occasional base for battlecruisers and light cruisers, it would exercise a very cramping influence upon the US navy, and amongst other things it would facilitate the protection of the Canadian communications. Submarines, mines, aircraft and machine guns render the defence of a small and isolated island easier than it was in pre-war days, and there can be little doubt that the development of Bermuda as a naval war anchorage and supply base is an important part of a war plan against the USA.[1]

21. One of the most difficult questions to decide in the event of a war with the USA is the policy to be followed in the West Indies. Not only are they valuable possessions, but they occupy commanding positions on the Panama and South American–US trade routes. It appears that the defence of Jamaica could not be seriously undertaken, for it is only 100 miles from Guantanamo, the USA naval base in Cuba, and very strong naval, military and air forces could be brought against it. A submarine flotilla based on Kingston might, however, act as a deterrent to such an expedition.

22. It is considered that arrangements should be made to hold one of the more distant, and therefore less vulnerable, of the British West Indies Islands as a base for raiding operations on the South American trade, and if it fell, to carry on operations by arranging secret rendezvous for supply ships. This would necessitate the deflection of strong protective forces from the US navy. Port Castries, St Lucia, is one of the few harbours available, but it would require considerable development before it could accommodate battlecruisers, light cruisers and submarines. Trinidad occupies an ideal strategical position, has oil supplies, and could probably be easily defended on account of the mountainous nature of the coast, but unfortunately it has no secure anchorage.[2]

Situation in the Pacific

23. The Panama Canal enables the USA to concentrate superior forces in the Eastern Pacific more quickly than a European Power, and therefore the Imperial Navy could only operate in that area at a considerable disadvantage. Therefore, trade with the West coast of North and South America would probably have to cease.

[1]The Admy ignored the fact that Bermuda, only a few hundred miles E of the US's principal ports, was ripe for invasion in such a conflict and could not be defended against a major assault.

[2]St Lucia was hardly more defensible, given US presence in Panama.

24. If the attempt were made to take Vancouver Island or invade the Pacific coastal region of Canada, freedom of sea transport would greatly facilitate the operation, and submarines based on a fortified Canadian port would undoubtedly act as a deterrent. If raiding attacks by surface ships and submarines were also carried out from such a port against the USA trade in the Eastern Pacific, it would probably cause considerable deflection of power from the US forces in the Atlantic. Vancouver and Esquimault are too close to the frontier, and a base further north would have to be provided. Bella Koola … seems to possess several advantages over Malcolm Island for a war against the USA. It is further north, and can be connected easily with the railway system. Ships would have to be berthed alongside [each other?].

25. In the Western Pacific, the handicap of time and distance would not be so greatly in favour of the USA, and Australia and India are close enough to influence materially the course of events. The problem in this area may be examined from two general points of view:

(a) That in which the USA fleet in the Western Pacific was superior to the Imperial fleet.

(b) That in which the Imperial fleet was superior to the USA.

26. With regard to (a): If a superior USA fleet was based on the Philippines, it could attack Imperial trade or territory in Far Eastern waters. Now the trade with China and Japan is valuable, but from the point of view of food and raw material, it is not of great importance. The trade with Malaya and Australia includes, however, rubber, tin, oil, cereals, meat, wool, etc., and its value would be accentuated during a war with the USA.

27. The main lines of communication are so far distant from American territory that an inferior fleet would be able to afford this trade a considerable degree of protection. Harbours in Australasia, Malaya and British Borneo would then have to be utilised as war anchorages, and Singapore, Colombo, and ports in Australia, [used] for purposes of docking and repairs. Hong Kong is unfavourably situated, and could fulfil no useful functions as a naval base under these circumstances.

28. There is also the possibility that the USA might launch an expeditionary army against British possessions. Hong Kong would be the most probable objective, and a fleet based on that port would be in a position of great disadvantage with a superior fleet flanking its only line of supply. In such circumstances, it is essential that the inferior fleet should maintain its liberty of action against the enemy's lines of communication by operating from anchorages to the north of the Philippines, with the resources of Australia in the background.

29. With regard to (b): If a superior British Imperial fleet occupied the Western Pacific, every effort should be made to deprive the USA of her

only naval bases in that area by the capture of the Philippines. The men and material could be provided from India and Australia, and Sandakan would be suitably placed with anchorages for transports and cruisers, with Singapore and Colombo as bases for docking and repair. Hong Kong is on the wrong side of the main line of communications. It is, however, well situated as a harbour of refuge and convoy collection port for trade with China and Japan, but the seizure of the Philippines would be the most economical and effective method of trade protection.

30. With regard to fleet anchorages generally, the Pacific is vast, and the circumstances of war so variable, that an organisation is also required which will enable any suitable anchorage to be quickly equipped as a temporary base for operations against the USA trade or military communications, and this will entail special provision for fuel, stores and depot ships.

Summarised Conclusions

31. The foregoing may be summarised by saying that if it is necessary to be prepared for a war with the USA:

(a) A first class naval base capable of maintaining and accommodating a large fleet should be developed in Canadian Atlantic or Newfoundland waters.

(b) Bermuda should be developed as a war anchorage and supply base, and adequately defended.

(c) Port Castries in St Lucia, or some other harbour in the more isolated West Indies Islands, should be developed as a base for raiding operations on US trade.

(d) Canadian naval resources would be best utilised in the Atlantic, but the development of a fortified harbour on the Pacific coast as a base for submarine operations would be fully justified. Bella Koola or some similar outlet would be suitable.

(e) Singapore and Sydney should be developed as first class docking and repair bases in the Western Pacific, Hong Kong only being suitable as a base for submarine operations.

(f) An organisation is also required so as to enable any suitable harbour to be quickly equipped as a temporary base with the necessary defences, supply and depot ships.

7. *Admiralty Memorandum: Naval Situation in the Far East*

21 October 1919

1. The Admiralty have been considering the question of naval bases in the light of after-war events, and more particularly the situation with regard to Hong Kong.
2. It would be of great assistance to the Board if information could be afforded as to what will be the probable attitude of the Government with regard to the renewal of the Anglo-Japanese Alliance in 1921. It is understood that the position is briefly as follows.
3. Japanese official attitudes will probably be in favour of renewal but the British Government may not desire to prolong an Alliance which might cause them to be embroiled with the US. If this presumption is correct the Treaty is not likely to be renewed, and in the event the Naval situation in the Far East will undergo complete alteration.
4. Should a cause of dispute arise with Japan and hostilities ensue, it is possible that we should find ourselves in alliance with America, but this cannot be counted upon. Similarly, should America go to war with Japan, it is possible that either on Canada's or Australia's account, we should find ourselves ranged alongside the US, but again, this cannot be counted upon.

...

8. *Memorandum for the Board of Admiralty by the Chief of Naval Staff*

7 January 1920

Size of Fleet

...

3. The Naval Policy and Expenditure as approved by the Board was placed before the War Cabinet in a Memorandum on 24 October 1919 [5].
4. In that Memorandum it was pointed out by the Admiralty that it was vital to the British Empire that the sea supremacy should not be sacrificed and that, if the US could not be induced to abandon or modify the 1916 programme, efforts would have to be made to undertake the construction required to counter-balance it.
5. After consideration of this Memorandum, the Prime Minister sent a telegram to the British Representative at Washington pointing out that

Great Britain had no desire to enter into Naval competition with the US but could not afford to ignore what they were doing and requesting information on certain points.[1]

6. To this telegram no satisfactory reply has been received. But, on the contrary, since the Admiralty Policy has been put forward recent estimates have been introduced in the US which indicate a further increase of two battleships and one battlecruiser over and above the original 1916 programme.

7. It therefore became necessary for the Board to reconsider their views on our Naval Policy and especially the means by which we can ensure maintaining our sea supremacy.

8. It appears that there are only two solutions open to us –

(a) For a definite approach to be made by the British Government to the Government of the US with a view to the limitation of Naval Armaments, or

(b) Ourselves to embark on a further building programme which will ensure that we are at least equal in material strength to the US Navy as at present budgeted for.

9. As regards 8(a) –

At the present moment we have an Alliance with the third great Naval Power, Japan. This comes to an end in 1921, and if it is renewed on an offensive and defensive basis, then we might view with equanimity the Naval expansion of the US. But is almost inconceivable for the British Empire to consider in the future an Alliance with Japan, which can only have for its object protection against the US, the country which is allied to us in blood, in language and in literature and with whom we share the mutual aspiration of maintaining the peace and progress of the world.

10. From motives of economy alone, but also from the far mightier motive of a union between the English-speaking nations of the World, it seems inevitable that our whole Naval Policy should be directed towards an Alliance or an Entente with the US, and that the British Empire and the US should then be able to advance hand in hand in their peaceful avocations, increasing happiness, contentment and prosperity.

An Alliance or Entente with the US based on an equality in Naval material is, in fact, required to reach the ideals we each aim at.

11. As regards 8(b) –

If such an understanding is politically not possible, it remains for this Empire to preserve its sea power and take the necessary steps vital to its existence. It will then be necessary definitely to lay down that a one power standard against the strongest naval power is the minimum compatible

[1]Sir Edward Grey (1862–1933): Lib MP; FS 1905–16; Amb to US 1919; Visct.

with our vast sea requirements, and that the British building programme in all types of vessel must be such that this one power standard is fully maintained.

...

9. *Admiralty War Memorandum*

12 January 1920

Political Situation

1. The Anglo-Japanese Alliance may not be renewed on its expiration in 1921. British interests in the Pacific and Far East generally are likely to be more closely allied to those of the US than Japan. Racial differences and the exclusive commercial policy of the latter may eventually tend to estrange Great Britain from Japan as they have already the US.[1]

...

4. In the event of hostilities between Japan and the USA it would probably not be to British interests to be allied or even sympathetically neutral to the former. Great Britain and the US may find themselves actively allied against Japan in defence of their common interests; but in view of the American constitutional objection to forming alliances, it is unlikely that such an alliance will precede the outbreak of war.

5. In these circumstances there may be no opportunity of arranging a combined plan of operations until the emergency actually arises, and ..., without a knowledge of the US's plans, it is impossible to say what form British co-operation would take. ...

10. *Speech to the Democratic National Committee, New York, by the Secretary of the Navy*[2]

6 February 1920

...

... We have never accepted, and never will accept, the un-American policy advocated by some that 'America should have the second largest

[1]Japan aimed to dominate E. Asian trade. The US had become a high tariff nation since 1862.

[2]A tub-thumping 'stump speech', this was almost certainly intended for domestic consumption, but can be seen as an inducement both to the American public and other nations to join the League of Nations – or see a major building programme.

Navy in the world' as if this great country should limit its protection and offensive [capability] and accept second place to any nation on earth.

We are to have a League of Nations with America making as large a contribution as any other country to a mobile police force afloat, or are we to have a Navy 'incomparably the most adequate in the world'. Which must it be? It must be one or the other.

11. *Memorandum by the First Sea Lord for the War Cabinet*

7 May 1920

Gas Warfare

...

2. It is impossible any longer to ignore the fact that the US Representatives at the Peace Conference having inoculated Europe to the idea of a League of Nations, have since approved the adoption in practice of an entirely opposite doctrine, viz., *rapid, thorough and vast preparations for War.*

Enormous expenditure has been sanctioned for the purpose after complete discussion in public and in Congress. The consequential result is that they are rapidly attaining an overwhelming position as a Fighting Power, as compared with nations of the European Continent, who have accepted the principles they [the Americans] have propounded.

...

6. From information available, it appears clearly established that the US had already adopted a lethal filling as a proportion of the burster for their turret armour-piercing shell.[1]

[1]There is no evidence for this assertion.

12. *General Board: Senior Member Present to the Secretary of the Navy*[1]

24 September 1920

Building Program for the Fiscal Year 1922

...

3. The Navy second to none recommended by the General Board in 1915 is still required today. But in addition, the great war has shown the importance of unimpeded ocean transportation for commerce. If either belligerent loses control of the sea the national fighting power and endurance is greatly affected. In times of peace a great and developing country needs a proportionately great merchant fleet of its own to ensure its markets and preserve its commerce from subservience to rival nations and their business. Our Navy and our merchant service are inextricably associated in the economic progress and prosperity of the people. A combatant Navy supporting and protecting a great merchant fleet such as the country requires both in peace and war appears to the General Board as an essential condition of national progress and economic prosperity.

4. Owing to the extent of our Coast line bordering as it does upon two great oceans, our widely separated possessions in the Pacific, including Alaska, the large increase in our merchant marine and our rapidly expanding commercial interests, the General Board believes that the policy so far as the Navy is concerned should be such that ultimately the US will possess a Navy equal to the most powerful maintained by any other nation of the world.

5. In urging that this become the continuing Naval policy of the US there is no thought of instituting international competitive building. No other nation can in reason take exception to such a position. In assuming it the US threatens no other nations by the mere act of placing itself on an equality with the strongest. It is an act of self defense which all will acknowledge as an inherent right and cannot justly be construed as a challenge. On the contrary, the pursuance of such policy of equal naval armaments may well tend to diminish their growth and would certainly work to lessen the danger of sudden war.

[1]The General Board was the US Navy's 'think-tank', set up in 1900 'to insure efficient preparation of the fleet in case of war and for the naval defence of the coast' and composed of senior officers. The Senior Member Present (at the time RAdm R. E. Coontz, US Navy (1864–1935): USNA 1881; ND 1917–19; CNO 1 Nov 1919–21 July 1923) signed reports made to the Secretary of the Navy.

13. *Memorandum for the War Cabinet by the First Sea Lord*

14 December 1920

Naval Construction

...

In the first place the following limiting facts must be stated –

(a) It takes from 15 to 18 months to advance a Capital Ship to the launching stage, and three years to complete her.

(b) There are only six berths in this country which could be used for the construction of modern capital ships, and of these only four can be conveniently used. To adapt other berths than these six would involve great expense and delay.

(c) There is only sufficient skilled shipbuilding labour, and only sufficient special armour, heavy gun, gun mounting and shell plant, to deal with four such ships a year. To expand these facilities would involve great expense and delay.

...

... the position in 1925, assuming that we lay down four capital ships both in 1921–22 and in 1922–23, will be as follows –

	Great Britain	US	Japan
Class A	9	12	8*
Class B	13	11	4
Class C	4	4	4
	26	27	16

* Eight others to be completed by 1928.[1]

If a decision is so delayed that we are unable to lay down four capital ships in 1921–22, it must be accepted that our facilities will not allow us to lay down more than four in 1922–23, quite apart from the obvious political objections to a greater programme. The position in 1925 would then be –

	Great Britain	US	Japan
Class A	5	12	8*
Class B	13	11	4
Class C	4	4	4
	22	27	16

* Eight others to be completed by 1928.

[1]Class A: post-WW I ships; Class B, pre-Jutland (1916); Class C, pre-war.

Several of the new US ships will be completed in 1923–24, and possibly some of the Japanese, and it would be easy for either or both navies, having established this lead, to match any subsequent shipbuilding by us and thus to relegate Great Britain permanently to third Naval Power.

Moreover, it cannot even be treated as certain that if the commencement of building is deferred until 1923–24, facilities for laying down four capital ships in a year will remain available in this country, unless exceptional steps are taken to ensure this. The Admiralty entertain on this point grave apprehensions, which are based on the following considerations –

(1) Special plant and machinery, different from those used for merchant ships, are required for warship construction and are already being scrapped to enable peace work to be undertaken.

(2) Specially skilled labour, accustomed to special warship work, is being dispersed, and the longer warship construction is put off, the more difficult it will be to find suitable skilled labour.

(3) The heavy gun, armour and gun mounting Firms are already asking for subsidies to keep their armour plant in existence, i.e., £500,000 *per annum*, or 6% of its value. If this plant is scrapped from lack of use and it is again required in one, two, or three years' time, it will require an expenditure of 10% times its original cost, i.e., £100,000,000.

In short, in delaying new capital ship construction until 1921–22, we have held our hand up to the last possible moment, and the loss of the year 1921–22 would be nothing less than disastrous to our chances of retaining our navy equal with the Strongest Naval Power.

The suggestion has been made that the result of hesitation on our part might be to encourage the US to modify their 1916 programme.

It is important, therefore, to point out that of the 12 US battleships classed above as 'A' five battleships are well advanced and due for completion in 1923–24.

One battleship and four battlecruisers are less advanced but due for completion in 1924–25.

Two battlecruisers are about to be laid down, material is being collected, and they are also due for completion in 1924–25.

It is inconceivable that the US would scrap the five battleships which are well on their way to completion, and most improbable that they would take off the slips the sixth battleship and the four battlecruisers actually laid down.

Any change of policy on their part would be likely, therefore, only to affect the two battlecruisers not yet laid down.

But assuming for the sake of argument that it extended to the whole of their battlecruisers, and that they not only abandoned the two not laid down, but removed the other four from the slips, such action on their part would not obviate the necessity for our laying down four capital ships for this year. By doing so we should barely maintain our supremacy, as is evident from the following figures, which would then represent the position in 1925 –

	Great Britain	US	Japan
Class A	5	6	8
Class B	13	11	4
Class C	4	4	4
	22	21	16

On the other hand the political objections to our laying down four capital ships *after* the US had abandoned six of theirs would be enormous. It might, in fact, pay the US to take this step, relying on the effect being to make it politically impossible for Great Britain to lay down any capital ships at all. The resulting position in 1925 would then be –

	Great Britain	US	Japan
Class A	1	6	8
Class B	13	11	4
Class C	4	4	4
	18	21	16

These figures suggest that the only wise course is to announce our policy before the US discuss any modification of their programme, assuming that any modification is in contemplation, in which case we shall be free subsequently to make whatever reductions are reasonable in view of their action.

14. *Limitation of Naval Armaments and Relative Naval Strength: League of Nations Proposals*

14 August 1920

Remarks by Deputy Director of Plans:[1]
Admiralty Policy and the League of Nations

...

The USA is not a member of the League and it cannot be clear whether or not she will become one until after the Presidential Elections, which take place in November 1920. The USA is the only Power which is financially able or willing to build a large fleet and which can hope to rival or surpass Great Britain as a Naval Power in the near future.

For this reason it is clear that until the USA defines her position in regard to Article 8 of the Covenant of the League, Great Britain must take the greatest care not to bind herself in any way whatever by any sort of agreement which can hamper her naval development. At the same time, as the principal naval signatory of the Covenant, she must show her faith in the League by being prepared with some policy in connection with its naval clauses.

It is therefore suggested that any proposals of Naval matters which Great Britain should originate or agree to in connection with the League should all be subject to a reserve that they do not hold unless, and until, the USA joins the League on the same terms as the other nations.

15. *Memorandum by First Lord for Cabinet*

25 January 1921

Naval Estimates

...

3. *Abolition of South American Light Cruiser Squadron.*
The importance of this small Squadron is primarily diplomatic and commercial. Its abolition would unquestionably reduce our prestige considerably in the South American States where important British trading interests are concerned, and importance is attached on this account to its retention by the Foreign Office, as will be seen from the following extract from a letter on the subject.

[1]DDP: Capt C. J. C. Little: ent RN 1897; Capt 1917; RA 1929; VA 1933; DCNS 1934–6; Adm 1937; 2SL 1938–41; Head, BAD, 1941–2; CinC, Portsmouth 1942.

'From the point of view of this Department, there can be no doubt that withdrawal of this Squadron would be most regrettable. The visits of HM Ships to South American ports are invariably productive of satisfactory results and international courtesies of this nature are highly valued by the Latin American countries. If the Squadron were withdrawn, attentions of this kind would continue to be paid by the US Government, while HMG would no longer be in a position to arrange for periodical visits at suitable moments. It is in fact not too much to say that the withdrawal of the Squadron would probably be resented in South America as an affront, and as implying that HMG did not consider these countries as being of any great importance, notwithstanding the fact that more than half the British investment abroad, say nearly one thousand million pounds, is invested in Latin America.

For these reasons, Lord Curzon would most strongly deprecate the withdrawal of the Squadron.'

16. *Hankey: Diary 1921*

London,
30 January 1921

… During the Paris visit a gramophone record of one of Harding's speeches had been turned on for the PM's delectation. It was a speech on Americanism and was so provocative that the PM said he felt like turning the Admiralty on to build all the capital ships they could as fast as possible in order to go for the Yanks. …

17. *Memorandum by the First Lord*[1]

28 February 1921

Naval Estimates, 1921–22

… the Naval Policy of this Government, as announced by my predecessor in the House of Commons last year, and recently confirmed by the Prime Minister (CID Minutes, 23 December 1920) [not reproduced] is to maintain a 'One Power Standard' – i.e., equal with any other power.

[1]Arthur Lee (1868–1947): Con MP, Fareham, 1900: Army 1888–1900 & 1914–15 (W Front); jnr min posts 1915–18; Pres, Bd of Agric & 1st M of Agric 1919–21; FL 1921–2; baron 1918.

… recognising the special financial difficulties of the Government [the Admiralty] have agreed to assume risks which, under ordinary circumstances, they would regard as unjustifiable.

How great those risks are of falling below the 'One Power Standard', is sufficiently indicated by the following comparative figures [for capital ships] of the three strongest navies:

Country	Post-Jutland	In Commission	Personnel	Ests 1921–22	Post-Jutland 1925
US	10 (a)	31	163,751 (c)	£113m (e)	12
Japan	8 (b)	12	76,600	£68.5m (f)	8
GB	1 (*Hood*)	16	137,760 (d)	£82.88m (g)	1+4 (h)

(a) two more sanctioned – about to be laid down
(b) eight more sanctioned and money voted
(c) actual strength February 1921
(d) not including Coast Guard or Boys
(e) latest information
(f) approved
(g) now submitted
(h) if present Admiralty proposals approved.

18. *Memorandum by Naval Staff*

1 June 1921

Naval Situation of the British Empire in the event of a War between Japan and the United States

…

Summary

27. The arguments in this paper may be summarised as follows:

(i) That the objectives of either opponent are strictly limited by long distance and lack of bases.

(ii) That Japan's immediate objective will be the seizure of the Philippines.

(iii) That under existing conditions the American fleet cannot be based westward of Honolulu.

(iv) That it will be to our advantage financially and otherwise to remain aloof from the war.

(v) That there are possibilities of friction with the US from the point of view of our trade with Japan, but that on the other hand, a permanent Japanese occupation of the Philippines is vitally opposed to British interests.

…

(vii) That if naval facilities are not provided in the Pacific and rapid reinforcement is not possible we may find ourselves in a war with Japan which might otherwise have been avoided.

Appendix I: Disposition of Fleet in a War between US and Japan.

1. Main Fleet:
Atlantic and Mediterranean Fleets concentrate in the Mediterranean. Capital ships with three-fifths complements to complete at once and join Main Fleet.

2. Reinforcements in Eastern Waters
The principle governing the size of the British Fleet in the East at the opening of a Japanese-American war is, that in order to make British neutrality respected and to safeguard our important interests, we should maintain in that part of the world as strong a fleet as possible; at the same time, the fleet in European waters must not be weakened to such an extent as would preclude its employment for operations in the Atlantic in the event of Great Britain being drawn into the war on the side of Japan.

19. *Memorandum by the Naval Staff for the CID*

5 October 1921

II. *Policy with regard to the Limitation of Naval Armaments*
2. … no scheme should be countenanced which would in any way jeopardise the naval security of the British Empire or endanger the safety of our sea communications.
3. … great results are expected by the world at large from the Conference and it is most undesirable that any failure to produce them should lie at the door of the British Delegation.
4. … they should restrict themselves to the consideration of the schemes brought forward by the US or other foreign Delegates.
5. Tactics apart, this is a logical attitude to adopt, as we have already lead the way in a reduction of naval armaments by the large diminution in the number of our warships since the Armistice and by our delay in putting forward a building programme; therefore, it is now for others to show us their good intentions.
6. No opportunity should be lost for maintaining the incontrovertible fact that the naval needs of the British Empire, extending to every ocean, are infinitely greater than those of any other nation, and that although the Government has accepted a position of equality in naval strength with the

US this is a concession to which their naval needs do not really entitle them.

…

10. The Naval Staff consider that it should be made quite clear to the US Government that the British Delegation are not empowered to discuss rules or methods of warfare on the sea.

…

15. (a) *A Naval Building Holiday*

This proposal cannot be entertained by us at the present time. We have already indulged in a five years' holiday, and have in consequence fallen considerably behind the One-Power Standard in modern Capital Ships, which was approved by the Government, and confirmed by the Imperial Cabinet, as the minimum standard required for the safety of the Empire.

To agree to a further holiday would place us in a position of permanent inferiority.

…

22. (h) *Limit to number of Capital Ships*

… on the whole this method holds out the greatest prospect of agreement and could be supported by the British Empire. …

…

34. From our point of view this basis would be very generous to the US, since the necessity for ear-marking a special percentage of naval strength to provide for a retention of a separate force in Home Waters does not apply to them.

35. Acceptance of even a total margin of superiority over Japan which we have indicated may, however, be considered impossible by the US in view of [the] Anglo-Japanese Alliance which causes them considerable apprehension.

This is a powerful argument in favour of an attempt to substitute a Tripartite Agreement for the present Anglo-Japanese Alliance.

…

20. *Reuter's Telegram*[1]

Washington,
16 November 1921

America's Proposal for Limitation of Naval Armaments.
… The US believes this plan safely guards the interests of all concerned. In working out this proposal the US has been guided by four general principles:

(a) The elimination of all capital ship building programmes either actual or projected;
(b) A further reduction through the scrapping of certain older ships;
(c) That regard be had to the existing naval strength of the conferring Powers;
(d) The use of capital ship tonnage as the measurement strength for navies and proportionate allowance for auxiliary combatant craft to be prescribed.

Proposal for Limitation of Naval Armament
Capital Ships
US

(1) The US to scrap all new capital ships now under construction and on the way to completion. This includes six battlecruisers, seven battleships on the ways and building [and] two to be launched.
(2) … The grand total of capital ships to be scrapped is 30, aggregating 845,740 tons.

Great Britain

(3) Great Britain is to stop further construction on four new battleships of the *Hood* class which have not yet been laid down but upon which money has been spent and which, on completion, would have a total tonnage of 172,000 tons.
(4) … The grand total tonnage of ships to be scrapped under this agreement would be 583,375 tons.

…

(10) If the terms of this proposal are agreed to then the US, Great Britain and Japan agree that their numbers three months after the making of this agreement shall consist of the following capital ships:

[1]Reuter's: a private British news agency. This report summarises Hughes' dramatic proposals of 12 November 1921.

US

Maryland, California, Tennessee, Idaho, Mississippi, New Mexico, Arizona, Pennsylvania, Oklahoma, Nevada, Texas, New York, Arkansas, Wyoming, Utah, Florida, North Dakota, Delaware.

Total: 18. Total tonnage: 500,650.[1]

Great Britain

Royal Sovereign, Royal Oak, Resolution, Ramillies, Revenge, Queen Elizabeth, Valiant, Warspite, Malaya, Barham, Benbow, Emperor of India, Iron Duke, Marlborough, Erin, King George V, Centurion, Ajax, Hood, Renown, Repulse, Tiger.

Total: 22. Total tonnage: 604,450.[2]

Japan

Nagata, Hiuga, Ise, Yamashiro, Fuse, Setsu, Kirishima, Haruna, Hiyie, Kongo.

Total: 10. Total tonnage: 299,700.[3]

[1] US Navy: *Florida, Utah*: 1909–10, 21,825t, 21k, 10×12in, 12×5in, 8×3in; *Utah* sunk Pearl Harbor, 7 Dec 1941.

Wyoming, Arkansas: 1911, 26,000t, 21k, 12×12in, 16×5in, 8×3in; *Wyoming,* gun trng 1932.

New York, Texas: 1912, 27,000t, 21k, 10×14in, 16×5in, 8×3in.

Nevada, Oklahoma: 1914, 27,500t, 20.5k, 10×14in, 8×5in; *Oklahoma* sunk Pearl Harbor, 7 Dec 1941.

Pennsylvania, Arizona: 1915, 31,400t, 21k, 12×14in, 8×5in; *Arizona* sunk, Pearl Harbor 7 Dec 1941.

New Mexico, Mississippi, Idaho: 1917, 32,000t, 22k, 12×14in, 8×5in.

Tennessee, California: 1919, 32,300t, 20.5k, 12×14in, 16×5in.

Colorado, Maryland, West Virginia: 1920–1, 31,800t, 21k, 8×16in; *Washington* sunk as target 1924.

Delaware, North Dakota: 1908, 20,000t, 21k, 10×12in; disposed of 1924.

[2] Royal Navy: *Royal Sovereign, Resolution, Revenge, Royal Oak, Ramillies*: 1915–16, 29,150t, 21k, 8×15in, 12×6in, 8×4in, 2×21in tt.

Queen Elizabeth, Warspite, Valiant, Barham, Malaya: 1915–16, 32,700t, 24k, 8×15in, 8–12×6in, 8×4in.

Emperor of India, Iron Duke, Benbow: 1912–13, 25,000t, 10×13.5in, 12×6in; *Iron Duke* harbour service 1932–46; others scrapped 1931–2.

Ajax, Centurion, King George V: 1911–12, 26,500t, 10×13.5in, 12×4in; *Centurion* target ship 1926–44; others scrapped 1926–7.

Renown, Repulse: battlecruisers, 1916, 26,500t, 6×15in, 17×4in, 2×3in, 32k.

Tiger: battlecruiser, 1913, 28,500t, 8×13.5in, 12×6in; scrapped 1932.

Hood: see note 12.

Marlborough: 1912, 25,000t, 10×13.5in, 12×6in; sold 1932.

Erin: 1914 (building for Turkey), 23,000t, 10×13.5in; scrapped 1923.

[3] Imperial Japanese Navy: *Settsu*: 1911, 21,433t; target ship 1924.

Fuso, Yamashiro: 1914–15, 12×14in, 30,600t; both sunk 25 Oct 1944.

Ise, Hyuga: 1916–17, 33,800t, 25k, 12×14in, 16×5.5in, 8×5in; both sunk 1945.

Nagato (and *Mutsu*): 1919–20, 33,800t, 25k, 8×16in, 18×5.5in, 8×5in; *Mutsu* exploded 1943.

Kongo, Hiei, Kirishima, Haruna: battlecruisers,1912–13, 27,000t, 25.9k, 8×14in, 16×6in, 4×3in, 4×21in tt; all sunk 1942–5.

Replacement

12(a) The tonnage basis for capital ship replacement under the proposal shall be as follows:

US: 525,000 tons; Great Britain: 525,000 tons; Japan: 315,000 tons.

(b) Capital ships 20 years from date of completion may be replaced by new capital ship construction. … the first replacement tonnage shall not be laid down until 10 years following the date of the signing of this agreement.

…

(d) No capital ship shall be laid down during the time of this agreement whose tonnage displacement exceeds 35,000 tons.

…

17. It is proposed that the total tonnage of cruisers, flotilla leaders and destroyers allowed to each Power shall be as follows:

US: 450,000 tons; Great Britain: 450,000 tons; Japan: 270,000 tons.

…

20. It is proposed that the total tonnage of submarines allowed to each Power shall be as follows:

US: 90,000 tons; Great Britain: 90,000 tons; Japan: 54,000 tons.

…

23. It is proposed the total tonnage of aircraft carriers allowed to each Power shall be as follows:

US: 80,000 tons; Great Britain: 80,000 tons; Japan: 43,000 tons.

…

25.(a) Cruisers 17 years of age from the date of completion may be replaced by new construction.

(b) Destroyers and flotilla leaders 12 years of age from the date of completion may be replaced by new construction.

(c) Submarines 12 years from the date of completion may be replaced by new submarine construction, …

(d) Aeroplane carriers 20 years from the age of completion may be replaced by new aeroplane carrier construction, …

(e) No surface vessel carrying guns of a caliber greater than 8in shall be laid down as a replacement tonnage for auxiliary combatant surface craft.

21. *Hankey to his wife*

Washington,
13 November 1921

… the announcement yesterday at the opening ceremony of the Conference of the American plan for naval disarmament. It is really magnificent and stunning. None but a very great nation would have conceived it. So far as I can judge it is a superb offer and I am glad to say that conference decided to accept it, subject to a few details.

22. *Views of the Admiralty Section for the British Delegation on American Proposals for Disarmament*

Washington,
13 November 1921

The British Delegation are fully in accord with the proposals of the US Government in regard to the capital ships to be retained, arrested in construction, and scrapped respectively by the British Empire, the US and Japan in the near future, and wish to record their sincere appreciation of the high motives which actuated the US Government in making these proposals which involve them in heavy relative financial losses. …

It follows that British Delegation would be prepared to accept the relative strengths in capital ships which is submitted in paragraph 10 of the Paper containing the US proposals.

As regards the proposal for a 10-year building holiday, however, while fully in agreement with the spirit of the desire, we feel that it is not in the best interests of the economical conditions of the countries to adopt this method of reducing armaments.

…

… and paragraph 12(d) contains a further proposal that no individual ship shall exceed a tonnage of 35,000. Thus the tonnage allowed to the British Empire and the US by paragraph 12(a) would permit of a minimum number of 14 capital ships. Now consider what would happen at the end of a building holiday of 10 years. All the special industries and plant devoted to the manufacture of large warships would have ceased to exist as private enterprise could not afford to allow all this material to be idle for such a long period. The only alternative would be such enormous Government subsidies as would defeat the economical object of the limitation scheme.

…

There would follow, therefore, a period of feverish activity in the shipbuilding world. Armour plate and gun manufactories would be revived at a great cost, and all the other specialised concerns whose products are required to equip a modern capital ship would be once more brought to life, the process of revivication being attended by considerable outlay thus defeating the plan.

This period would last for six or seven years in order to enable the last ship to be completed within the permissible time for replacement. This would entail the simultaneous construction of six capital ships out of a total programme of 14 ships, allowing for a period of three years for the completion of one ship. …

In Great Britain the number would amount to 12.

…

Such a spasmodic existence is neither economical nor likely to lead to a settled and peaceful atmosphere amongst naval nations.

…

23. *Notes by Admiralty Section of the British Delegation*

Washington,
13 November 1921

Auxiliary Combatant Craft

It is suggested that the tonnage of Auxiliary Combatant Craft allowed to each nation in the US proposals bears a definite relation to the battleship strengths and is the tonnage of these types of craft necessary as adjuncts to the Battle Fleet.

… in arriving at the figure of 450,000 tons … no regard has been taken to the vital question of the safeguarding of food supplies. … In this respect Great Britain's position is unique, the US broadly speaking does not rely on the sea at all for the feeding of her population and Japan to a far less extent than Great Britain and with comparatively short sea communications.

The distribution of Light Cruisers, Sloops and Gunboats on foreign stations since the Armistice has been as follows (for reasons of economy certain of these have since been withdrawn): [all in displacement tons]

China Station	38,235
Australia	42,575
New Zealand	10,375
South America	22,050

North America	23,940
Africa	17,620
Canada	5,500
East Indies	19,970
Total	180,265 tons.

... so wide is the field and so little known are the dangers which may threaten our merchant ships in 10 years' time that we cannot be bound by any restriction in regard to the light craft of whatever suitable type we may require to build for this purpose.

In regard to paragraph 30 of the US proposals we are at present in the act of preparing 50 suitable merchant vessels to mount six or eight 6in guns for commerce protection in war. ... Owing to the especially precarious position of Great Britain in respect of her food supply and the subsequently enhanced value of her merchant marine in war we cannot and should not be tied in respect of any measures we may consider it necessary to take for its self-protection.

...

24. *Rear Admiral Chatfield to the First Sea Lord*

Washington,
15 November 1921

... you should ask the US advisors for further details how they propose to give effect to their proposal of a 10 years' holiday. That it would appear to involve very extensive considerations, both naval and political, economic and industrial, and you will therefore be glad if they will therefore, as a first step, enlarge on the subject.

Should they reply that they realise that the proposal has gone too far and invite you to make a better proposal, I suggest that you should say that you naturally have views on this very important subject, that you do not consider spasmodic building as a practical thing. ... If the US advisors agree generally with the principles of what you announce, I suggest you should invite them to redraft their proposals on that line, ... This will keep the initiative with the US, which is very desirable.

Should they, on the contrary, ask you to prepare proposals, I suggest that you should consent to do so, provided that they are prepared to state at the next public conference that we have done so at their request and that they owned that their proposals failed.

... I would suggest that you should say that we do not like the tonnage basis, if only for the reason that tonnage cannot be seen but numbers can.

It will then be necessary to explain how we read their proposals as to tonnage, … i.e., by dividing 500,000 by 35,000.

You will be asked for your opinion on the 35,000 [ton] limit. … we should, if necessary, accept a maximum limit of tonnage for the capital ship, if only for the reason that it is most undesirable that you should take up any position which you cannot maintain, and it is my serious opinion that you cannot maintain either technically, publicly or politically the attitude of wishing to have no limit to the size. The most important consideration in fixing the limit is that the battleship shall not be reduced in size so far that she is seriously menaced by [other] forms of attack, such as air or submarine. …

Now with regard to actual size can we accept the 35,000 ton limit? My opinion is that we must necessarily, because of public opinion, but also that you cannot meet the argument satisfactorily that it is the same for everybody. …

25. *Note by the Director of Plans*[1]

17 November 1921

Further Considerations on the American Proposals

Whilst giving full credit to the US for the sacrifice of such a large amount of naval material by the process of scrapping, it cannot be too clearly realized that the remainder of their proposals operate entirely for their own advantage, and to the comparative disadvantage of the British Empire.

If the American proposals are adopted capital ships remain in their existing condition. In cruisers and other smaller craft, and also in the important matter of aircraft carriers, we are at the present time well ahead of the US. By their present proposals we lose this advantage, and they are enabled to build up to an equality with ourselves modern vessels in all these classes with all the advantages entailed by having the British experience to assist them in design.

If the British Government are determined, for reasons of policy, to accept the proposal for a 10 years' building holiday, then it would be more to our advantage that this holiday should be made a general holiday in all classes of vessel. … It is for consideration whether it would not be a good tactical move for the British Delegation to make this proposal saying that

[1]DP: Capt Barry Domvile (1878–1971): ent RN 1892; Capt 1916; DP 1920–2; CoS, Med F, 1922–5; *Royal Sovereign* 1925–6; DNI 1927–30; RA & VA, 3CS, Med F 1931–2; Pres, RNC, Greenwich, 1932–4; Adm & ret 1936.

they wish to go even further than the US in the direction of a cessation of warship building.

It must be realised that if this policy is adopted it will have the desirable effect of retarding the progress in invention of a considerable number of weapons to which a capital ship is especially vulnerable, and would thus make less dangerous one of the principal disadvantages of the 10 years' holiday, which is whilst capital ships remain as at present all the weapons by which they can be attacked are not subject to similar strictures, nor can means be devised by which they could be satisfactorily controlled.

26. *Notes on US Proposals*[1]

18 November 1921

The US proposals are based on a 10 year holiday in the construction of capital ships but no holiday in the construction of light cruisers, TBDs, submarines and aircraft carriers.

...

2. In regard to the replacement of Light Cruisers and TBDs, Great Britain is placed in quite a different and unenvious position *vis-à-vis* the US and Japan.

Great Britain has already scrapped or placed on the disposal list all her ships in these categories built prior to the war.

She cannot therefore under the US scheme lay down any replacements for about six years.

The US and Japan can, owing to the fact that they will have still a certain number of old Cruisers in commission, commence laying down replacement tonnage at once and with other ships falling due in subsequent years, keep up a steady flow of shipbuilding and gun manufacture thereby avoiding subsidies and keeping alive the art of warship design, etc.

3. The US and Great Britain after completing present submarines on the stocks will each have almost reached their quota of submarines at 90,000 tons. The US will have 7689 tons to build to complete to that figure and Great Britain 9524 tons.

Japan, on the other hand, owing to her small submarine fleet can lay down 23,226 tons to complete her quota of 54,000 tons and thus materially improve her submarine position.

[1]Very likely an Admy source.

4. In regard to aircraft carriers it is understood the US do not include their two Seaplane Carriers the *Langley* and the *Wright* in this category {and] can therefore lay down the full 80,000 tons allowance.[1]

Japan can lay down 38,500 tons.

And Great Britain only 2560 tons.

These vessels, however, are not from their form of construction warships, and do not therefore materially affect armament firms.

5. In conclusion by accepting the US proposals as they stand we are broadly speaking committed to a complete cessation of warship production in Great Britain for six or seven years whereas both the US and Japan can with care nurse their yards with the construction of light war vessels until the capital ship replacement burst commences in 1932.

27. *Hankey to the Prime Minister*

Washington,
17 November 1921

... Lord Beatty asked Colonel Roosevelt, in connection with the naval holiday, what America proposed to do with her shipyards, in order that they might be available and efficient at the end of the 10 years' holiday.[2] Colonel Roosevelt replied that they would have plenty to do building cruisers and seaplane carriers. Lord Beatty then asked about the armour plate plants. Colonel Roosevelt replied, 'Oh, they will be kept busy reconditioning our old battleships'. Lord Beatty then turned to Admiral Coontz and said, 'Are you really going to reconstruct your old battleships?' Admiral Coontz looked very embarrassed and said, 'Of course we are not'. Colonel Roosevelt then said, 'Oh, yes we are, and we are going to begin with the *Delaware*'.

[1]*Langley*: collier 1912; carrier 1922; seaplane tender 1937; 12,700t, 15k, 4×5in.
Wright: ex-freighter, converted to seaplane tender, 1920, 8,400t, 15k, 2×5in, 2×3in.

[2]Col Theodore Roosevelt, Jr (1887–1944): son of Pres Theodore Roosevelt; businessman and investment banker; Capt, US Army, France, 1917–18; Repub; Asst Sec N 1921–5;Govr of Puerto Rico 1929–32; Govr of Philippines 1932; publisher; Brig-Gen 1941–4; N Af, Italy, France; d. of heart attack 12 July 1944.

28. *Memorandum by Naval Staff for CID*

21 November 1921

…

2. (a) Great Britain has already had a five years' 'Naval Holiday' in Capital Ship construction since the laying down of the *Hood*.

(b) Great Britain would be adversely affected for the reasons given under (a) should the 10 years' holiday proposed by the US be accepted.

(c) It must also be borne in mind that the position of the Capital Ship at the end of the 10 years' holiday will have depreciated enormously in comparison with new submarines and aircraft.

With regard to attack from the air as well as long range gunfire, the 10 most recent US battleships will be at a great advantage compared with the five 'Royal Sovereigns' and five 'Queen Elizabeths' which have weak decks, whereas these 10 US ships have 3.5in and 3in armour decks.

(d) Although European navies were purposely omitted in the original US proposals, it is assumed from Mr Hughes's remarks that he anticipated that such Powers as France and Italy would eventually come into line. It is obvious that if these countries refuse to restrict the development of their fleets, Great Britain will have to reconsider the extent to which she can proceed in the reduction of her naval armament.

3. It is the opinion of the Naval Staff that not only does the US not lose by scrapping 15 ships of the 1916 programme, but if thereby British new construction is stopped she (the US) puts herself in a much better position than she would otherwise occupy. The grounds for this assertion are that slow progress has been made on 12 ships of the 1916 programme and that of these 12 six are Battlecruisers of admittedly poor design. Shortly after the US ships had been completed they would have been rendered obsolescent by our new construction of eight ships.

4. The proposals dealing with Light Cruisers, Aircraft Carriers and Submarines would, if carried out, be much more unfavourable to Great Britain with her world-wide commitments than to either the US or Japan.

5. It must be said that, after a careful examination of Mr Hughes's proposals, the Naval Staff has come to the conclusion that the latter are, in almost every detail, much more favourable to the US than to ourselves.

29. *Hankey to the Prime Minister*

Washington,
25 November 1921

...

13. Mr Hughes has explained that the American plan for capital ships was based on no principle. It was a rough-and-ready rule of thumb based roughly on a continuance of the existing relative position of the Powers and scaling gradually down to an equality between the British and American fleets. Once the nations stated a scale of their precise needs, Mr Hughes felt that discussion would never end. We accepted his proposal because we want limitation of armaments and it does not jeopardise our security.

30. *Note by Captain C. J. C. Little*

1 December 1921

Notes on USA in respect of Treaty obligation guarantees.

... the agreement is a great advantage to us under existing conditions. It is a great thing getting rid of all the new American ships when we really have nothing on the stocks ourselves. It sounds almost too good to be true.

31. *Hankey to the Prime Minister*

2 December 1921

...

Still, if we can bring home with us an agreement which removes the American post-Jutland programme of capital ship construction, together with a settlement of the Anglo-Japanese Alliance, I shall feel that we have done as much as could be hoped for here, and shall not feel dissatisfied. This much I believe we shall accomplish.

32. *Hankey to his wife*

Washington,
10 December 1921

… we are about to announce in plenary session the quadruple treaty to replace the Anglo-Japanese Treaty. …

… We were faced with violent antipathy between the Japanese and the Yankees, and a strong feeling in America against the Anglo-Japanese Alliance. In order to create an atmosphere in which a lasting settlement could be achieved on disarmament we had to find some substitute for the alliance, which would conciliate both parties. This we have succeeded in doing and all has gone through successfully. So we are very bucked, as it is the direct result of the work we did on the voyage.

33. *The Washington Naval Treaty*

6 February 1922

I. The Contracting Powers agree to limit their respective naval armaments as provided in the present Treaty.

II. … the US may complete and retain two new capital ships of the 'West Virginia' class now under construction. On completion of these two ships the *North Dakota* and *Delaware* shall be disposed of …

The British Empire may … construct two new capital ships not exceeding 35,000 tons … On the completion of the said two ships the *Thunderer*, *King George V*, *Ajax* and *Centurion* shall be disposed of …[1]

III. … the Contracting Powers shall abandon their respective capital ship building programmes, and no new capital ships shall be constructed or acquired by any of the Contracting Powers …

IV. The total capital ship replacement tonnage of each of the Contracting Powers shall not exceed in standard displacement, for the US 525,000 tons; for the British Empire 525,000 tons; for France 175,000 tons; for Italy 175,000 tons; for Japan 315,000 tons.

V. No capital ship exceeding 35,000 tons standard displacement shall be acquired by, or constructed by, for or within the jurisdiction of, any of the Contracting Powers.

VI. No capital ship of any of the Contracting Powers shall carry a gun with a calibre in excess of 16in.

VII. The total tonnage of aircraft carriers shall not exceed in standard displacement, for the US 135,000 tons; for the British Empire 135,000

[1]*Thunderer*: battleship, 1911, 25,870t, 21k, 10×13.5in, 16×4in; sold 1926.

tons; for France 60,000 tons; for Italy 60,000 tons; for Japan 81,000 tons.

VIII. … all aircraft carrier tonnage built or building on 12 November 1921, shall be considered experimental, and [any carrier] may be replaced, within the total tonnage limitation prescribed, … without regard to its age.

IX. No aircraft carrier exceeding 27,000 tons standard displacement shall be acquired by, or constructed by, for or within the jurisdiction of any of the Contracting Powers.

However, any of the Contracting Powers may, provided that its [i.e., each Power's] total tonnage allowance of aircraft carriers is not thereby exceeded, build no more than two aircraft carriers, each of a tonnage of 33,000 tons standard displacement, and in order to effect economies any of the Contracting Powers may use for this purpose any two of their ships, whether constructed or in the course of construction which would otherwise be scrapped under the provision of Article II.[1]

X. No aircraft carrier of the Contracting Powers shall carry a gun with a calibre in excess of 8in.

XI. No vessel of war exceeding 10,000 tons, other than a capital ship or aircraft carrier, shall be acquired by … any of the Contracting Powers. [AMCs] shall not be within the limitations of this Article.

XII. No vessel of war of any of the Contracting Parties, hereafter laid down, other than a capital ship, shall carry guns with a calibre in excess of 8in.

…

XIX. The US, the British Empire and Japan agree that the *status quo* at the time of the signing of the present Treaty, with regard to fortifications and naval bases, shall be maintained in their respective territories and possessions specified hereunder:

1. The insular possessions which the US now holds or may hereafter acquire in the Pacific Ocean, except (a) those adjacent to the coast of the US, Alaska and the Panama Canal Zone, not including the Aleutian Islands, and (b) the Hawaiian Islands.
2. Hong Kong and the insular possessions which the British Empire now holds or may hereafter acquire in the Pacific Ocean, east of the meridian of 110° E. longitude, except (a) those adjacent to the coast of Canada, (b) the Commonwealth of Australia and its territories, and (c) New Zealand.
3. The following insular possessions and territories of Japan in the Pacific Ocean, to wit the Kurile Islands, the Bonin Islands,

[1]*Lexington, Saratoga*: 33,000t; converted battle cruiser hulls.

Amami-Oshima, the Loochoo Islands, Formosa and the Pescadores, and any insular territories or possessions in the Pacific Ocean which Japan may hereafter acquire.

The maintenance of that *status quo* under the foregoing provisions implies that no new fortifications or naval bases shall be established in the territories and possessions above specified. …

XXIII. The present Treaty shall remain in force until 31 December 1936.

34. *Resolutions Offered by Mr Elihu Root Regarding the Use of Submarines*

February 1922

I. The Signatory Powers declare that among the rules adopted by civilized nations for the protection of the lives of neutrals and non-combatants at sea in time of war, the following are to be deemed an established part of international law.

1. A merchant vessel must be ordered to submit to visit and search to determine its character before it can be seized.
   A merchant vessel must not be attacked unless it refuses to submit to visit and search after warning, or to proceed as directed after seizure.
   A merchant vessel must not be destroyed unless the crew and passengers have been first placed in safety.
2. Belligerent submarines are not under any circumstances exempt from the universal rules above stated; and if a submarine cannot capture a merchant vessel in conformity with these rules the existing law of nations requires it to desist from attack and from seizure and to permit the merchant ship to proceed unmolested.

…

IV. The Signatory Powers recognise the practical impossibility of using submarines as commerce destroyers without violating, as they were violated in the recent war of 1914–1918, the requirements universally accepted by civilized nations for the protection of the lives of neutrals and non-combatants, and to the end that the prohibition of the use of submarines as commerce destroyers shall be universally accepted as part of the law of nations, they now accept that prohibition as henceforth binding as between themselves and they invite all other nations to adhere thereto.

35. *Memorandum by Admiralty Plans Division*

5 April 1922

...

11. The Root Resolutions in regard to submarine warfare, although admirable in intention, cannot be relied upon when formulating war plans for the defence of commerce. Pretext may always be sought and found for enabling a combatant to attack his opponent in his most vital spot – in our case sea-borne commerce – and resolutions made in the harmonious atmosphere of the Conference Room vanish at the stern test of war.

36. *Rear Admiral Sims, US Navy, to Rear Admiral Andrews, US Navy*[1]

Office of the President,
Naval War College,
Newport, RI,
30 March 1922

...

... It seems to be the general opinion that the [Washington] Conference was called through an understanding between the English-Speaking peoples to check the growing power of Japan and her influence in the Far East. I believe the main lines of the Conference were pretty well decided before it met, and I believe this is the beginning of a thorough understanding between the English-Speaking peoples as to the development of the Far East.

[1]R Adm Philip M. Andrews (1866–1935), US Navy: USNA 1886; Actg RA & chief, Bu Nav 1912; Capt 1913, *Montana*; *Maryland* 1914; Cmdt, N Trng Sta, S Francisco 1915; *Mississippi* 1918; i/c Cardiff US N Base 1918–19; cdr, US N Forces, E Med 1919; US N Det, Adriatic 1920; Cdt, 5th N Dist & Norfolk NY, Va 1921–3; Actg VA & cdr, US N Forces, Eur 1923–5; Cdt, 1st N Dist & Boston NY, Mass 1925–30; ret 1930.

37. *US Navy: General Board: Senior Member Present to the Secretary of the Navy*[1]

29 November 1922

Superiority of the British over the US in the Fighting Strengths of the Capital Ships (excluding airplane carriers) resulting from the Treaty Limiting Naval Armament.

2. … The [Naval] War College finds that the ratios of fighting strengths of the British and American capital ship fleets at the ranges noted are as follows:

	15,000 yards	20,000	24,000
American Fleet	100	100	100
British Fleet	144	141	255

The Bureau of Ordnance finds the following ratios of capital ship strength assuming a somewhat different fire distribution:

	15,000 yards	20,000	24,000
American Fleet	100	100	100
British Fleet	140	150	90

…

5. At ranges greater than 21,000 yards most of the US inferiority arises from the lack of our ability to elevate a large percentage of our guns beyond 15°. This is a correctable defect of our fleet. A similar defect that existed in the British fleet has already been corrected.

6. The penetration factor has an important bearing on the ratio of strengths at ranges less than 20,000 yards. Increases in deck protection of the older US capital ships and an increase in the ballistic qualities of the 14in/45 caliber guns of the US ships would probably place the two fleets in approximate equality at these ranges. The British capital ships have already undergone extensive modification in these respects.

…

[1]SMP: R Adm Harry McL. P. Huse (1858–1942), US Navy: USNA 1878; Capt, *Nevada* 1907–08; Capt, Philadelphia NY 1908–11; *Vermont* 1911–13; NWC 1913–14; CoS, Atl F 1914–16; RA 1916; ND 1916–19; Cdr, F Train 1919; armistice supvn 1919–20; Actg VA & Cdr, US N Forces Operating in Eur Waters 1920–1; Cdt, 3rd N Dist, New York 1921; Gen Bd 1921–22; ret 1922.

Sec of Navy: Edwin L. Denby (1870–1929): law, business; enlisted US Navy 1898 & Major, USMC Res 1917–18; Repub Reprv, Indiana, 1903–11; Sec of Navy 1921–4, resigning over naval oil reserve scandal (Teapot Dome), innocent but naive.

10. The General Board believes from its own studies and from its analysis of the War College computations:

(1) That the present capital ship Treaty fleet of Great Britain is at least 30% superior to the present capital ship Treaty fleet of the US.

(2) That this disparity of strength can be practically overcome by the modernisation of US capital ships.

…

12. The General Board considers it essential to the … US:

(1) That the angle of elevation of all turret guns be increased to 30%.

(2) That heavier deck protection be installed on the present coal-burning battleships.

(3) That thorough investigation be made and action taken regarding further improvements in the battle strengths of existing US capital ships.

38. *Captain W. V. Pratt, US Navy: 'The Real Value of the Naval Treaty'*[1]

4 May 1923

…

5. The treaty undoubtedly resulted in a closer relationship between Great Britain and ourselves.

6. It effected, by arbitration, an allotment of sea power commensurate with national interest and prestige.

…

8. It gave to the US a definite policy, one which she had never had before in her history as an independent state. This policy is, in effect, that though the US did not desire to exceed the navies of other countries it felt that its dignity and its safety demanded a navy second to none; one which was balanced in the ratio set by the American proposal for a limitation of armaments.

9. It enabled both naval men and legislators to plan for naval needs in the way of a balanced navy, as they had never been able to before.

We are too apt to consider that we are the only people that made a sacrifice. We may have paid more, but if we did, it is also to be remembered that we called the conference; that we made the first proposal; and that we were in a better position to make concessions than any other country which sat with us at the conference.

[1]In *Japan Advertiser.*

What we gave up, in our right to fortify, was probably more than offset by the goodwill resulting from the concessions made by all three nations entering into the various contracts. …

39. *Admiralty Minute by Alex Hunt*[1]

13 August 1923

The Naval Section at Washington under the instructions of the Admiralty and the CID aimed at a limitation of Capital Ships being governed by numbers and not by tonnage. The statement of the Agreement reached by Great Britain, USA and Japan which was made on 15 December 1921 dealt with tonnage and not with numbers. This was in distinct conflict with the Naval Section's views, and the Naval Section protested to the British Delegates.

France and Italy always adhered to tonnage not to numbers. … Thus the British Empire in 1931 can only lay down two ships, and cannot divide the tonnage – 70,000 – in such a way that say six ships might be laid down whose total did not exceed 70,000 tons.

…

[1]Alex Hunt: Asst. Sec., Admy.

PART II

THE GENEVA CONFERENCE
1922–1927

It was not to be expected that a multilateral treaty of such great import, and on such an unprecedented subject, as the Five Power Treaty of Naval Limitation signed at Washington in 1922 would enjoy a smooth life. It raised, firstly, the question, for both the British and the Americans, of how to defend their positions in the Pacific, since they were forbidden to add to their fortifications in the western Pacific and, in effect, they had ceded naval supremacy there to the 'local' great power Japan, which already possessed defended and developed bases in the area. The Americans, whose remote Pacific possessions had never prompted Congress to appropriate money for their defence, merely shrugged their shoulders and concentrated on building up Pearl Harbor, far distant from the threatened islands. The British embarked on the long saga of developing a naval base at Singapore, sufficient to house the 'main fleet' and near enough to the western Pacific to deter Japanese imperial ambitions [41, 58].[1]

There was, secondly, an American programme, ultimately accomplished, to raise the elevation of their battleships' main armament, which drew British objections, though it was a moot point as to whether it was prohibited by the treaty. British ships had a 20° elevation whereas the older American ships had a 15° elevation, raised to 30° after Washington; only a few British ships were raised to this elevation in 1935–37. The Americans happily adopted a 'stand pat' position on the treaty as regards capital ship gun calibres and displacement and evidently enjoyed substantial battleship building facilities, in contrast to the British [42, 56, 62].

Although the treaty had specified total tonnage amounts in submarines for each of the signatories and the Root Resolutions had endeavoured to pin submarines to the historic rules on cruiser warfare, the British were disappointed that no other nation had supported their heartfelt (but scarcely realistic) proposal for total abolition of a weapon which had brought Britain almost to her knees in the spring of 1917. The Americans, vaguely sympathetic to the British plea in 1921–22, now became covert opponents, since they were developing a new kind of ocean-going submarine, equipped for either mine, torpedo or surface warfare and able

[1]See B. McL. Ranft (ed.), *The Beatty Papers, II (1916–1927)*, Part V, pp. 357–413.

to operate close to Japanese trade routes and coasts, though Rear Admiral Hilary P. Jones's hymn of praise to the modern submarine was rather overstated [44, 45, 48].[1]

Both nations aspired to closer relations but the United States was passing through a phase in her foreign policy between the relative 'isolationism' of the nineteenth century and the full blown internationalism of the post-Pearl Harbor era. This was a phase in which the United States dipped one foot in the water of international relations but was averse to getting the other one wet in the causes of arms limitation and disarmament as well as global peace. It set a fine moral example but abjured the use of force and even economic sanctions. Rear Admirals Hilary P. Jones and William Veazie Pratt exhibited this national mood of pride in achievement and high principle without the will or means to impose it [45, 50]. There was, in fact, a naivety about the American approach to world affairs, especially Anglo-American relations. The British, concerned to hold what they had, believed that the Americans were all talk and no action and therefore, wisely, did not count on the Americans for military assistance in the cause of world peace. The tone of the Admiralty documents is severely pragmatic, a prim dowager in genteel poverty apportioning its scanty assets with care.

As a result of America's unwillingness to commit herself in advance, the British also clung firmly to belligerent rights, seeing blockade of the enemy as one of their principal weapons, insisting on the search and seizure of neutral shipping suspected of carrying contraband [66]. This had brought her into diplomatic, political and press conflict with the greatest neutral trader, the United States, between 1914 and 1916. The Americans, who did very well out of a greatly increased trade with the Allies, were reluctant to go to war over the issue – and Sir Edward Grey, the Foreign Secretary, played them like an adroit fisherman. The conflict over 'freedom of the seas', of neutral rights versus belligerent rights, continued intermittently until 1940. The dispute did, however, spark Wilson's policy of building 'a navy second to none' [43, 66].[2]

Britain felt that it was inconceivable to fight the United States but that if war came it would damage the British Empire more than the USA. She

[1]R Adm Hilary P. Jones, US Navy (1863–1938): USNA 1884; Spanish war 1898; cmded *Rhode Island* 1911–12; Cmdt, Washington NY, 1913–14; *Florida* 1914–16; RA 1917; CinC, Atl F 1919; Adm & CinC Fleet 1922; Gen Bd 1923; LN disarmament 1926; ret 1929; London N Conf 1930.

[2]Neutral and Belligerent Rights have been well addressed in two recent Society volumes: John D. Grainger (ed.), *The Maritime Blockade of Germany in the Great War: The Northern Patrol, 1914–1918* (Aldershot: NRS, 2003), and Nicholas Tracy (ed.), *Sea Power and the Control of Trade: Belligerent Rights, 1854–1970* (Aldershot: NRS, 2005). I am also indebted to my former PhD student, Dr J. S. Rofe.

had conceded parity to the Americans as long ago as 1919, at first grudgingly, in the 1920s with resignation. Old Britannia, in straitened circumstances, could not afford competitive building with young Columbia, which could say 'We've got the ships, we've got the men, we've got the money too'.[1] The Americans, however, did not seem to quite believe Britain's acceptance of parity, despite its enshrinement in the Washington Treaty, though that delineated it fully only in the case of capital ships. On several occasions thereafter, the Americans returned to the issue, seeking assurances that Britain really meant that all classes of warship were covered. Their claim was based initially on Wilson's exasperation with the 'stop, search and seize' policies pursued by the British in 1915, and there were echoes of this in the 1920s. They contended, for example, that they should not 'be at the mercy of any country that may dictate terms as to what neutrals might trade with us and what might not' [50, 59, 65]. By the post-war era, Americans argued also that a large navy was necessary to defend two long coastlines, overseas possessions, lengthy trade routes, a rapidly growing commerce, and a burgeoning merchant marine [40, 53]. They believed, too, that a major fleet was 'for the ultimate good of civilization' [50]. As the decade wore on, however, the dominant note seemed to be that parity accorded with the nation's new-found power, wealth, dignity and glory. The British were sceptical of the Americans' claim for equality, believing it to be a matter merely of prestige, or the 'favourite sport of twisting the lion's tail' [66]. They believed further that the Americans were 'unable to justify a claim to equal numbers on any other ground save that of parity' as a moral principle [52, 57, 60]. Since the USA seemed to present little threat to them, the British readily granted parity, aware that in practice they could do no other [40–43, 46, 48, 50–52, 57, 59, 64–6]. There was, however, one respect in which they felt that parity could not apply – cruisers.

The years from 1922 to 1930 are concerned chiefly, therefore, with the issue of cruisers. The Washington Treaty had provided that they should have a maximum displacement of 10,000 tons and a maximum gun calibre of 8.1in but said nothing about total tonnage or numbers. The maximum quickly became the norm, for now that new battleships (other than those to complete the ratios) were not to be constructed, a 'naval race' in cruisers took the place of the one in dreadnoughts. Japan was quick off the mark in building cruisers of the largest size and Britain and America, both of whom entertained suspicions of Japan's ultimate ambitions in Asia and the Pacific, felt they had to follow suit. There was

[1]Music hall song, by G. W. Hunt, popular at the time of Britain's dispute with Russia, 1878.

therefore something of a 'free for all' in cruiser building and plans in this decade.

The British case was that their far-flung possessions and trade, coupled with their dependence on a high volume of imports of food, raw materials and fuel – and the exports to pay for them – demanded a substantial cruiser force. The Admiralty produced figures to show that British tonnage at sea on a given day was two to three times the American amount. Most of Britain's trade, moreover, was carried in her own bottoms [48]. The Admiralty attempted to quantify the minimum number of cruisers required to defend this trade. Allowing 25 for fleet work, another 54 were necessary for trade protection. Most of these should be light cruisers displacing about 5,000 tons and carrying 6in guns, based on the Empire's numerous bases and therefore short-legged [51]. Ideally, the Royal Navy would have stuck to the 6in gun, even if requiring a displacement of about 7,500 tons for fleet cruisers. It would not have built 8in gun, 10,000 ton cruisers at all, even if the US Navy had plumped for them, but as the Japanese Navy, the only conceivable enemy, had gone promptly for the maximum size and gun calibre, Britain felt obliged to create a heavy cruiser force at least three units larger than that of the Japanese. It argued at Geneva in 1927, therefore, for a heavy cruiser entitlement of 15 vessels and was prepared to make do with 45 modern light cruisers for trade protection, plus about 10 or 20 over-age ships (over 20 years old) and a few armed merchant cruisers (usually large liners of high freeboard, unhandy and armed with obsolete 6in weapons) [63]. Britain was adamant about the absolute need for small trade protection cruisers, a figure reached by strategic requirements, not an arbitrary, universal quota which would be fixed at an unacceptably low figure. The Prime Minister at the time of Geneva, Stanley Baldwin, a suave and astute politician, expressed the policy succinctly: 'We stand for a one-power navy sufficiently equipped with cruisers to protect our trade routes.'[53].[1] Rear Admiral Hilary P. Jones, however, in 1927, castigated the Admiralty for an 'astronomical' building programme, at which Beatty would have raised a bushy eyebrow; in 1925–29 (Churchill's time at the Treasury), the Royal Navy lived on iron rations [64].

The American situation was completely different. Their principal focus was on the Pacific (implying that they trusted British sea power to keep the Atlantic safe for them). The few bases they had in that vast ocean were widely scattered and poorly equipped. What seemed to be required were large vessels of great endurance, of substantial offensive power and as

[1] Stanley Baldwin (1867–1947): ironmaster; Con MP 1908–37; Fin Sec to Treasury 1917; Pres, Bd of Trade 1921–2; CEx, 1922–3; PM, 1923, 1924–9, 1935–7; LPC 1931–5; Earl, 1937.

well protected as could be managed on 10,000 tons. The Americans envisaged some 25 of these; in addition they had already 10 'Omahas', of 7,050 tons armed with 6in guns. This would give them about 325,000 tons, whereas Britain claimed between 375,000 and 420,000 tons, and possibly more if old cruisers were counted. The Americans really wanted to get the parity tonnage for cruisers down to 250,000–300,000 tons but were prepared to accept 400,000 tons, about 60 ships each, for the period up to 31 December 1936, when the Washington Treaty came to an end. They argued for freedom to install guns of up to 8in in all their cruisers [49, 54, 55, 57, 59, 61].

The British suggested that the Americans could get sufficient protection and endurance in a cruiser of 7,500 tons – provided they armed it with 6in guns; the Americans, however, stuck stubbornly to their 10,000 ton, 8in gun design [58, 59]. Britain felt the necessity to protect its overseas trade, on which the United Kingdom was dependent, but while the Americans affected to acknowledge this, in practice they refused to accept Britain's need for a large number of small trade protection cruisers. It may have seemed on the surface a straight fight between the Admiralty and the Navy Department but the real problem was the Japanese, the spectres at the conference table. The Washington Treaty had not limited the numbers and total tonnage of cruisers and destroyers – much to the secret delight of the British – but it was likely that they would form the subject of subsequent negotiations in a decade driven by peace, goodwill and lower armaments bills. The Japanese had taken advantage of Washington's vagueness in this respect to build 12 10,000 ton 8in gun cruisers and by the time of Geneva these were either built or in hand. The only way in which the western countries could lower their demands was to come to at least an entente, never a realistic possibility. Japan, therefore, profited by the inability of the 'satisfied' powers to combine to safeguard their interests in Japan's backyard.

The American desire for a settlement of the flotilla craft issue was genuine, though neither the President, Calvin Coolidge, a famously taciturn but shrewd politician, nor Frank B. Kellogg, his Secretary of State, lacking the authority and subtlety of Hughes, exercised sufficient control over the Geneva negotiations.[1] Hugh Gibson, about to move embassies from Berne to Brussels, was named chief delegate, but he too lacked control of his fellow-delegates, mostly naval men, who dominated

[1]Calvin Coolidge (1872–1933): Repub; small town lawyer; Govr, Mass, 1919; V Pres 1921–23; Pres 1923–9.

Frank B. Kellogg (1856–1937): Repub: Kansas Sen; Amb to UK; Sec of State 1925–29; supposed author of Kellogg-Briand 'Pact of Peace', 1928, but a reluctant bridegroom.

the American party.[1] The principal spokesman was Rear Admiral Hilary P. Jones, an able officer who was currently the senior member on the General Board. Jones, though prepared to make small concessions, was inflexible on the principle of parity and was backed by much of the press, industrial interests and much of Congress, to whom he was a patriot [58]. Gibson, a decent man prepared to make meaningful compromises, struggled to control his over-mighty subject [60].

The British were also genuinely in favour of limitation – but on their own terms, which meant that they were happy to let the Americans have what cruisers they wanted so long as they could have enough smaller ships to protect their trade. The conference, held in a city famed for its dissenting disputations though now the home of the League of Nations and the doves of peace, lurched unavailingly through the humid June and July of 1927. The Americans seemingly left the British and the Japanese, at that time willing supporters of limitation and even their own lower ratio, to arrive at a compromise formula, hinting that they would probably accept its main features. The British Cabinet, headed by Baldwin and a somewhat belligerent Churchill, latterly the Royal Navy's scourge, was then perturbed lest their chief negotiators – the First Lord, Bridgeman, and the notable League apologist and possibly the world's foremost dove, Lord Cecil – concede too much to Japan and recalled their Delegation. A somewhat chastened and chagrined Bridgeman and Cecil returned to Geneva a few days later, to find all hope of getting the Americans on board had evaporated.[2]

Geneva was probably doomed to fail. American pronouncements prior to the conference exhibited a staunch determination to stand fast for parity and a somewhat twisted interpretation of British policy [40, 43, 45, 46, 48–50, 53–5, 57, 61, 64]. The British, painstakingly demonstrating their dependence on ocean trade, obstinately clung to an irreducible number of small cruisers [47, 51, 53]. They were puzzled by the American attitudes, the principal British naval advisor, Vice Admiral Field, saying that he 'found the Americans very trying to deal with' [58–60].[3] The Americans, it seemed, were fickle and divided but after Bridgeman and Cecil returned from London, the Americans felt the British were intransigent. The Japanese, as the junior party, could hardly be expected to show the major powers the way to a treaty, and the French and the

[1]Hugh Gibson (1883–1954): diplomat; Minr to Switzerland 1924–7, to Belgium & Luxembourg 1927–33, 1937–8; member of US Delegn, London N Conf 1930.

[2]William C. Bridgeman (1864–1935): Unionist MP 1906–29; Parl Sec, M of Lab 1916; Bd of Trade 1919–20; Sec for Mines 1920–2: HS 1922–4; FL 1924–9; Visct 1929.

[3]AoF Sir Frederick Field (1871–1945): 3SL & Cntrlr 1920–3; VA & Special Service Sqdn (Pr of Wales's world tour) 1923–4; DCNS 1925–8; Adm & CinC Med 1928–30; FSL 1930–3.

Italians, for reasons of general European security and the unsolved problems of land and air arms, which were of greater concern to them, declined invitations to attend. Anglo-American relations actually worsened in the wake of Geneva, though not simply because of its failure. The two countries had been like ships that pass in the night – but there were those in both countries who learned lessons from the abortive conference and were determined to bring about an agreement.

40. *General Board of the US Navy: Senior Member Present to Secretary of the Navy*[1]

31 May 1922

Naval Policy: Building Program for the Fiscal Year 1924

...

2. Since 1915 the General Board has consistently advocated a naval policy that 'The Navy of the US should be equal to the most powerful maintained by any other nation of the world'. The [Washington] Treaty for the Limitation of Naval Armament gave formal international recognition to the principle of an American Navy second to none, which has thus become the national policy. This policy expresses America's estimate of the minimum strength of its navy that is necessary properly to support its policies and its commerce and to guard its continental and overseas possessions.

3. Although the size of the chief maritime nations as well as the direction of growth open to them has been limited, nevertheless, the purpose of navies and their place in the scheme of national life has not been modified by the agreements of the recent Washington Conference.

4. We hope that as a result of the Washington Conference a spirit of mutual confidence and frankness between nations may grow and develop, but until such a spirit has given serious evidence of life and endurance in the face of warring interests, it would be folly to risk the future of this great nation by accepting a policy of partial naval disarmament or of a limitation of naval armament below the strength of any other power whatever. Within the limitations of the Treaty we must have a navy at least equal to any other in material and number of personnel, and superior to all others in efficiency.

...

6. As the General Board has repeated for many years, the US Navy in peace and war protects US commerce, and in so doing it raises the standard of living of the American citizen. It gives not only military protection in war but economic protection in peace and war. America is passing by rapid stages to an industrial status that requires for the prosperity of our people an assurance of the maximum stability in the foreign demand for our products. Our great merchant marine supported by a navy at least as great as that of any other power is the surest guarantee we can have that foreign markets will remain open to us. When foreign

[1]The Fiscal Year [FY] ran from 1 July 1924 to 30 June 1925. The Senior Member Present was probably the CNO, Rear Admiral Coontz.

markets close to us, American prosperity ends. An efficient navy suitably maintained is a necessary national contribution to our own economic prosperity. Moreover, it is the outward and visible force to ensure to the US its ability to preserve for itself and for the world a rule of law, of order, and of justice.

7. America occupies a position of geographical isolation. No great power can reach America except by way of the sea. No great power can reach American outlying possessions except by way of the sea. No American supposes or desires that, if we become engaged in war, the war will be waged on American continental soil. The navy must see to it that the enemy's guns expend their ammunition remote from our shores. This requires a navy always in readiness with appropriate bases from which to operate.

...

31. *Summary [of 1924 programme]*

1924:

Battleships	Liberal appropriation for modernisation
Cruisers	8 [of] 10,000 tons
Gunboats for Chinese rivers	6
Minelaying submarines	3
Cruiser/scout submarines	3
Airplane carriers	1 [of] 27,000 tons
Airplanes	$19.5m
Personnel	120,000 enlisted men.[1]

41. *CID: Standing Defence Sub-Committee*

30 November 1922

The First Sea Lord stated that ... he wished to place on record a warning as regards the naval situation in the Pacific. He wished it to be clearly understood that since the Washington Conference the situation from the naval point of view had altered in the Pacific. The US were now incapable of naval action in the Western Pacific, thus leaving the British Empire the sole Power to counter with naval forces any aggressive tendencies on the part of Japan. We exist in the Far East on sufferance of another Power.

[1]Cruisers: *Pensacola, Salt Lake City*: 1929–30, 9,097t, 32.5k, 10×8in, 8×5in.

Minelaying submarine: *Argonaut*: 1927, 2.878/4,045t, 13.65/7.43k, 4×21in tt, 2×6in, 60 mines; lost 10 Jan 1943.

Scout submarines: *Nautilus, Narwhal*: 1927 & 1930, 2,987/3,960t, 17.5/8k, 6×21in tt, 2×6in.

Aircraft: a much greater sum than the FAA could contemplate.

Gunboats: not authorised until FY 1925.

This had already been pointed out to the CID, and a decision had been taken that the naval base at Singapore should be proceeded with. Without Singapore we should be swept out of the Western Pacific and have no means of countering a naval offensive by Japan. There was reason to believe that if the war had taken a definite turn against us, Japan would have thrown over the Allies and associated herself with Germany, and that even during the war Japanese agents were in touch with Indian agitators. Japan might fall to a similar temptation in the future, when, by encouraging a revolt in India and raising the banner of Asia for the Asiatics, it would be no exaggeration to say that Japan would be able to wrest from us our position in India. The British Navy under existing conditions without a base at Singapore, would be able to do nothing to counter the activities of Japan in the Far East. The CID had agreed to the construction of a naval base at Singapore.

42. *General Board of the US Navy*

2 November 1924

Explanation of the needs of the Navy

Battleships.
The Building programme for 1926 recommends the appropriation of \$6.5m for increasing the elevation of the turret guns of 13 of the battleships in order that none of our battleships may be inferior in gun range to those of our strongest rival. The [Washington] Treaty Limiting Naval Armaments has received the most careful study, and in the opinions of all the signatories except England contains no hint that such change in the elevation of our guns would violate in the slightest the spirit or letter of the treaty. … but they appeal to its spirit to forbid this change. In no sense would the spirit of the treaty be violated but attention is invited to the unwisdom of permitting the treaty to be interpreted in any respect on such debatable grounds, when the letter thereof is so clear.

43. *General Board of the US Navy: Senior Member Present to Secretary of the Navy*[1]

3 June 1925

Further Limitation of Naval Armament

…

5. …

(2) The dominant sea power ultimately dictates the world's navigation laws in peace as well as in war. In this connection it must be remembered that Great Britain, as a belligerent in the last war, swept aside the Declaration of Paris [1856] and the Declaration of London [1909], nullifying all the efforts of a hundred years towards establishing neutral rights on the high seas advocated by the US. Any further limitation of naval armament may increase Great Britain's power to ultimately dictate to the US what our domestic navigation laws shall be.

44. *Memorandum by Rear Admiral H. P. Jones, US Navy*

15 January 1926

Re: Preliminary Conference on Reduction in Armament

The question of submarines will, undoubtedly, come before the Conference and, judging by the past, Great Britain will strongly advocate the complete abolishment of submarines and France will be strongly opposed to such a proposition. In my opinion the US should, in the strongest possible manner, oppose the abolishment of submarines and stand firmly on the 5: 5: 3: 1.66: 1.66 policy in regard to submarines just the same as for any other unit of naval armament.

The position of England in regard to submarines is easily conceivable owing to her geographic location and for similar reasons Japan may take the same view as England. But for the US the situation is a totally different one. The role of the submarine in naval warfare has been very materially changed since the last war as the great increase in size, speed and radius of action have materially altered the employment of these vessels. They are now regarded as a vital element in any well-balanced fleet. The use of the submarine for scouting and to support air attacks is essential and it

[1]Senior Member Present: Rear Admiral H. P. Jones. Secretary of the Navy: Curtis D. Wilbur (1867–1954): Repub; Chf Justice, Calif Sup Ct; Sec N, March 1924–March 1929, perhaps an accidental choice.

must be recognised that the position of the submarine today is quite different from 1914 and 1918. They are now practically in a class with cruisers and can not be considered as differing essentially as they carry guns and may, in the future, carry airplanes and are capable of operating effectively even without the use of torpedoes or making undersea attacks. The question in the public mind seems to have been largely due to the improper use of the submarine by one country in the late war. It would be just as possible today to use improperly (in violation of the rule of International Law) other units of the fleet and it should be recognised that the submarine properly used in its legitimate field of work is just as necessary as the destroyer and airplane and no more open to suspicion as being an illegal means of warfare. Airplanes or destroyers could be used to bomb and destroy defenceless merchant vessels and could follow the same methods as employed by the Germans in their submarine campaign. The point at issue is not the weapon but the method of employment. A single destroyer could just as easily have sunk the *Lusitania* as the submarine and could not have removed her personnel to a place of safety.[1]

45. *Rear Admiral Hilary P. Jones, US Navy, to Rear Admiral William V. Pratt, US Navy*

1 February 1926

...

I have always been a great advocate of a real entente between us [the US and UK] but do not believe in written alliances. As I think I have told you in the past, Great Britain makes me pretty hot under the collar sometimes, but I admire the nationalism that is always manifest in all that they do. If ever we could get them really at heart to recognise that the US must be treated as a co-equal and must march in international affairs shoulder to shoulder with her, it would go a long way to straightening out questions between us. I realize that there is a very decided attitude in this country of resentment against England, but I believe that is largely fostered by the feeling that England is always trying to keep one lap ahead of us. If we could get both countries really to realize that we stand for Anglo-Saxon control and are, in reality, the only two countries that do stand for civilization as we know it, and that united we can carry that civilization on but divided it must fall, much for world peace will be gained.

[1] *Lusitania*: Cunard liner, 1907, 30,936t, *c.*30k; torpedoed by *U20*, 7 May 1915, off SW Ireland while on normal New York–UK service; 1,201 lives lost, 128 American but Wilson, though protesting, eschewed hostilities.

… I have heard the suggestion several times that we might profitably trade off battleships for an agreement on the part of Great Britain to the 5: 5 [ratio] in cruisers. This does not appeal to me, as I believe that if we do away with battleships we definitely put ourselves in a position of inferiority, even with an equality in other types. I am not sure that the submarine question should be treated separately from tonnage in a consideration of any further limitation of armament, but as you say, it may be impossible to talk to France and Great Britain around any council table when submarines are considered together with other types and inseparable. It seems to me that it is a question that must answer itself as the conference proceeds.

46. *Rear Admiral Pratt, US Navy, to Rear Admiral Jones, US Navy*

3 February 1926

…

The British factor, which is purely naval, … is more indirect [than the problem of continental military power]. Its purpose seems to be more to insure economic security and preponderance of economic power. It is indirect in acting in this way. England's economic assets are so widely scattered that security for them must be the *sine que non* of preponderance in the economic factor. If the above be true, I can understand why France will not accept a cut in her military without considering resources and other factors, and by the same token I also see why England might be ready to accept our point of view as to arbitrary measures of military strength. For so long as she maintains equality or preponderance with us and preponderance of sea strength against any possible European combination of naval powers, she can remain secure in what is to her vital – the economic factor. I imagine that our point of view is a rather simple common sense one – that if you wish to cut you have got to cut and if you intend to cut there is only one way to do it and that is on the arbitrary basis. I see no other way out of it and as the US is already the proponent of that scheme in the 5: 5: 3 [ratio] there seems no logical reason why we should ever depart from it. Regardless of good or bad for the Navy we did it and out of the agreement we secured the 5: 5: 3 [ratio] and equality with England, or rather equality with the leading sea power of the world whoever that may be. This position should never be given up.

By all means never give up the 5: 5: 3 [ratio] in battleships. We have a just claim for [equal] cruiser tonnages without that. England should never make the mistake of 1776 with America again. Hence equality in cruisers and all else. …

47. *Admiralty Memorandum*

30 June 1926

Mercantile Tonnage

Completed Ships of 100+ tons.

Country	*Ships*	*Tonnage*
British Empire	2821	17,111,074
USA	1636	9,656,178
Japan	519	2,699,045
France	409	2,457,192
Italy	462	2,597,038

Imports and Exports

	Year	*Total Imports*	*Food*	*Raw Matls.*	*Exports*	*% own ships*
GB & NI	1926	1,242,854,000	512,773,000	392,685,000	777,458,000	69.60
USA	1925	875,270,000	150,138,000	329,682,000	997,892,000	28.85
Japan	1925	217,604,000	33,158,000	126,281,000	195,014,000	61.77
France	1924	650,446,000	110,894,000	250,306,000	670,406,000	26.78
Italy	1925	215,203,000	not known	not known	150,274,000	42.00

[all values in sterling]

48. *Memorandum by Rear Admiral Hilary P. Jones, US Navy*

London,
10 November 1926

…

Before leaving I said to the First Sea Lord, ‘Now, let us understand each other perfectly so that there can be no doubt as far as the US is concerned: Great Britain accepts equality in all categories. In any conference we would establish a level of armaments in all categories in which each nation would have an equality.’ He agreed to that unequivocally.

…

Lord Beatty realized the futility of pressing for the abolition of the submarine and fully agreed with me that unless such abolition could be made wholly universal the submarine would not be abolished, and that such universality is impossible.

Our talk was very open and frank …

49. *Memorandum by Rear Admiral Hilary P. Jones, US Navy*

7 January 1927

The maximum tonnage fixed by the Washington Conference for cruisers is 10,000 tons, which may be accepted as the maximum tonnage for that class of vessel in any future Conference for the Reduction and Limitation of Armaments that may be held. After a careful study of her actual fleet requirements and also of her overseas units in protecting lines of communication between overseas dominions and the home country and between the dominions themselves, Great Britain decides that she will need 60 cruisers. In view of her extensive chain of bases over the world, it is not necessary that her total allowance of cruisers shall be of the maximum size and therefore she finds it more desirable to distribute her tonnage in cruisers of varying sizes, ranging from the maximum size of 10,000 tons to 5000 tons. On the other hand, the US, owing to lack of bases, would require cruisers of maximum sea endurance and maximum protection possible to be obtained within the maximum unit tonnage allowed, and therefore the US will demand that the great proportion of the total tonnage allowed shall be in units of the maximum unit tonnage. In the Conference it is agreed that the limit of the total tonnage of cruisers shall be 400,000 tons and the number of cruisers shall be limited to 60. Under this agreement, in accordance with (a) ['Limitation of the total tonnage and also the total number of units in each class'] the US could build, if she so desired, 40 cruisers of 10,000 tons and, of course, Great Britain could do the same. However, Great Britain may decide that 20 cruisers of the maximum size and 40 cruisers of 5000 tons would be more desirable for her than 40 cruisers of the maximum size. In such case the US may well decide that 30 cruisers of the maximum size would be sufficient for her requirements in cruiser strength and would constitute a sufficient parity with Great Britain to warrant such distribution. In any case both nations should outline the general policy that it is intended to carry out during the life of the agreement in order that no uncertainty shall exist as to the intentions of either during such agreement.

50. *Rear Admiral Pratt, US Navy, to Rear Admiral Coontz, US Navy*

Office of the President,
Naval War College,
Newport, RI.
10 March 1927

…

About a future conference, I am not too sanguine about a future conference. I sincerely hope though as long as we had to enter the last, that the 5: 5: 3 [ratio] will be pushed through to a successful termination. I have already expressed myself definitely to the effect that I personally do not care to have any more connection with a conference, but whoever our delegate may be, he should have the support of the Administration to admit of nothing but 5: 5: 3. …

The 5: 5: 3 [ratio] is, so far as the American people are concerned, much less a ratio between capital ships than it is an expression of principle. 5: 5 is what America stood for in the War of Independence. We fought for 5: 5 then and we are never going to accept anything less. As for 5: 3, it was an exceedingly generous gesture for us to make in view of the magnitude and strength of our country. We certainly should never agree to anything which reduces that ratio. I hope that every Administration will always back those sentiments up. We made great concessions when we attempted that. If we could hold to it, we are reasonably safe. If we do not, no one can tell what may happen.

I have noted lately a great deal of propaganda to the effect that we do not have the same extent of trade routes to guard that other nations have and for that reason we ought to be content with a smaller ratio in the matter of cruisers. That is an extremely fallacious argument. So long as wars are likely, and I see no immediate prospect of their being forever taboo, we, as a great trading country have got to be able to protect our trade, not only to our own colonies and outlying bases, few as they are, but we have got to be able to protect our trade interests to neutral ports and to safeguard the trade of neutrals to us in time of war as well as in time of peace. For these reasons I can see no force in the argument that we should not maintain a cruiser force and a Navy second to none. We cannot as the greatest trading country in the world ever admit to the plea we should be at the mercy of any country that may dictate terms as to what neutrals might trade with us and what might not. That to my mind is one of the replies to the argument that we have no trade routes of our own to guard comparable to the interests of others. Moreover, the question of equality with the best, as I have said before, is a matter of principle, a principle which it is of the most extreme importance for America to maintain. If our people and particularly Congress were once to get the idea that any other country proposed a plan affecting the sea which forbade equality on the sea with any other country, they would rise in arms. We are in a position now where we cannot and will not brook any inferiority in matters which vitally affect our interests as a great and growing world state.

No nation in the world is apt to use its influence and power more generously and more leniently than the US. I have nothing but praise to give England for the way she has used her sea power in the past, but I do maintain that America is just as well qualified to use that sea power for the ultimate good of civilization as are other world powers. One thing I think we may be sure of is, that if an attempt were made to deny equality to us, never again would such fair and generous terms be offered as America offered at the Washington Conference when she established the principle of the 5: 5: 3 [ratio]. We would then feel, after having made this fair and generous offer, that the spirit in which the American proposal was being made was being violated and, if it is to be violated, no country is able to do it and put a preponderant sea force on the water than America. Once let our people get the idea that we are denied equality and never again will we offer it. …

51. *Memorandum by Admiralty Plans Division*

17 March 1927

Limitation of Armament: Cruisers

It is clear that in regard to cruisers, the British Empire cannot accept a 5: 5: 3 ratio *vis-à-vis* the US and Japan. At the same time, it appears necessary to have a reasoned basis on which we can put forward proposals, and the following is an attempt to produce such a basis.

2. The Cruiser Force of a sea power has two principal functions –
(a) Fleet Work.
(b) Control of sea communications.
Of these, (a) Fleet Work, is equally important to each of the principal naval powers and a ratio corresponding to battleship strength appears equitable and would be acceptable.

The minimum number of cruisers required for a well-balanced fleet is five for every three capital ships. This formula applied to the Washington agreement in regard to capital ships gives the following –

	No. of Capital Ships allowed	*No. of cruisers required for Fleet work*
British Empire	15	25
USA	15	25
Japan	9	15
France	5	9
Italy	5	9

3. In regard to (b) – Control of sea communications, the number of cruisers required is dependent upon the length of the sea routes to be defended and the density of the trade normally using the routes, this latter being a measure of the importance of the route to the Nations whose ships traverse it.

On 1 April 1926, the total tonnage, including all vessels of 3,000 g.t. and upwards actually at sea was as follows –

	On clearly defined ocean routes	*In areas [of concentration]*	*Total*
British Empire	7,211,700	2,446,000	9,657,700
USA	3,557,500	153,000	3,710,500
Japan	1,014,500	200,000	1,214,500
France	1,151,500	22,400	1,173,900
Italy	1,357,200	n/a	1,357,200

By multiplying the tonnage at sea on defined Ocean routes by the length of routes to be traversed from port to port, a factor which may be termed 'Ton Mileage' is obtained as follows –

British Empire	27,229,492,000
USA	12,379,311,000
Japan	3,757,721,000
France	3,481,711,000
Italy	3,448,407,000

These figures fairly represent the relative need for cruisers in so far as the control of the defended routes are concerned. Assessing two cruisers for every one million ton miles the numbers of cruisers required for this purpose would be –

British Empire	54
USA	25
Japan	7
France	7
Italy	7

4. In regard to the tonnage in areas, it thought that since the areas are in all cases adjacent to or at terminals of the distinctive routes, it is reasonable to assume that no further allocation of cruisers is necessary for its protection. It should be noticed, however, that this assumption is one that handicaps the British Empire *vis-à-vis* all the other nations.
5. Lastly, it has to be recognised that the defence of the trade routes has to be continuous and that therefore only the cruisers actually available at any time can function for this purpose. It would be reasonable to allow a substantial margin for refits and time necessarily spent in harbour, but since this would affect all nations in proportion to their needs, it is not proposed to take this into account.
6. On this basis the requirements of the five principal powers for cruisers is as follows –

	Fleet Work	*Trade Protection*	*Total*
British Empire	25	54	79
USA	25	25	50
Japan	15	7	22
France	9	7	16
Italy	9	7	16

52. *General Board of the US Navy: Senior Member present to Secretary of the Navy*[1]

25 April 1927

Further Limitation of Naval Armament

3. In formulating its conclusions the General Board will take as its guide the Basic Naval Policy of the US, which is:

'The Navy of the US should be maintained in sufficient strength to support its policies and its commerce, and to guard its continental and overseas possessions.'

[1]Rear Admiral H. A. Wiley, US Navy (1867–1943) [and also for documents 53–7]: USNA 1888; Capt 1915; *New Jersey, Wyoming* 1916–18, 6th BS, GF; Actg RA 1918; RA 1921, Bat Divs 1919–20; NWC 1920; Cdt, 1st N Dist & Boston NY 1921–3; Actg VA & Cdr, Bat Divs, Bat F 1923–5; Gen Bd 1925–7; Adm & CinC, US Fleet 1927–9; ret 1929; govt & ND posts 1933–43.

53. *General Board of the US Navy: Senior Member Present to the Secretary of the Navy*

21 April 1927

Further Limitation of Naval Armament

National Policies of Great Britain.

(a) Naval support for the defense of the Empire and for the development of other imperial policies.

Note: Mr Amery, 30 March 1924:[1] What should be the standard of our naval power? For us, depending as we do for our very existence upon the continued maintenance of the sea, it is essential that as against any other power or combination of powers, whose armaments or policy might constitute a real and definite menace to our security, we should maintain a substantial margin of supremacy.

The one-power standard, however, is a standard which refers to the strengths of the fighting fleets as measured in capital ships. There can be no similar reference and ready standard for cruisers and smaller craft, the requirements in respect of which … must depend upon the peculiar defense problem of each power.

Mr Baldwin: We cannot allow, and we will not allow, any weakening at present of the defensive forces of the Empire. We stand for a one-power navy sufficiently equipped with cruisers to protect our trade routes, and sufficiently equipped bases throughout the world to make our fleet mobile and capable of action wherever the call may come from.

(b) Domination of world markets and world carrying trade.

(c) Opposition to the domination of the continent of Europe by any single power.

The above policies involve subordinate policies, which are:

1. Mercantile maritime supremacy.
2. Control of communications (cable and radio).
3. Acquisition or control of sources of fuel.
4. Military control of narrow waters near important trade routes throughout the world.
5. A world wide system of naval and commercial bases.

The National Policies of the US:

(a) No alliances.

[1]L. S. Amery (1873–1955): Con MP; Parl U-Sec for Colonies 1919; Parl U-Sec, Admiralty 1921; FL 1923–5; Dominions Sec 1925–9; SSt India 1940–5.

(b) The Monroe Doctrine.[1]
(c) The Open Door.[2]
(d) Maintenance and strengthening of American merchant marine.
(e) Exclusion of Asiatics.
(f) Limitation of other immigrants by quotas.[3]

54. *General Board of the US Navy: Senior Member Present to the Secretary of the Navy*

25 April 1927

Further Limitation of Naval Armament

…

7. A proposal to limit all of the above mentioned class of vessels [cruisers] by a single total tonnage limitation, is not consistent with the interests of the US, because it would operate to retard or prohibit our building of cruisers in sufficient numbers to meet our national needs. We have so far confined ourselves to a very limited cruiser program, not because we did not need the cruisers, but because those in authority desired to avoid the appearance of competition with foreign powers, and desired also to avoid excess economy in expenditures for new construction. This is a further and very potent reason for not including all of the above class of vessel in a single total tonnage limitation.

[1]Monroe Doctrine (1823): Actually the work of John Quincy Adams, Secretary of State under President Monroe, it forbade the establishment of new European colonies in the Western Hemisphere, while recognising those already established. An attempt by a European state or states to establish new colonies in the New World (specifically Latin America, then just about completing the expulsion of Spanish and Portuguese imperial authority) would be regarded as a hostile act. The US was unable to enforce the doctrine before at least 1898 and relied on Britain sharing the same attitude, enforcing it with the Royal Navy.

[2]Open Door (1899–1900): a unilateral American policy, it recognised China's sovereignty over its own customs, equal commercial rights for all nations, and Chinese territorial integrity. 9 Power Treaty of Washington, 6 Feb 1921–2, obtained a general but qualified international adherence to the Open Door, but no one, including the Americans, had any intention of fighting for it, and it left China unsatisfied. It always had a moral strength to it and the US could not help maintaining a semi-detached attitude towards China; she was always America's 'ward of court'.

[3]National Origins Act (1924): effectively closed the 'open door' to immigrants, especially Asiatics, notably Japanese, thus upsetting that proud nation and nullifying goodwill resulting from Washington Conference, building on pre-war insults in California.

55. *General Board of the US Navy: Senior Member Present to the Secretary of the Navy*

4 May 1927

Further Limitation of Naval Armament

Summary.
24. In view of all the foregoing the General Board concludes:
...
(e) That the most acceptable total tonnage of the cruiser class, less than 20 years old from date of completion, is:

US	300,000 tons.
UK	300,000 tons.
Japan	180,000 tons.

(f) That the most acceptable total tonnage of the destroyer class, less than 15 years old, is:

US	250,000 tons.
UK	250,000 tons.
Japan	150,000 tons.

56. *General Board of the US Navy: Senior Member Present to the Secretary of the Navy*

13 May 1927

Further Limitation of Naval Armament

Section III
48. The General Board concludes that:
(a) The abolition of capital ships, or any reduction in their present allowed maximum displacement, or any limitation which materially diminishes the importance of capital ships in the scheme of naval warfare, would be disadvantageous to the US.
(b) The general aim of a limitation of naval armament would best be furthered by leaving the questions related to capital ships for consideration by the 1931 five power conference.

57. *General Board of the US Navy: Senior Member Present to the Secretary of the Navy*

2 June 1927

Further Limitation of Naval Armament
General Consideration of National Policies as related to the question of the limitation of armaments

Great Britain

(a) The continued acceptance of the 5: 5: 3 ratio in capital ships and aircraft carriers.
(b) A demand for a greater cruiser strength than that of any other power.
(c) A demand for freedom to take counter measures in naval construction against the French naval program.
(d) A similar but less urgent demand for freedom to take counter measures against the Italian naval program.
(e) A demand for a greater than a 5: 3 ratio in cruisers with relation to Japan.
(f) Freedom to create and extend naval bases within the limitations of the present [Washington] Treaty Limiting Naval Armaments.
(g) A probable proposal to progressively decrease the number of capital ships while maintaining present ratios.
(h) A probable proposal to postpone the replacement program of capital ships as laid down in the present [Washington] Treaty.
(i) A proposal for the abolition of submarines or for more limited employment of submarines.

United States

(a) To create, maintain and operate a Navy second to none and in conformity with the ratios for capital ships established by the [Washington] Treaty for the Limitation of Naval Armament.

58. *Third Conference of the British Empire Delegation*

Geneva,
24 June 1927

. . .

Lord Cecil stated that there was no question in his mind that the Americans desired the results of this Conference to be based on two big principles.[1]

(1) to keep the Japanese allowance as low as possible; and

(2) to have equality with us.

He had heard from a journalist on the previous day that there was a large campaign being organised in America to prevent a reduction in armaments. This propaganda was being organised chiefly by the big steel and armaments manufacturers, and his informant had stated that the Bethlehem Steel Co. were prepared to spend up to $1m in propaganda. No doubt this was an exaggeration, but there was certainly an element of truth in the story.[2]

Lord Jellicoe said that, in conversation with the Americans, he had ascertained that what they required of their cruisers was a large radius of action owing to their scarcity of bases in the Pacific.[3] He told them that if they would agree to give up the 8in gun cruiser, the 7,500 ton ship would give them sufficient radius of action. He asked them why they liked the 8in gun ship, but could get no answer.

59. *Fourth Conference of British Empire Delegation*

Geneva,
29 June 1927

Admiral of the Fleet Lord Jellicoe: the Americans had, in fact, given away their position by the figures which they had announced on the first day of the Conference. They had estimated the total tonnage for cruisers as being between 250,000 and 300,000 tons, and, since they had proposed building up to the 10,000 ton standard, it was obvious that they anticipated their requirements would normally be some 25 to 30 cruisers. In view of this statement, they would find it very difficult to justify building up to our requirements. He had little doubt that at the back of their minds was a

[1]Visct [Robert] Cecil of Chelwood was a member of the British Empire Delegn.

[2]W. B. Shearer, a steel industry lobbyist, was active at Geneva.

[3]Lord Jellicoe, former Govr Gen of New Zealand, was a member of the British Empire Delegn.

feeling that the freedom of the seas with regard to commerce in war-time was at stake, and was the root of their objections to our necessarily larger [British] cruiser programme. In other words, what they were afraid of was that cruisers employed on the protection of our trade routes were in a position to be a menace to the trade of others.

...

Lord Jellicoe pointed out that the Americans had never explained the importance which they attached to the 8-in gun. If they would agree to accept a 6-in gun in its place, they could obtain the same radius of action with a 7500 ton cruiser as with a 10,000 vessel. He believed that at the back of their minds they were apprehensive about the number of our merchant ships capable of mounting 6-in guns, although in debate they had intimated that they preferred to leave merchant ships generally out of the question.

60. *Fifth Conference of the British Empire Delegation*

Geneva,
1 July 1927

...

Admiral Field said that for us the problem was not so much one of total tonnage as of numbers. When our requirement in numbers had first been stated to the Americans, they had been aghast, but they had since realised, and had admitted, that we had made out a good case for them. The Americans, being unable to justify a claim to equal numbers on any other ground save that of parity, had suggested an alternative method of approach, i.e., that each of the three Powers should agree to limit its construction on the basis of a definite building programme up to the year 1936. [Admiral Field] told the Americans Mr Bridgeman was only prepared to consent to this plan on the understanding that the number of 10,000 ton cruisers would be definitely limited and that they would accept the 6in gun for all others.

Admiral Field went on to say that he found the Americans very trying to deal with. He thought he had got them to agree to something and at the next meeting he found they simply reverted to their own original proposal. ...

...

Lord Cecil stated ... a divergence of view existed in the American Delegation. He thought it probable that the American naval officers were pressing Mr Gibson over the cruiser question. ...

61. *Statement Read to the Technical Committee by Rear Admiral Hilary P. Jones, US Navy*

Geneva,
5 July 1927

The position of the US Delegation is that we cannot discuss cruiser figures in excess of 400,000 tons for the period ending 31 December 1936.

That during that period we would require full liberty of action to build 10,000 ton cruisers up to a total of 250,000 tons, recognising at the same time the right of other Powers to build cruisers of similar characteristics up to tonnages in accordance with the principles of the Washington Treaty.

That we have no intention or desire to replace the 10 cruisers of the 'Omaha' class carrying 6in guns, except in the case of loss of one or more of those units.[1]

That in an effort to meet the British view-point regarding a limitation in the number of large cruisers we are willing, for this period and without prejudice to future action, to limit our further construction within a total limitation of 400,000 tons to vessels of a smaller tonnage, to be agreed upon.

We do not see any reason for limiting the calibre of gun in the smaller class of cruisers to anything different from that in the larger class.

We believe that each Power should have full liberty in the design and armament of a smaller class of cruisers, should such a class be adopted for the period in question.

This statement of American policy should be considered as our maximum effort to meet the British view-point.

We greatly prefer that within a total tonnage limitation and within the characteristics of cruisers provided for in the Washington Treaty, that each Power enjoy full liberty of action.

We invite attention to the fact that our original proposal was for a total limitation in the cruiser class of between 250,000 and 300,000 tons. We still ardently desire that the total tonnage limitation of cruisers to be agreed upon shall be very much lower than 400,000 tons, as we believe that an agreement on such a figure would be an extremely useful service to the cause of limitation. If it was found possible to agree upon a figure materially lower than 400,000 tons, the American arrangements regarding cruisers of the larger class could be revised downward.

[1] 'Omaha' class: 1920–5, 7,050t, 34k, 10 or 12×6in, 8×3in, 6×21in tt.

Any limitation on the basis of a cruiser tonnage in excess of 400,000 tons we regard as so ineffective a limitation as not to justify the conclusion of a treaty at this time.

62. *Admiralty Memorandum*

n.d., *c*. July 1927

Defended Naval Ports of the USA

Atlantic Coast

New York	Brooklyn NY can build 2 capital ships simultaneously. Battleships (not battlecruisers) can be docked. All repairs can be executed.
Hampton Roads, Va.	Norfolk NY can build 1 battleship and 1 destroyer. Largest ships can be docked. Mines are manufactured at this yard.
Philadelphia	NY can build 2 capital ships simultaneously. Largest ships can be docked. All repairs can be executed.
Boston, Mass.	NY can dock and repair all classes of ships. There was a destroyer and submarine base at Squantum in Boston Harbour but this is now inoperative.
Charleston, SC	NY builds and repairs destroyers. Earlier dreadnoughts can be docked and minor repairs to battleships can in an emergency be undertaken.
Portsmouth, NH	NY builds and repairs submarines. Earlier dreadnoughts can be repaired.
Washington, DC	Naval gun factory. No construction or repair work undertaken.
New London, CT.	Submarine base. Minor repairs to submarines undertaken.
Naragansett Bay, RI	Naval training and torpedo station at Newport, RI.

Key West, Fla.	Naval operating base chiefly used by destroyers, submarines and aircraft. The Yard is now inoperative but could be opened again as machinery is well tended. Emergency repairs to submarines could be undertaken.

Pacific Coast

San Francisco, Calif.	NY can build 1 battleship and 3 destroyers simultaneously. Largest ships can be docked. All repairs can be executed.
Puget Sound, Wash.	Bremerton NY can build 1 battleship. Battleships (not battlecruisers) can be docked. All repairs can be executed.
San Diego, Calif.	Naval operating base. Minor repairs to destroyers can be executed.
Astoria, Ore.	There is a destroyer and submarine base at Tongue Point but this is inoperative.
Los Angeles, Calif.	There was formerly a destroyer and submarine base at San Pedro but this is now closed.
Pearl Harbor, Oahu Island, Hawaii	NY contains a dock to take largest ships. It will eventually be able to execute all repairs but the yard is not yet fully developed. There is a submarine and aircraft base.
Balboa, PCZ	There is a dock to take the largest ships. Major repairs to cruisers can be undertaken.
Colon, PCZ	Submarine and aircraft base.
Manila, Philippine Islands	Naval station. Minor repairs to ships of Asiatic Squadron can be undertaken at Cavite, in Manila harbour.
Guantanamo [Cuba]	(It is not certain if this port is now defended). Very minor repairs can be undertaken.

Guantanamo is chiefly used for training purposes.
It was defended before the 1914–18 war with two 6in batteries.

63. *Conference of British Empire Delegation*

Geneva,
11 July 1927

Admiral Field: stated that under our proposal we should have only 15 big cruisers and the rest would be 6in gun ships. The Americans pressed for 25 big cruisers with no limitation as to the size of the gun in the remainder. He stated that the offensive power of the 8in gun was 2.5 times greater than that of the 6in gun, and, therefore, there was no question that the American proposal would provide a force of much greater offensive character. …

64. *Rear Admiral Hilary P. Jones, US Navy, to the Secretary of the Navy*

Geneva,
21 July 1927

…

… So far, all of the proposals that have come from the British are merely in the form of some disguise or other by which they may approach their enormous building program which they submitted to us some time ago. In our Technical Committee when they suggested such figures I characterized them as 'astronomical' in size. I do not think they have yet forgiven me for using the term 'astronomical' in describing their tonnage demands. …

65. *Hankey: Diary 1927*

12 October 1927

Sir A. Chamberlain told me that he had information to the effect that following the breakdown of the Geneva Conference he had learned that the real reason why the Americans were so keen on parity with us in cruisers was that they were determined never again to put up with the interference with their commerce to which they were subject as neutrals in the first two and a half years of the great war.[1] He thought that, in order to remove this reason, we might be able to come to terms with them on the question of rules of blockade. I at once felt anxious and settled down to write a Memorandum giving the reasons against such a negotiation. … If the Americans demand Freedom of the Seas we should be in a fix. To accept would put us in difficulties with the League [of Nations] and be an abandonment of our essential belligerent rights. To refuse would only cause further estrangement. Any possible agreement would involve on our part a sacrifice of some belligerent rights. …

66. *Mr Alexander Flint: General Remarks on Enquiry into Belligerent Rights at Sea*[2]

30 November 1927

Any negotiations with the USA on these rights are a leap in the dark.

…

5. … with the growth of their Navy a considerable body of American opinion, Naval and otherwise, leans towards the American Navy carrying out the British practice in the Great War. All the same the bias of executive opinion in the past has been towards restricting belligerent rights and this is a natural attitude of self-interest on America's part. She is the great exporting nation and her geographical position militates on the whole, against the exercise by her of drastic pressure on the commerce of most nations.

6. We have, apart from rights under Blockade, a long established and indefeasible right recognised in International Law of seizing enemy ships and enemy cargo with the exception of cargo under a neutral flag (which we gave up by the Declaration of Paris [1856], except as regards contraband). Our wars have demonstrated that the relinquishment of this right would mean the abandonment of our chief, and in some cases, sole means of bringing pressure to bear on the enemy. The value of the right has been demonstrated by Sir Julian Corbett and Captain Mahan.[3] The property is not seized in the aspect that it is the property of individuals but rather that is a part of the commerce from which the enemy State derives its resources. The property is natural in effect and prevention of

[1]Sir Austen Chamberlain (1863–1937): Con MP; SSt India 1915–17; War Cabinet 1918–19; C Ex 1919–21; LPS 1921–2; FS 1924–9; FL 1931. Baldwin assured Hankey belligerent rights were safe with him.

[2]Alex Flint (1877–1932): Pmnt Asst Sec, Admy, 1901.

[3]Sir Julian Corbett (1854–1920): lawyer; historian, naval writer, educator, strategist.

Capt Alfred Thayer Mahan, US Navy (1840–1914): naval historian, defence strategist; Naval War College; RA (ret).

its circulation demoralizes or complicates the individual, the life and power of resistance of an enemy. …

It is presumed that there will be no concession on this matter of capture of enemy private property. …

7. … What justification is there for thinking that America will depart now from the attitude she took up in 1915 and 1916? Her views are on record and it is foolish to expect at this time a measure of compliance with British practice. In the matter of 'detention', i.e., the diversion of a ship into a port for further examination, the USA strongly upheld visit and search must be carried out on the spot and that only available evidence for seizing the ship was to be taken from the ship's papers and what could be discovered on board. There is little justification yet for thinking that America would depart from this opinion, yet we rightly contended that unless the ship could be sent in for further search and examination, and unless the evidence could be supplemented by information on shore from intercepts and censored documents, belligerent rights were flouted. The modern trader is too cute and the modern commercial systems so elaborate that the ship's papers are the last place to disclose any evidence that the ship or the cargo is really liable to seizure.

8. As to continuous voyage the Americans themselves in their Prize Court admit the principle for contraband, …

…

14. To agree to limiting belligerent rights is really to agree to an attack on this country. To volunteer to initiate steps seems defeatism. The whole scheme of defence of the Empire is based on sea supremacy and no steps should be taken which rest on the theory that we are no longer safely predominant at sea. American bluff should not be allowed to gain an easy victory; they have threatened us with their Mercantile Marine and yet the Marine is so far a failure. It is premature to accept the present American Press Campaign as any more than propaganda. The Americans are not a militant nation. The President does not rush into a war until he has the country behind him, and if it is a war and America is neutral, whilst some individuals may suffer from the exercise of belligerent rights, the country as whole, by the selling of its goods whilst a neutral, is likely to make fabulous profits, which profits would be lost by a war.

The present outcry is bluff associated with the favourite sport of twisting the lion's tail: in connection with the propaganda to secure a big navy in order to protect American exports in war (on the theory that industrial life must not in any way be deranged), there is a threat or bluff in the demand that belligerents shall allow all normal trade to proceed as well as the abnormal export boom immediately established with the belligerents on the outbreak of war. For the sake of part of her trade the war is to be prolonged and if we use our legitimate weapons against the enemy we are threatened with American might. It would be the worst defeatism to bow to the threat. …

…

21. There is no firm basis for agreement with the USA. Nobody has the slightest idea of what the USA would ask if approached. In any case, she is afraid of being hoodwinked by us, and will probably make her terms severe. We have not really any grounds for thinking there are possibilities of agreement. If there were one or two agreed points, they would merely throw into stronger relief the points on which no agreement had been reached and more harm than good would have been done. The time for approaching USA is after USA has been at war and has probably adopted the belligerent practices of the Allies in the Great War.

Note by the Fourth Sea Lord on Belligerent Rights[1]

…

It would appear to be a reasonable line to take that as the USA and Great Britain are now the paramount powers at sea it to the interest of both in pursuit of their common ideals that the rights and privileges attached to sea supremacy should be safeguarded. Every inroad on the power of the British Fleet is *a priori* a weakening of the American Fleet at the same time.

England in peace time conceded the absolute freedom of the sea to all nations. American doctrine does not do so. Certain trade is definitely reserved for US ships and no other may participate. Before discussing freedom of the seas in war America might well be asked to concede its operation in peace.

[1]4SL: VAdm Sir Vernon Haggard.

PART III

THE FIRST LONDON NAVAL CONFERENCE 1927–1930

The Geneva Conference had failed because neither the British nor the American Governments gave it close enough attention, largely eschewing preliminary negotiations, which would have flagged differences, and did not choose appropriate delegations. It suffered also from the undue prominence, in the American delegation, of naval officers, notably Rear Admiral Hilary P. Jones. Towards the end, Churchillian opposition to cruiser parity led to the temporary recall of the British Delegation, a death blow to an already fading conference.

By 1930, different men headed governments and navies and, spurred by a clause in the Washington Five Power Treaty of 1922 that there should be a review of capital ship and aircraft carrier provisions in 1931, they resolved to subsume that with a renewed attempt to resolve the problems thrown up by Geneva in a conference at London early in 1930. The proposed naval discussions ran in tandem with other talks on preparations for a World Disarmament Conference. The President of the United States from March 1929 was Herbert Hoover, the leading international philanthropist of his day, and anxious to go down in history as a great peacemaker.[1] Since June 1929 the Prime Minister of the United Kingdom had been the pacific Ramsay MacDonald.[2] Their arrival in office was the signal for a fresh attempt at friendlier Anglo-American relations and a commitment to secure world peace and disarmament. Their basis was the so-called 'pact of peace', the Pact of Paris (more commonly known as the Kellogg-Briand Pact) of 1928–29, which proposed to renounce war as an instrument of national policy and gained the ready signature of most powers.[3] Both leaders made gestures towards limitation by cancelling ships. The conduit between these two men of peace and goodwill was the new American Ambassador to London, the ebullient and energetic Charles

[1]Herbert Clark Hoover (1874–1964): mining engineer; Eur relief aid, 1914–17; War Food Adminr, 1917–18; Repub Sec of Commerce 1921–28; President 1929–33.

[2]James Ramsay MacDonald (1866–1937): Lab MP; leader Lab Party 1911–14, 1922–31; pacifist, WWI; PM & FS 1924; PM 1929–31; PM of Natnl Govt 1931–5; LPC 1935–7.

[3]Kellogg-Briand Pact (Pact of Paris), 1928–9; concluded by US SSt Frank B. Kellogg and French FM Aristide Briand. It was part of an on-going French attempt to lure US into guaranteeing French security – and an equally prolonged US attempt to avoid commitment.

Gates Dawes.[1] Most of the extensive preliminary discussions were carried on by MacDonald, via the enthusiastic Dawes, and Hoover's Secretary of State, the austere Henry L. Stimson, a commanding figure, experienced in public service and a member of the internationally minded 'East Coast Establishment'.[2] Both Stimson and MacDonald were determined to keep discussions firmly in their own hands. The issues were aired in a frank exchange of views and sealed by MacDonald's visit to Hoover in October 1929, a meeting that would be termed later a 'summit' conference. By the time the conference proper opened on 21 January 1930, its skeleton had been laid down [67–97]. Although the British and the Americans stage-managed the conference, the Japanese, French and Italians also attended. The Japanese, apart from arguing for an increase in the Washington ratio to 70 per cent for auxiliary craft, were co-operative and conciliatory but the French and Italians, eyeing one another's Mediterranean ambitions suspiciously and in any case more concerned with overall security, were unable to sign up to the eventual treaty.

The British feared that the Americans would renew their historic call for 'the freedom of the seas' and pit their neutral rights against Britain's equally traditional belligerent rights, which the British regarded as one of their principal weapons of war, but although there were one or two scares for them, the Americans, mercifully, did not press the issue, nor the parallel subject of allowing food ships through a blockade (a Great War concern of Hoover) [92, 95]. They were more vocal on the potential threat of Britain's western hemisphere bases to the USA's security but it was really a round in the national political sport of tweaking the lion's tail. The British kept the matter in low key but were quite firm on holding on to the (rather run-down) bases, pointing out that they might be required in a future war against powers other than the United States [84, 87, 92–6].

Capital ship and aircraft carrier concerns were addressed to some extent by the London Naval Conference of January to April 1930. There was some abortive haggling over capital ship displacement and tonnage [100, 105, 106, 112]. Nine old ships were scrapped but the principals agreed to postpone battleship replacement until 1936 and left the Washington ratios undisturbed [78]. The Americans made much noise about the superiority, at least in numbers of flight decks and their aircraft capacity, of Britain's naval air arm; however, this so-called advantage was more apparent than

[1]Charles Gates Dawes (1865–1951): Chicago banker; Gen 1917–18; Dawes Plan, refunding German reparations, 1924; V Pres 1925–9; Amb to UK 1929. Known as 'Hell and Maria' Dawes.

[2]Henry L. Stimson (1867–1950): lawyer; Repub; Sec of War 1909–13; Gov Gen, Philippines 1928–9; SSt 1929–33; Sec of War 1940–46.

real. In fact, the Americans, who had a 1,000-plane programme, were about to surpass Britain, the pioneer, in tactics, ship capacity, quality of aircraft and qualified officers. The Americans made much of the handicap under which their service laboured of having two over-large carriers, the *Lexington* and *Saratoga*, but at Washington they had pressed to retain two battlecruiser hulls for these carriers – and in the coming Pacific war these proved their worth [68, 97, 99, 110]. On the submarine question, Britain wanted the abolition of a weapon which exposed her soft underbelly; failing that, the British argued for a restriction on submersible numbers, total tonnage and unit size, along with a refinement of the 'Root Resolutions' of 1922, compelling submarines to adhere to the rules of 'cruiser warfare' [73, 77, 78, 84, 109]. Destroyers caused little discussion, America offering to scale its numbers down to the British level, along with submarines – if the British would be more amenable on cruisers [73, 74].

The main business, as at Geneva, was parity in cruisers. In contrast to Geneva, however, negotiations were carried on in a more amicable spirit, with naval officers reduced to mere advisors who were rarely consulted (and felt aggrieved that their entreaties were ignored), and, crucially, there was more flexibility in each side's position [73, 75–8, 80, 82]. Even Churchill acknowledged that 'the growth of friendship and mutual trust among the English-speaking peoples remains the supreme object of world politics' [71]. He had been disconcerted by the deterioration in Anglo-American relations since (but not solely because of) Geneva, and the then-Prime Minister, the emollient Stanley Baldwin, and his Foreign Secretary, Sir Austen Chamberlain, had endeavoured to mend fences with the Americans between 1928 and 1929. Stimson was animated by the same desire to restore harmony to Anglo-American relations. There was abroad in both countries a vague sense that America and Britain should establish an informal condominium, under whose benign direction universal peace and order should reign, and that they should act as exemplars.

American naval documents nevertheless exhibit an obsession with parity with the Royal Navy and treat Britain almost as a potential enemy [67, 69, 70, 109]. Britain, though agreeing cheerfully to parity in all classes, was trying to manage a vast Empire, long trade routes and economic recovery in reduced circumstances; even where money was available, appropriations for defence had to compete with a widespread desire in all parties for expensive social welfare [71, 73–7, 80, 81, 83]. If it was 'guns or butter' in Britain, in America there was for the most part an indifference to world affairs; concerns over parity seemed to be cast in a vacuum. The deepening Great Depression merely focused the attention of the Atlantic world even more sharply on economy in national expenditure, though it led to dictatorship, revanchism and militarism elsewhere.

The British were quite prepared to extend parity to cruisers. America, they felt, could have as many cruisers as she wanted and of any type permitted – but an initial American demand for 25, then 23 and ultimately 21, 10,000 ton 8in gun cruisers was strongly resisted because, the British pointed out quietly, it would mean an automatic increase in the Japanese number and they, too, could have 15, the same as Britain, who did not want any more and preferred to have a large number of small 6in gun ships for policing and trade protection. The Americans, anxious to restore transatlantic harmony, agreed eventually to 18 large units, plus the 10 existing 'Omahas' (7,050 tons and 6in guns), and 10 new 6in gun cruisers (if required), with Britain having 15 8in gun cruisers and 35 of smaller size armed with 6in guns (including, for their lifetimes, the four 'Hawkins' ships, armed with 7.5in guns). Much to the chagrin of the US Navy, they succeeded in splitting the cruiser category into two ('heavy', 8in gun; and 'light', 6in gun). Japan was left with her 12 8in gun ships (effectively 70 per cent for the life of the treaty, as the Americans were slow to build up to treaty strength) and her ratio in 6in gun cruisers and smaller warships was edged up to 70 per cent, while in submarines she achieved parity. Parity, in this formulaic way, was to be achieved by 31 December 1936, by which time another conference would have been called. The British, dealing with real or likely scenarios, had reduced their Geneva demand for 70 cruisers to 60, and then, determined to mend fences with the Americans, to 50, citing the benevolent world situation. The Admiralty, though sceptical about the worth of the Kellogg-Briand Pact, accepted 50 rather unwillingly but, realistically, could not have hoped for more, with or without limitation.[1] They were somewhat mollified by the fact that the treaty would be short-lived. They agreed subject to other navies being limited and called for replacements of ageing ships at a rate of three a year. The Americans were pleased that they had achieved virtual parity and Pratt relieved that he could now pursue a rational policy (though most American admirals regarded him as a self-serving traitor). The less compromising Jones had returned to the United States early because of illness but his admirers in Congress put up a debate lasting into July, when Hoover at last secured American ratification. The Japanese, however, were somewhat disappointed that they did not rise (officially) to a 70 per cent figure in heavy cruisers [70–72, 74, 75, 78, 82, 83, 86, 88–91, 98, 101–4,

[1] G. C. Peden, *British Rearmament and the Treasury, 1932–1939* (Edinburgh: Scottish Academic Press, 1979), p. 15.

107, 108, 112, 113]. Their Prime Minister, Hamaguchi Osachi, had accepted the treaty, believing that Japan could not compete in a naval race with Britain and America and that she could not afford to unite the western powers against her. For this reason, he was assassinated about a year after the Conference, an event which may be said to mark the beginning of the slide into another world war.[1]

The London Treaty of 1930 was a definite achievement. A pact completing the work at Washington in several directions [111], it led to some disarmament and much limitation. In an age lulled by the balm of the 1920s, it seemed another major step on the road to universal and eternal peace but was, however, flawed. The principal driving force for MacDonald and Stimson was a better relationship between their countries; naval considerations were of little consequence, a policy made possible by an apparently cloudless global sky. As in most international negotiations, potentially awkward compromises had been made. The treaty was destined for a very brief life (a major calculation everywhere in its acceptance), expiring on 31 December 1936. The French and Italians (worryingly for the other Mediterranean power, Britain) were unchecked in the auxiliary classes. The Japanese lurched into a decade of assassination, government dominated by the military, and fractured responsibility (which made it hard to know who spoke for Japan). They posed problems for the next round of naval limitation talks, intended to extend the agreements made at Washington and London into the 1940s.

[1]D. Borg & S. Okamoto, eds., *Pearl Harbor as History: Japanese–American Relations, 1931–41* (New York: Columbia University Press, 1973), *passim.*

67. *Rear Admiral Frank H. Schofield to Rear Admiral Hilary P. Jones, US Navy*[1]

24 February 1928

…

3. As to the conference at Geneva where three powers only were represented, Great Britain had for her basic strategic policy her determination to maintain British superiority on the high seas. Her problem was, therefore, to shape negotiations so that that superiority would not be greatly disturbed by any agreement which she might enter into. … She, therefore, had to seek some method of getting the necessary numbers without too great an expense. … She undoubtedly estimated that the best way of doing this was to attempt a limitation in types of cruisers such that the types determined upon and standardized would be more useful to her than to anyone else. … Her delegates saw that the 8in cruiser, if built, even in less numbers than her smaller cruiser would make the operation of her small cruiser extremely hazardous operations; that the larger cruiser might interfere seriously with her control of the sea, – her attempt to direct neutral commerce, or to interfere too greatly with belligerent commerce.

…

8. The situation, then, is that Great Britain with its system of securely defended bases is in a position at the very outbreak of war to interrupt all of the great lines of sea communication throughout the world, and the only way that this interruption can be met is by superiority in types of ships as to fighting power and by types of ships having sufficient cruising radius to go after these vessels of the British Navy that are disturbing commerce in focal areas.

…

11. … They came to Washington with one principal mission, which was undoubtedly to get rid of our marked predominance in capital ships.

[1]R Adm Frank H. Schofield, US Navy (1869–1942): USNA 1890; ONO 1916–17; head of Sims' planning staff, 1917–18; *Texas* 1919–21; Gen Bd 1921–4; RA & *Omaha* & Destroyer Sqdns, Bat F 1924–6; ONO 1926–9; Geneva Conf 1927;cdr, Bat Div 4 1929–30; Actg Adm & CinC, Bat Force 1930–2; Gen Bd 1932–3; ret 1933.

68. *General Board Memorandum*

14 September 1928

US Naval Aircraft

… The proposed distribution as regards assignment, approved by the Navy Department, March 1928, is as follows:

Afloat	474
Overseas	204
Training	192
Marines	91
Total	1,000

Deficit in allowance of 1000 planes, June 1930:

VO	175
VT	62
VF	45
VN	47
VP	30
VTa	2[1]

69. *General Board Memorandum*

6 October 1928

General Naval Policy

To create, maintain and operate a navy second to none, and in conformity with the ratios for capital ships established by the Washington Naval Treaty limiting Naval armament.

To make war efficiency the object of all training and to maintain that efficiency during the entire period of peace.

To develop and to organise the Navy for operations in any part of either ocean. To make strength of the Navy for battle of primary importance.

To make strength of the Navy for exercising ocean-wide control of the sea with particular reference to the protection of American interests, and overseas and coastwise commerce next in importance.

[1]When Britain went to war in Sept 1939, the FAA had 232 aircraft. The first figures add up to 961 and the second to 361.

To encourage and endeavor to lead in the art and material of naval warfare.

To give every possible encouragement to civil aviation with a view to advancing the art and to providing aviation and aircraft production facilities available for war.

To cultivate friendly and sympathetic relations with the whole world by foreign cruises.

To support in every possible way American interests especially the expansion and development of American foreign commerce and an American merchant marine.

To maintain a Marine Corps of such strength that it will be able adequately to support the Navy by furnishing details to vessels of the Fleet in full commission, guards for shore stations, garrisons for outlying possessions, and by the maintenance in readiness of an expeditionary force.

To cooperate fully and loyally with all departments of the Government.

Building and Maintenance Policy

To build and maintain an efficient and well-balanced Fleet in all classes of fighting ships, in accordance with the capital ship ratios, and to preserve these ratios by building replacement ships and by disposing of old ships in accordance with continuing programs.

To make superiority of armament in their class an end in view in the design of all the fighting ships.

To provide for great radius of action in all classes of fighting ships.

Capital Ships

To prepare and maintain detailed plans for new capital ship construction.

To replace existing capital ships in the years specified in accordance with Treaty provisions.

To keep all retained capital ships modernized as far as Treaty terms permit, and good practice justifies.

Aircraft Carriers

To build and maintain aircraft carrier tonnage allowed by the Washington Treaty for the Limitation of Naval Armament.

To prepare detailed type plans for the rapid conversion of suitable merchant vessels to aircraft carriers.

To design aircraft carriers with hangar space such that the maximum number of heavy class planes may be carried.

Cruisers

To support the Fleet and protect our commerce, replace all old cruisers with modern cruisers of 10,000 standard ton displacement carrying 8in guns and, in addition, to build similar cruisers at a rate that will maintain effective cruiser tonnage in conformity with the capital ship ratios.

Small Cruisers and Gunboats

To build no small cruisers.
To build replacement gunboats as required.

Destroyers

To build and maintain effective destroyer tonnage in conformity with the capital ship ratios, giving priority to destroyer leaders.

Submarines

To build and maintain effective submarine tonnage in conformity with the capital ship ratios.

Auxiliaries

[Intention to build and maintain various classes]

Aircraft: Heavier-than-Air

To direct the development and employment of Naval Aviation primarily to the fulfilment of its principal mission, namely, operations at sea with the Fleet.

To direct the development of heavier-than-air craft primarily in the two classes that can operate from ships, *viz.*,

(1) Light Planes for fighting, spotting, tactical scouting, and dive bombing.

(2) Heavy Planes for torpedoes, heavy bombs, and long-distance scouting.

To combine as many functions in a single plane in each class as can be done with efficiency.

To continue the development of a seaplane of long range for sea operations from a ship or from a naval base.

[Lighter-than-Air craft: chiefly rigid airships, to be developed].

Organization Policy

…

To organize the Navy as far as possible so that expansion only will be necessary in time of war.

To decentralize administration as far as indoctrination permits.

To organize fighting ships permanently by classes.

To assign units as required from the permanent organization to task groups for special operations and training.

Operating Policy

…

To maintain a general scheme of progressive education and training for the Navy.

To assemble the active Fleet at least once a year for a period of not less than three months.

To keep in commission, fully manned and in active training, all fighting ships possible.

To keep airplane carriers fully manned and operating with the Fleet.

To put vessels assigned to reserve in condition for active service.

To make foreign cruises as international conditions warrant, thereby cultivating good will and educating the personnel.

To operate a navy train sufficient for the upkeep of fighting ships and expeditionary forces.

To make every effort, both ashore and afloat, at home and abroad, to assist the development of American interests and especially the American Merchant Marine.

[There follow sections on Personnel, Base and Shore Stations, Communications, Inspection, Information, and Publicity].

70. *Rear Admiral Hilary P. Jones, US Navy, to the Secretary of the Navy*[1]

18 June 1929

…

… we have not advanced the claim for preponderant combatant tonnage over Great Britain but have merely insisted on as nearly an equitable parity in such tonnage as can be arrived at under conditions actually existing.

[1]Charles F. Adams: lawyer, banker, celebrated yachtsman; scion of famous Boston family; Sec Navy 1929–33. Quietly opposed Hoover & Stimson.

It may not be inappropriate at this point to invite attention in regard to Great Britain's essential food lines and her demand for cruisers to insure their integrity. The plea that if she were shut off from the sea it would mean starvation in a short while for her whole population is very convincing to her people and appealing, apparently, to a large section of ours. But if this plea is examined from the standpoint of actual geographical conditions a certain fallacy will become apparent, certainly insofar as we are concerned. The essential food lines of Great Britain itself lead across the Channel and North Sea to north continental Europe and through the Strait of Gibraltar into the Mediterranean to southern continental Europe and on through the Suez Canal to the East; or they lead across the Atlantic to North and South America and the West Indies. In the former case here food lines could not be seriously menaced by us even if we possessed a decidedly preponderant cruiser strength. In the latter case, naturally, it would be decidedly to our interest that they not be interrupted. Therefore, it seems to me, that as between Great Britain and ourselves the integrity of her essential food lines need not enter the problem.

The situation is materially different in the case of the far-flung sea lines of commerce along which the volume of our trade is as great as hers and is rapidly becoming even greater; in addition to which there are many lines leading into our ports which are practically food lines for us in that raw material absolutely essential to our land transportation facilities flow over them. It seems to me that this situation renders our demand for as nearly an equal opportunity on the high seas as it is possible to attain unanswerable.

71. *US Naval Attaché, London, to Office of Naval Intelligence, Navy Department*[1]

2 July 1929

Mr Winston Churchill: 'Equal Fleets Not Equality'

'A question which seems to require urgent attention affects the safety and power of this country, and the whole life and cohesion of the British Empire. I mean the maintenance of the British Navy at the minimum strength necessary to enable us to guarantee the security of our food

[1]Naval Attaché, London: Capt W. W. Galbraith (1878–1955): Capt & Asst Dir N Intelligence, 1924; Dir N Intelligence 1925–6; Cdr, Destroyer Div 25, N Fcs, Eur 1926–8; N Att, London, 1928–31; ret 1932.

supplies and our trade, and to preserve the necessary contact with the world-spread Dominions and Possessions of the British Crown.

At the Washington Conference of 1921 we agreed with the US to abandon altogether that supremacy at sea which we had enjoyed for at least 100 years, which we had never abused, and which in the late war, enabled the US to participate in the general victory of the Allies. We abandoned that position willingly and sincerely, and we accepted the new principle that Britain and the US should be equal Powers upon the sea. I was one of those principally responsible for that decision. It was a tremendous decision, and it is irrevocable.

But that decision implied two conditions. The first was that special regard should be had to the entirely different circumstances of this crowded island, which can be starved in a few weeks, and the great continent in which the people of the US dwell so safely and so prosperous.

It would not, in my opinion, be a fair interpretation of the principle of equal powers upon the sea if a mere numerical measure of the two fleets, each the replica of the other, were to be made the rule. Then we should not have equality, but under the guise of equality an absolute and final authority. Such a result I intend to resist, and I shall claim your support in so doing.

The second condition, which seems to me to be vital to the faithful and successful carrying into effect of the doctrine of equal power upon the sea, is that any agreement between Great Britain and the US must be based upon a tolerant and good-hearted spirit towards naval affairs on both sides of the Atlantic. If naval equality is to lead to a jealous and suspicious scrutiny of every ship and gun and every armour-plate between the two navies, it would be much better to have no agreement at all and for each of us to go our own way, acting sensibly and soberly, and in a neighbourly fashion, but free and unfettered.

Since Mr Hoover became President of the US it has seemed to me, at any rate, that a more comprehending and sympathetic spirit has been imparted to the policy of the US, not only towards this country, but towards Europe in general.

It was the intention of the late Government and particularly of Mr Baldwin and Sir Austen Chamberlain, to make sure that a similar contribution of good will and fair play should be forthcoming from the British Empire. After all, the growth of friendship and mutual trust among the English-speaking people remains the supreme object of world politics, and is today the surest means of the final and utter expulsion from the thoughts of men of the hideous tragedy and hateful processes of war.'

72. *General Board: Senior Member Present to Secretary of the Navy*[1]

13 July 1929

Actual and Rated Tonnages of Auxiliary Surface Combatant Vessels of the US and the British Empire

. . .

3. The vessels used in the two tables [not reproduced] are:
(a) For the US –
Cruisers and destroyers built and building and the five cruisers recently contracted for of the 15 cruiser program.
(b) For the British Empire –
Cruisers and destroyers built and building for [the Royal Navy].
This has been necessary because two British cruisers have recently been 'contracted for' and it is not known if they are actually under construction.

4. The General Board invites attention to the position of hopeless inferiority of the US shown by both tables.

The US would have 23 cruisers and 280 destroyers of a total combined actual tonnage of 487,545.

The British Empire would have 59 cruisers and 173 destroyers of a total combined actual tonnage of 565,031, an excess in favour of the British Empire of 77,488 actual tons.

Table No. 1 shows an excess of 82,431 rated tons and Table No. 2 an excess of 85,357 rated tons in favour of the British Empire. This excess of tonnage in either case amounts to more than eight 10,000 ton cruisers.

5. Moreover, destroyers cannot and should not be compared with cruisers in combatant value; their mission and functions are totally different; and one cannot perform the duties of the other. It would be a very grave error and could put the US in a position of hopeless inferiority to use any evaluation on any such basis.

6. These computations are based solely on an arbitrary assumption as to relative values, and further violate the principle which we have constantly maintained, *viz.*, that cruiser tonnage should not be divided into two distinct classes of cruisers, which would compel us to build small cruisers of a type that are unsuited to our needs and would deprive us of the privilege of building cruisers of a larger type best suited to our needs. Both of the tables support the British thesis. …

[1]SMP: probably the CNO, Adm Charles F. Hughes, US Navy (1866–1934): CinC, Battle F, & US F: CNO 14 Nov 1927–17 Sept 1930.

73. *Ambassador Dawes to Secretary of State Stimson*

US Embassy,
London,
18 July 1929

[Enclosing letter from the Prime Minister, James Ramsay MacDonald]

…

'The position of our conversations up to now seems to me to be as follows:

1. We both agree that the Washington arrangements regarding first class battleships and aircraft carriers will not be disturbed.

We agree that there will be a parity between us as regards cruisers. Hitherto there have been difficulties between our experts on this subject arising out of the distribution of tonnage between large and small craft. We have agreed however that the somewhat differing situations of our two countries will be resolved by the construction of a yardstick and I am waiting for your proposals regarding this. Pending this you and I on behalf of our governments have agreed that we shall not allow technical points to override the great public issues involved in our being able to come to an agreement.

… [Atherton says] 'Fourteen approximately the same type of cruisers (as the US are laying down) have been completed by the British who apparently have in construction or otherwise 10 more.'[1] These figures have been taken apparently from an out of date white paper. Since then alterations have been made and the position today is number built and building 15; number projected three; these three include the two I have slowed down. … I have slowed up the preparations for laying down the two cruisers included in the 1928 programme and have done so not merely for the purpose of lengthening out the time for the completion of that programme but in the hope that it is the first step towards a reduction.

3. We agree to parity in destroyers and in submarines[,] parity in this case being equal gross tonnage in each of the two categories. I ought to tell you however that as soon as the Five Power Conference meets [at London, 1930] I shall raise again the use of submarines and state my desire that they may be eliminated altogether. I know that I am in a somewhat weak *debating* position as regards this because the submarine is exactly the arm that can do Great Britain the most damage in the event of a naval war against us breaking out. My motive however

[1]Ray Atherton: long-serving Counselor, US Emb, London.

is not that at all. I base myself on the fact that though all war is brutal and ruthless the way in which the submarine is used raises that brutality and ruthlessness to a very much greater height than has been known.

74. *Stimson to Dawes*

State Department,
Washington,
21 July 1929

…

… parity should consist of equal gross tonnage and it is our suggestion that this should be achieved by the scrapping of destroyer tonnage on the part of the US until it is equal to the present tonnage of the British. This determination may encounter public opposition in this country, inasmuch as the US now has clear preponderance over Great Britain in the destroyer class, and this is the only such class. However, when fleet parity is actually in sight, this is a real contribution towards armament reduction which this Government is able and prepared to make.

We also agree with MacDonald as to parity in submarines, to consist of equal gross tonnage and to be arrived at by the scrapping of present submarine tonnage on the part of the US until it has become equal to existing submarine tonnage of Great Britain. As to the Prime Minister's desire to abolish the use of submarines and the reasons he gives for this wish, we are in agreement. This position of the two countries as to submarines may be influenced by the attitude[s] of other nations. The drastic steps, as to submarines and destroyers, supported by this Government are predicated by drastic action with regard to cruisers by the British. …

75. *Dawes to Stimson*

US Embassy,
London,
22 July 1929

[Enclosing Speech to House of Commons by Mr MacDonald]

'… A visit by me to the President of the US is now the subject of conversation so that it will take place when it is most helpful to promote the cordial relations of our two countries and in particular advance the ends of disarmament and peace which we hold in common.

… and the general outlook is such as to justify us in reviewing our own programme. Our predecessors did this from time to time as the outlook brightened. Therefore not only as proof of our sincerity but as a duty imposed upon us to guard the expenditure of national money we have decided as follows:

To suspend all work on the cruisers *Surrey* and *Northumberland.*

To cancel the submarine depot ship *Maidstone.*

To cancel two contract submarines.[1]

To slow down dockyard work [and] other naval construction.

As regards the 1929–30 programme, in any event no commitments would have to be entered into before the autumn and no steps will be taken to proceed with it until the matter has received further consideration.

The Government of course recognizes that substantial reduction in the naval building programme must have a direct effect on employment in the dockyards but I am glad to say that as a result of special rearrangements suggested by the Admiralty it is hoped to secure the absorption of a large amount [of] labour which would otherwise be discharged from the royal dockyards. The representatives of dockyard labour will at once be consulted.

We are indebted to the Board of Admiralty for the help which they have rendered and, I desire to state that having expressed their technical view on the minimum armaments they consider to be necessary they have furnished us with loyal help in achieving our object with the least possible dislocation and hardship.'

76. *Stimson to Dawes*

State Department,
Washington,
23 July 1929

[Enclosing Statement by President Hoover]

'… The Prime Minister introduces the principle of parity which we have now adopted and its consummation means that Great Britain and the US henceforth are not to compete in armament as potential opponents but to cooperate as friends in the reduction of it.'

[1] *Surrey, Northumberland*: 10,000t, 30k, 8×8in, 4×4in, 8×21in tt; scheduled completion 1932; suspended, then cancelled 14 Jan 1930.

Maidstone: a submarine depot ship, same name, was built in 1937–8.

Royalist, Report: scheduled completion 1930; 1475/2030t, 17.5/8.8k, 1×4.7in, 8×21in tt. Four other 'R' class built.

77. *Stimson to Dawes*

State Department,
Washington,
25 July 1929

[Review of the present state of negotiations]

…

1. We have agreed that the conference shall be inaugurated as a consequence of the Kellogg-Briand Pact.
2. We have agreed on parity in combatant strength.
3. We have agreed that this parity should be separately by categories of capital ships, aircraft carriers, destroyers, cruisers and submarines.
4. We have agreed not to disturb the provisions of the Washington Treaty, thereby fixing ratios of capital ships and aircraft carriers but see paragraph (a) *infra* under second point.
5. We have agreed that a yardstick shall be adopted by which comparative value of the ships within the categories shall be measured.
6. The American Government agrees, subject to reaching agreement on other questions, to scrap excess destroyers and excess submarines down to the British level either at present or by 1936.
7. We agree with Mr MacDonald as to the principle of total abolition of submarines in international war. We realize with him that it may be impossible to secure consent of other nations, but we should make a mutual effort in this direction.

Second point – There are left the following points which we would like to have settled in principle as necessary to assure the success of a conference.

(a) We should like an agreement that all replacements of capital ship under the Washington Treaty shall be postponed until after 1936. This will give a holiday from major naval construction (capital ships and aircraft carriers) until after that date, and as at that time under that Treaty it will be necessary to revise the programme, that would be an appropriate date at which again to seek a further general revision of naval strength downward.

(b) Entirely in accord with the suggestion that we must have a yardstick, we consider it essential that we should agree upon certain principles upon which the yardstick shall be based before we can present a definitive series of figures. It is our suggestion that in the cruiser

category, for instance, we should take the new 10,000 ton, 8in gun cruiser as representing the standard, and that we should in measuring the relative combatant strength of other ships in the cruiser category, consider the elements of the yardstick at
Displacement
Age
Guns.

Our general view is that protection, speed, habitability, etc., are entirely relative to the other factors, and do not require special consideration. No doubt these factors may deserve different weight for other categories.

(c) We suggest that for cruisers we should adopt 20 years of age as the scrappable age, for destroyers 16 years, and for submarines 13 years.

(d) It is our impression that we should seek to equate our cruiser, destroyer and submarine tonnage as at 1936 instead of today, as this will better accommodate the British situation.

(e) If the principles of paragraphs (b), (c) and (d) can be adopted, we have resolved technical questions purely into the question as to the discounts from the standard that are to be allowed for age and gun caliber. …

(f) We are of course anxious to arrive at a situation which will allow us to reduce our authorized cruiser program, which would imply arriving at a theoretical tonnage in 1936 of somewhere from 200 to 250,000 tons. We have made some rough calculations as to our own and the British fleets, taking into account age and gun caliber and taking into account the number of ships that would be scrapped by 1936 under the 20 year agc limit, and taking into account the cessation of the three new 8in cruisers and the two projected 6in cruisers of the British Navy, and we believe that we could work it out quantitatively at about these limits.

(g) Our view is that if we can agree to these principles a preliminary conference should be had in London, representative of the Five Powers, seeking their adherence to such of these principles as concern them.

(h) Under the Washington Arms Treaty we are compelled tó hold a conference of the five naval powers by 1931. We could by mutual consent merge these conferences into the one proposed for December [1929] and avoid the necessity of holding two conferences on much the same subjects.

(i) A formal conference should be called in December [1929], following Mr MacDonald's visit. The result of that visit undoubtedly will be to further the building of good will and to pave the way for mutual understanding.

78. *Dawes and Gibson to Stimson*[1]

US Embassy,
London,
29 July 1929

...

Mr MacDonald, with the full agreement of the First Lord of the Admiralty, then stated that he felt a minimum of 45 6in cruisers is essential, due to the need for numbers of small vessels on distant stations and for long lines of communication and this made it difficult to comply with the idea of not replacing small cruisers which would become obsolete by 1936 under the 20 year age limit.

The following memorandum embodying his views as to how parity might be achieved in the cruiser class was then written by Mr MacDonald. He emphasised the fact that this was an entirely personal and tentative proposal which he would submit tonight to his Admiralty and upon which he would be glad to have your views.

General Agreement as to Cruisers

1. The British Government would be satisfied with a large cruiser strength of 15 and would agree to the American Government building up to 18.
2. The British Government would ask for an equivalent (to be measured by the yardstick) in 6in cruisers so that their total in that class should be 45.
3. As regards the *Hawkins* group of four cruisers, an agreement will be come to that for purposes of classification they shall, during their lifetime, be counted as among the 6in class and then replaced by ordinary 6in ships.[2] Consideration will be given to having this equation completed by 1936.
4. In order to arrive at parity the US may construct up to 10 6in ships.

Mr MacDonald made it clear that in the above memorandum it was his idea that the equivalent of 45 6in gun British cruisers would be constituted

[1]Hugh P. Gibson: leader of Delegation, Geneva 1927, & member 1930 Delegation.

[2]'Hawkins' class: 1918–25, 9800t, 30.5k, 7×7.5in, 4×4in, 4×21in tt; considerable modifications in 1930s.

by 10 additional American 6in gun cruisers to be constructed should we so desire them, the three additional American 10,000 ton cruisers and our 10 *Omaha* cruisers.

Also the Prime Minister kept in mind, it seems evident, the possible intentions of the other naval powers in laying down this need for 45 6in gun cruisers. Mr MacDonald stated that he would submit his proposals to the First Sea Lord tonight and that if any material modifications were suggested he would communicate them to me before his departure for Scotland on his vacation.[1]

The best possible spirit on the part of the British was exhibited in the conduct of the Conference. Save reserving the question of the replacements of small cruisers, no objection was made by them to the suggestion of abandoning all future new cruiser construction. Our readiness to support the movement for the suppression of submarines and our readiness to defer replacements of capital ships until 1936, when they agreed that an excellent opportunity would be afforded to make renewed efforts for more definite reduction, met with particular gratification on their part.

We wish also to call attention to the fact that the suggestion of our having preponderance in 10,000 ton cruisers came spontaneously from them, as did the suggestion that we be authorized, should we so desire, to build 10 additional 6in gun cruisers.

That reduction in all classes of ships was one of the ideas uppermost in the President's mind, we did not fail to point out and for that reason we urged that they give consideration as to how far they could go in refraining from replacing, as they became obsolete, 6in gun cruisers.

79. *Notes on the Cruiser Situation by the Director of Plans*[2]

1 August 1929

Question: If agreement is reached with the US alone, can we reduce our cruiser requirements from the number 15 8in and 45 smaller cruisers?
Answer: We are not in a position to suggest that our ultimate cruiser requirements should be less than this. Although agreement may be reached with the USA, we have to consider the other naval powers, Japan, France and Italy. Making every allowance for reductions on their part, which

[1]AoF Sir Charles Madden: brother-in-law of Jellicoe; Capt *Dreadnought* 1907; NS to FL 1908; 4SL 1910; R Adm 1911; Home F 1911–14; CoS to Jellicoe 1914; V Adm 1BS 1916–19; CinC Atl F 1919–22; FSL 30 July 1927–30 July 1930.

[2]DP: Capt R. M. Bellairs: DP 1929–31; RA ret 1932; British N Reprv, LN; ABC talks with US, Jan-March 1941. D-day planning 1944.

appear [not?] to be at all likely in any agreement, we require about 60 cruisers to meet the bare needs of our security.

It may be pointed out, however, that for the purposes of negotiating an agreement over a term of years it is perhaps unnecessary to insist on this number 60 since under a steady replacement programme of three cruisers a year we cannot have more than 50 effective cruisers in 1940, and by a suitable replacement timetable during the intervening period we can average that this number 50 is approximately the figure of our strength.

It is considered necessary, however, that the terms of any agreement should not prejudice our ultimate requirements of 60 cruisers and our right to increase our building programme to achieve this in emergency.

80. *Dawes to Stimson*

US Embassy,
London,
1 August 1929

[Enclosing letter to Dawes from MacDonald]

'…

The President and I are striving to do two things. He wants parity in strength with Great Britain and to this I heartily agree; we both in addition wish to reduce naval armaments. The combination of both gives us a specially difficult practical problem.

2. … I am in the ridiculous position therefore of appearing to be grudging in my negotiations because my country had not been assuming that yours was a potential enemy.

3. I am sure that the President, in the exercise of that fine understanding mind of his, will see that when, as a practical person, I have to face the question of the standard upon which parity is to be secured I must turn my thoughts from America and direct them to the rest of the world. These two predominant facts confront me: 1) There are three other naval powers armed very effectively and in a position to damage my country and the people for whose existence I am responsible.[1] 2) There are our dominions with their needs and their fears. I must take these things into account. If I did not my existence as Prime Minister would soon be [ended?] and no agreement which I should make with your President would be worth the paper upon which it was written. He and I would be pursuing a vain thing.

[1]Japan, France & Italy.

The standard upon which parity is to be based must therefore allow me to fulfil my obligations.
4. I am determined to make that standard lower than it is at present. Indeed I wish to begin a policy which will reduce it to zero by making nations secure by other means than armament. But obviously my ability to do so depends for the moment not upon my country and yours but upon agreements which in co-operation with each other we can persuade the other powers to make mutually.' …

81. *Stimson to Dawes*

State Department,
Washington,
2 August 1929

…

1. … Candidly we are doubtful that Great Britain's need is as great as he [MacDonald] seems to think and also we are doubtful of the necessity, if Great Britain has a fleet of small cruisers, of her even nearly matching the US's strength in 10,000 ton cruisers.

   …

4. …

   In paragraph three of his communication Mr MacDonald refers to three other naval Powers effectively armed to which he must give consideration besides the US.

   It is difficult for us to imagine such a political combination as he refers to and still more difficult to imagine that it will be balanced or made possible by the number of units of small cruisers that he is discussing.

   It does not seem likely that the addition of 12 small cruisers to Britain's existing fleet would affect the situation should he, in truth, find Great Britain surrounded by a host of enemies in 1934 when his fleet might begin to decrease in numbers.

   …

82. *Dawes to Stimson*

US Embassy,
London,
4 August 1929

[Enclosing copy of letter from Gibson]

'...

Our problem, fundamentally, is to discover some means of reducing the cruiser strength of Great Britain in cooperation with a man who, if its political practicability can be demonstrated to him, is honestly willing to carry it out. He is naturally cautious on account of the great responsibility resting upon him. I am nevertheless convinced that it will be possible, without endangering British security, to reduce British cruiser strength and that, by dealing directly with MacDonald, you and the President can give him this same conviction.

It will be the expectation of every political party in England that an agreement with us will be reached before the November meeting of Parliament. It is obvious that MacDonald realizes this pressure and it is unlikely that so auspicious a time will present itself again. For this reason I feel that this problem should be taken up directly and as soon as possible by the two leaders.'

83. *Dawes to Stimson*

US Embassy,
London,
9 August 1929

[Enclosing copy of letter from MacDonald]

'...

3 (a). The British Fleet is not one unit. If it were I could reduce [it] considerably. It is scattered into different and remote divisions each with functions to perform relating to peace and not to war conditions. I know that if war broke out concentration would naturally take place but that cannot be helped. I really cannot neglect peace duties in order to avoid the suspicion that war is in our minds all the time. Let me state what the cruiser disposition today is so that what I now say may be plain:

(1) With our two main fleets – the Atlantic and the Mediterranean – there are three 8in and 12 6in cruisers (in September there will be four and 11 respectively).

(2) On foreign stations (China and Australia) there are seven and 12 respectively.
(3) Two are at home on instructional duties.
(4) 14 are in reserve or undergoing large repairs.
(5) Four are in care and maintenance.

You will at once see how this division of the whole fleet necessitates the maintenance of figures higher than if the fleet operated as one unit.
(b) Put it another way. Australia, New Zealand and the numerous islands for which we are responsible in the southern Pacific, are policed by four cruisers in commission and two in reserve and remember these are the only resources we have in the event of civil trouble or lawlessness breaking out. India, Burma, the Malay Straits, Somaliland, Kenya, the Persian Gulf, the Indian Ocean islands are policed by three cruisers and a few sloops which can barely make one visit a year to necessary ports. When one visualizes what the function and necessary work of the cruisers are and when my high figures are apportioned to duties one begins to see the difficulty of a drastic reduction.
(c) The cruiser category for me is therefore only partly a fighting category and is to a considerable extent a police category. (That gives us a possible chance of an agreement if we could decide upon police units which, however, must be habitable in the tropics as I must consider the comforts of the men.)
4. I have been working at a scheme which would make British figures in 1936 the standard of parity. Then without replacement in the meanwhile we should have 15 8in and 34 6in ships, a total of 49. I hope you will see in the light of the above functions of cruisers that there is not much margin for reduction unless in the meantime by our united efforts we can make the world *feel* peace. But I must deal with today and it is quite impossible for me to think of figures now which are remote from today – say beyond 1936. I shall, however, steadily reduce as national security is found by other means than arms and I shall continue to work for that other security. *Whether it is possible to fix as a first resting place upon the 1936 position depends upon an international agreement.*
5. If your President would agree to the 1936 position as being a temporary maximum goal to be worked for I can see my way to meet him subject to the proviso I have made. That position is reached by the ordinary operations of scrapping but as I really feel the practicability of an absolute naval commitment as a *business* proposition I would propose to scrap each year one cruiser which I would not otherwise scrap and replace it by a scheme of building which would leave us with 50 cruisers and no more.

6. I ought to say that that will leave me in a bit of a fix between 1936 and 1940 as cruisers fall out in bunches during these years to a total of no less than 23 but again that would be a matter of arrangement in manipulation of building. That might at times appear to be an increase but of course the whole scheme would be published so that mischief makers might be disarmed.
7. I again press for the production of some sort of yardstick to let us see where we are in actual effective strength. Every textbook and naval report I have consulted in order to be prepared for these conversations show that the 8in cruisers are worth in the event of a fight almost an infinity of smaller craft and guns. You in your 8in ships have more guns than are in ours and so in your 'Omahas'. It is not profitable to talk of these ships as though their tons were of the same value. Let us know where we are. The constant reference to absolute tonnage in your recent messages stands in the way of a clear vision of either quantitative or qualitative negotiation. Your declaration at Geneva was very specific upon this point.
8. I emphasize the obligations placed upon me by my geographical position which the US does not have to bear.'

84. *The Assistant Secretary of the Admiralty to the Under Secretary of State, Foreign Office*[1]

26 August 1929

2. My Lords concur with Mr Secretary Henderson that this [AMCs] is hardly a practical question at the present time.[2] They consider that the old right of arming merchant vessels for defence is too valuable to be abandoned in return for Sir E. Howard's condition, namely, that 'All Naval Powers would forego the right to make use of submarines in a naval blockade'.[3] This would certainly not be sufficient *quid pro quo*.

In addition we require to arm merchant ships for other purposes.

…

5. With regard to Sir E. Howard's suggestions in the same Despatch [not reproduced] concerning the defence arrangements in the West Indies, it was only as recently as 24 July last that the First Lord of the Admiralty repeated the declaration made by Sir Austen Chamberlain on 8 February

[1]Alex Hunt to R.L. Craigie.

[2]Arthur Henderson (1863–1935): Lab MP; Pres, Bd of Educ 1915–16; War Cab 1916–17; HS 1924; FS 1929–31; Pres, World Disarmament Conf 1932–5.

[3]Sir Esmé Howard (1863–1939): FO 1885–92; S Af War; Amb, Spain 1919–24; Amb, US 1924–30; Baron Penrith 1930.

1928, that 'preparation for a war with the US has never been and never will be the basis of our policy in anything'.

If an assurance as suggested by Sir E. Howard were desirable this declaration of the policy of HM Government should be amply sufficient. A unilateral declaration or gesture towards the US in regard to our naval bases in the Western Atlantic, it is considered, should not be entertained. These bases are necessary to the navy in such a war as might arise as a consequence of our Locarno commitments, and we should therefore give no one-sided undertaking to a foreign power as to their defence arrangements.[1]

My Lords consider that we cannot entertain any limitation of our sovereign rights in the West Indies islands.

85. *Admiral William Veazie Pratt, US Navy, to Maurice Gertlin*[2]

C-in-C,
US Fleet,
27 August 1929

… in 1916 matters began to look bad for the Allies, and it behoved the US to take heed to be in a position to defend herself, in case the necessity arose. This, and not the Challenge to British Naval Supremacy, was the reason why this program was planned.

… I should not call his [President Woodrow Wilson's] viewpoint anti-British, but I do think it was pro American with no hyphen in it. [He concluded] that the only way to make America respected … was to possess a Navy sufficiently strong to have its rights and its opinions regarded.

… [The 5: 5: 3 ratio was] aggressive towards none and a just definition of America's position, one which gives her a reasonable position of preparedness in case of war, and makes her status as a neutral respected.

They [naval officers] realize as well as others that war between England and America would be a crime leading perhaps to world revolution, which no thinking men of either country would permit, but understanding each other better than outsiders understand us, we do not worry so much about hostility even if we do not always agree in details, and we are all in accord that there is too much talk on the subject from the unresponsible.

[1]Locarno Treaty: 7 Dec 1925: non-aggression pact – France, Belgium, Germany, guaranteed by Italy & UK.

[2]Gertlin was Literary Editor, *Portland Evening News*. Probably Portland, Me., as Pratt came from nearby.

86. *Stimson to Dawes*

State Department,
Washington,
28 August 1929

…
11. The cruiser strength of the British [Empire] should be reduced [by] 31 December 1936 to 50 units which will have a total displacement tonnage not to exceed standard tons 330,000. Fifteen of these units shall be 8in cruisers aggregating 146,800 standard tons, four shall be 7.5in gun cruisers aggregating 39,426 tons and 31 are to be 6in gun cruisers aggregating 143,774 tons of which not more than seven all with 6in guns are to be constructed before 1936.
12. Cruiser strength of the US is to be brought to parity with the cruiser strength of Great Britain as stated above, taking into account the effect upon the navies of both of the elements of displacement, and guns as evaluated by the yardstick, and age. …

87. *First Sea Lord to First Lord*[1]

5 September 1929

I suggest that an authoritative statement be made that John Bull is not selling up the Empire just yet.

88. *General Board: Senior Member Present to Secretary of the Navy*[2]

11 September 1929

Further Proposals on Naval Disarmament

…
3. The General Board now understands:
(a) That on 31 December 1936 the British cruiser category will consist of 50 units totalling 339,000 tons and no more. Also that these 50 units will be as follows:

[1]Albert V. Alexander (1885–1965): local govt; Capt, Artists' Rifles WW I; lay preacher, leader in co-op & union movts; Lab MP, Hillsborough, Sheffield, 1922–31, 1935–50; Parl Sec, Bd of Trade 1924; FL 1929–31 & May 1940–Dec 1946; M Defence 1946; Chllr, Duchy of Lancaster & Visct 1950; Lab leader, Lords 1955; Earl 1963.
[2]SMP: the CNO, Adm Charles F. Hughes.

13	10,000 ton 8in cruisers	130,000	standard	tons
2	8,400 ton 8in cruisers[1]	16,800	"	"
14	6,500 ton 6in cruisers (new replacements)[2]	91,000	"	"
21	older 6in cruisers	101,200	"	"
50	Units	339,000	"	"

(b) That the following cruisers will be scrapped by 31 December 1936:

Name	Std Tons	Year Completed
Vindictive	9,996	1918
Hawkins	9,800	1919
Frobisher	9,860	1924
Effingham	9,770	1925[3]
Dartmouth	4,860	1911
Lowestoft	5,120	1914
Birmingham	5,120	1914
Cleopatra	3,895	1915
Carysfort	3,895	1915
Comus	3,895	1915
Calliope	3,920	1915
Champion	3,920	1915
Castor	3,920	1915
Brisbane	5,120	1916
Constance	3,920	1916
Canterbury	3,920	1916
Cambrian	3,920	1916
Centaur	4,120	1916
Concord	4,120	1916
Caradoc	4,180	1917
Calypso	4,180	1917
Caledon	4,180	1917[4]
Total	115,631	

(c) That the *Conquest* and *Yarmouth*, now on the sale list, are considered already disposed of.[5]

[1]*Exeter, York*: 1931, 8400t, 32k, 6×8in, 4×4in.
[2]Probably the new 'Leander' class.
[3]The first four constitute 'Hawkins' class.
[4]*Dartmouth*: 1910, 5250t, 8×6in; BU 1930.
Lowestoft, Birmingham: 1913, 5440t, 9×6in, 1×3in; BU 1931.
Brisbane: RAN; 1915, 6,000t, 8×6in: BU 1936.
'C' series: 1914–17, 3750–4870t, 2–5×6in, 8×4in, 2×3in; BU 1930–6.
[5]*Conquest*: 1915, 3750t, 2×6in, 8×4in: BU 1930.
Yarmouth: 1911, 5250t, 8×6in: BU 1929.

(d) That the following constitute the 21 older 6in cruisers to be retained:

Name	*Tonnage*	*Year Completed*
Cardiff	4,290	1917
Curlew	4,290	1917
Ceres	4,290	1917
Danae	4,850	1918
Dauntless	4,850	1918
Dragon	4,850	1918
Carlisle	4,200	1918
Coventry	4,290	1918
Curacoa	4,290	1918
Delhi	4,850	1919
Cairo	4,200	1919
Calcutta	4,200	1919
Colombo	4,200	1919
Dunedin	4,850	1919
Durban	4,850	1921
Adelaide	5,100	1922
Diomede	4,850	1922
Despatch	4,850	1922
Capetown	4,200	1922
Enterprise	7,580	1926
Emerald	7,550	1926[1]
Total	101,480	

(e) That on 31 December 1936 the foregoing 339,000 standard tons is to be the strength in the British cruiser category, composed as outlined in sub-paragraph (a) of this paragraph.

4. The Prime Minister has requested a statement of the concrete composition of the American cruiser category on 31 December 1936, which we consider would achieve parity.

...

17. The General Board still adheres to its opinion:

(a) That limitation should be based upon total tonnage in categories with full freedom for each signatory power as to size of units and caliber of guns within the restrictions laid down by the Washington Treaty.

[1] 'C' series: 1917–18, 4,120–4,200t, 29k, 5×6in, 2×3in, 8×21in tt. Several were converted to AA cruisers in mid-1930s.

'D' class: 1918–22, 4850t, 29k, 5–6×6in, 3×4in, 12×21in tt.

'E' class, 1926, 7550t, 32k, 7×6in, 3×4in, 16×21in tt.

Adelaide: RAN; 1918, 5440t, 9×6in, 3×4in.

(b) That categories should not be divided into separate classes as to unit size and caliber of guns.
(c) That 8in gun cruisers are best suited to the needs of the US.
(d) That in any agreement provision should be made that no replacement for vessels whose age limit expires after 31 December 1936 should be laid down prior to that date.

18. The General Board is further of the opinion that if all of these principles be included in any agreement that during the period of such an agreement the US may, in a spirit of concession, agree.
(a) To accept the 339,000 standard tons proposed by the Prime Minister as the maximum tonnage in the cruiser category for the US and the British Empire.
(b) To the proposal by the Prime Minister to scrap the four *Hawkins* 7.5in gun cruisers and three 6in gun cruisers, that will be less than 20 years of age by 31 December 1936, prior to that date and to replace them by new 6in gun cruisers.
(c) Not to exercise the freedom of choice of unit size and gun caliber and to agree to build not more than 210,000 standard tons of 10,000 ton 8in units and agree to utilize the remaining available tonnage, namely, 58,500 standard tons, in building not more than eight cruisers armed with guns not exceeding 6in in caliber.
…
21. In order that substantial parity between the US and the British Empire may be achieved by 31 December 1936, the General Board recommends as follows:
(a) That the Prime Minister's proposal of 339,000 standard tons as a standard of parity in the cruiser category to be achieved by 31 December 1936 be accepted.
(b) That composition of the cruiser category of the British Empire on 31 December 1936, as outlined by the Prime Minister, be agreed to.
…
26. The General Board, in an earnest endeavour to reach an agreement on the basis of the proposed British cruiser category of 339,000 standard tons as of 31 December 1936, is willing for this purpose to accept as representing parity with that category on that date a cruiser category of the US consisting of:

	Standard Tons
10,000 ton, 8in gun cruisers	210,000
7,050 ton, 6in gun cruisers ('Omaha' class)	70,500
Five new 6in gun cruisers	*c*.35,000
Total	*c*.315,500 standard tons.

89. *General Board: Senior Member Present to Secretary of the Navy*[1]

11 September 1929

. . .

16. The General Board is of the opinion that this novel application of Washington Treaty ratios to numbers instead of to category tonnage is inconsistent with the American position as set forth in para. 5 above [not reproduced] and is one to which the US cannot consistently subscribe.

. . .

19. The General Board is of the opinion, taking into consideration all of the elements of sea power, including the very important ones of bases and fast merchant ships readily convertible into auxiliary cruisers, in both of which the British Empire possesses an enormous preponderance over the US, that the needs of the US during the terms of this agreement demand a minimum of 21 10,000 ton, 8in gun cruisers and no agreement contemplating a lesser number of 10,000 ton, 8in gun cruisers should be considered.

20. Attention is invited to the fact that with the tonnage available to the US there could be built 27 8in gun cruisers aggregating 268,500 tons, which, with the 10 6in gun cruisers of the 'Omaha' class aggregating 70,500 tons, would make a grand total in the cruiser category of 339,000 tons.

21. In order that substantial parity between the US and the British Empire may be achieved by 31 December 1936, the General Board recommends as follows:

. . .

(d) That the yardstick be not used.

(e) The American position has been and the General Board has consistently maintained:

(1) That no question of limitation can be properly solved except on the basis of total tonnage in each category, and

(2) That in the cruiser category there can be complete freedom as to the size and armament of units except as limited by the Washington Treaty.

[1]SMP: probably CNO, Adm Hughes.

90. *MacDonald to the First Lord*

n.d., *c.* September 1929

I discussed generally the Naval Programme with the Chancellor yesterday.[1] We shall not get it through especially the replacement part. I shall go to America with it as it is and use it as a working basis and discuss the question with the President without agreeing to any modification. But here you will have to examine with the Cabinet Committee:

1. the scrapping proposals.
2. the 6,500 [ton] 6in [gun cruiser] number with a view to economy. I also find that statements made at Washington and Geneva have been found and will be used[,] the argument being that if under certain conditions the Admiralty on a certain fighting strength assumed security they must, if the conditions are restored, return to lower figures. I have replied that that will be the business of the Five Power Conference and that we are discussing with the USA existing conditions. This means, however, an offer of great reduction at the Five Power Conference and a drastic cut in Naval Estimates. One saving we can effect is not to build in anticipation of the shortage and scrapping after 1936 but leave that for later consideration. The sooner this is faced the better, so the Cabinet Committee will work in my absence and be ready to report to me what it proposes when I return.

91. *Note by the Director of Plans on the General Trend of conversations to date between the Prime Minister and Mr Hoover*[2]

20 September 1929

...

It was made clear to us that parity, in order to be understood by the public of the USA, must be expressed in terms of total tonnage showing no great difference between the nations, and that the yardstick could only be considered as equating the small differences which exist between the two total tonnages. A yardstick for the use of explaining the small difference was all it was considered possible for public opinion in the USA to accept.

...

[1]Philip Snowden (1864–1937): Lab MP; CEx 1924 & 1929–31; LPS 1931–2; Visct 1932.

[2]DP: Capt Bellairs.

… the difference between us on this yardstick question is that whereas we are prepared to consider, for the sake of argument, that 10,000 tons of 8in is equivalent to 21,800 tons of 6in, the USA consider that 10,000 tons of 8in is equivalent to 13,800 tons of 6in. The difference between us is therefore large.

…

We know that Japan intends to claim 70% of the 8in tonnage of the strongest naval power. If the USA insist on the figure of 21 8in ships this means that Japan will claim 147,000 tons of 8in ships which would enable them to build four more 8in ships of the larger size, making 16 8in ships in all. This would compare with our number [of] 15. Even if we could insist on Japan being limited to the 5: 3 ration of the Washington Treaty she would still, on the USA figures, be in a position to claim 126,000 tons of 8in cruisers, enabling her to build at least one more, making 13 in all. We are not able to come to any agreement which gives Japan more than her present 8in ships so long as we are limited to 15 of this class. If Japan is limited to 12 ships we feel that it is impossible to frame any agreement which gives the USA more than 18 ships.

The reply of Mr Hoover to this difficulty of the Prime Minister is to ask the Prime Minister if he cannot reduce the tonnage figure for 1936 from 339,000 tons to 300,000 tons. Our position in this respect is that we have reached bed-rock in the figure of 339,000 tons.

92. *Hankey: Diary*

7 October 1929

… The gist was that Hoover had prepared a draft communiqué regarding the conversation, … which *inter alia* was to include a statement to the effect that the Americans agreed that the bases in the West Indies were not a threat to them; we were to announce that we would not increase them materially, while they were to undertake to have no bases in the eastern hemisphere. In addition, and even more important, they were to announce conversations were to begin on the question of belligerent rights – or 'rights and immunities at sea' as they were termed – and, most important of all, Hoover was, in the communiqué, to express the hope that foodstuffs would, as the result of the conversations, be excluded from the scope of blockade, food ships being treated like hospital ships.

93. *Hankey: Diary*

8 October 1929

10.00. Meeting of COS who prepared a telegram to the Prime Minister asking him not to accept the West Indies proposal, as our garrisons, for financial reasons, were reduced to a nucleus, and, if the international situation changed, we might, quite irrespective of the Americans, want to put them back. Also deprecating the raising of belligerent rights, and urging strongly that the foodstuffs proposal should not be raised.

94. *General Board Memorandum*

8 October 1929

British Naval Bases in the Western Hemisphere

1. The General Board has been asked if it could subscribe to the following statement:
'With the view to reducing fear and the friction that comes from fear, we have obtained the opinion of our General Board of the Navy, that the existing military and naval bases of Great Britain in the Western Hemisphere are not in a condition to be a menace to the US.'
2. The General Board cannot subscribe to the foregoing statement.
3. The General Board is of the opinion:
(a) That the military value of military and naval stations lies in their position and natural physical characteristics rather than in the military condition and state of development.
(b) That the present military condition and state of development of the existing military and naval stations of Great Britain in the Western Hemisphere minimize but cannot wholly eliminate the menace inherent in their position and natural physical characteristics.
(c) That so long as these stations remain in their present condition they are not an appreciable menace to the US.

95. *Hankey: Diary*

17 October 1929

... Then Baldwin's Government was defeated; MacDonald came into office and at once began his conversations with General Dawes with a view to a naval disarmament agreement. ... We were all very astonished and I was very shocked when we learned that the whole subject [belligerent rights] [was discussed] at MacDonald's Sunday conversation at Hoover's lumber camp.[1]

96. *Naval Attaché to the Chargé d'Affaires*[2]

28 November 1929

...

The *New York World* says that 'apart from Senator Reed of Missouri, there is not, so far as we know, anybody in America who takes seriously the British Naval Bases at Bermuda and Jamaica, or regards them as a threat actually or potentially against the security of the US.[3] ... The proposal to dismantle them is regarded as a gesture, but the value of this gesture could never have been more sentimental, and the decision of Great Britain not to make the gesture has no bearing whatsoever on Anglo-American relations.' The *World* then goes on to say that 'the striking thing about the British Military position in this hemisphere is not that there are trifling defences at Bermuda and Jamaica, but that there are no defences at all in most of the British possessions. ... No better evidence could be adduced of the completeness with which successive British Governments have ignored the possibility of war with the US in arranging their naval and military policy in this hemisphere.'

The *New York Herald-Tribune*, a 'Big Navy organ', takes a different view. It ignores all references to the defence arrangements of these bases, but points out the value of naval bases in general for the repair and refuelling of naval forces, and how the British West Atlantic bases have a distinct value to Great Britain. It calls attention to the amount of British freight passing through the Panama Canal, which, in American ships, is two times as much as carried in American ships elsewhere, and regretfully points out that America has no bases in the Eastern Atlantic or on the Suez route corresponding to Great Britain's bases on the Panama route. It ends up by saying that 'everyone should realise that the Conference starts with a limited object – the attainment of equality in auxiliary vessels – but does not attack the broad question of equality in total manpower'.

The view of the *Herald-Tribune* is undoubtedly that of the Navy Department, which was put forward so forcibly at Geneva in 1927, the

[1]Camp Rapidan, Md.

[2]NA, Washington: Capt J. S. M. Ritchie (1884–1955): ent RN 1899; Capt 1923; NA, Washington 1928–31; Dir Trng 1931–3; *Furious* 1933–5; R Adm & ret 1935; Cdre RNR 1939; FOIC Liverpool 1941–4; FO Norway 1945.

Chargé: Ronald I. Campbell (1890–1983): FO 1914; Paris, Cairo; FO 1923–7; Washington; Belgium; Washington 1941–5; Asst U Sec 1945; Amb, Egypt 1946–50.

[3]Sen J. Reed : Dem Senr, Mo., 1911–29.

absence of bases being their main argument for the large and offensive type of Cruiser as opposed to the smaller type armed with 6in guns.

Moreover, the Big Navyites (as I have heard one Admiral say more than once) believe that Naval bases should be taken into consideration in measuring parity. On the other hand, the Navy Department do not seriously consider the British Naval bases and merchant marine in the Atlantic in any way a menace to the US, and it believed that they would not favour any gesture on the part of Great Britain towards dismantling the present defences, as this might create an awkward precedent.

The point of view of the *New York World*, I venture to suggest, is probably that taken by the majority of instructed opinion in the country. …

97. *Rear Admiral William A. Moffett, US Navy, to the Secretary of the Navy*[1]

4 December 1929

…

11. … considering total tonnage and total number of flight decks the relative air strength of the navies of Great Britain and the US would appear somewhat as follows:

Great Britain

Ship	Tonnage	Aircraft	Remarks
Argus	14,450	40	Experimental
Hermes	10,850	40	"
Eagle	22,600	52	"
Furious	22,450	72	"
Courageous	18,600	72	
Glorious	18,600	72	Commissioning Feb 1930
Totals: 6	107,330	348[2]	

[1]R Adm W. A. Moffett, US Navy (1869–1933): USNA 1890; Spanish War 1898; Capt 1917; trng cmd 1914–18; *Mississippi* 1918–20; Dir N Aviation 1921; R Adm & Chief, Bur Aeronautics 1921–33; lost with airship *Akron*, 4 April 1933.

[2]*Argus*: 1918, 14450t, 20k, 20 aircraft, 6×4in.

Hermes: 1923, 10,850t, 25k, 12 aircraft, 6×5.5in; sunk, Ceylon, 9 April 1942, Japanese aircraft.

Eagle: 1923, 22,000t, 24k, 21 aircraft, 9×6in, 4×4in; sunk, Med, *U73*, 11 Aug 1942.

Furious: 1917–18, 22,450t, 31k, 33 aircraft, 12×4in.

Courageous, *Glorious*: 1924–30, 22,500t, 30k, 48 aircraft, 16×4.7in; *Courageous* sunk, *U29*, Irish Sea, 17 Sept 1939; *Glorious* sunk, off Narvik, 9 June 1940, by German battlecruisers.

All except *Hermes* were conversions.

US			
Langley	12,700	36	Experimental
Saratoga	33,000	90	
Lexington	33,000	90	
Totals: 3	78,700	216	

Based on comparative dimensions of flight decks and the number of planes which it is estimated these decks are capable of supporting.

12. On a basis of total plane operating capacity the above figures place the ratio between Great Britain and the US at 1.61 to 1.00. Moreover since Great Britain possesses six carrier decks to our three, this disparity is, in effect, much greater since mobility and flexibility are greatly superior.

...

14. Referring to the table in paragraph 11 above, we note that Great Britain has four experimental carriers totalling 70,350 tons while the US has only one of 12,700 tons. Great Britain can, therefore, replace a total of 97,800 tons of the total 135,000 tons allowed while we can replace but 69,000 tons. If each country were to expend this remaining tonnage in carriers of 13,800 tons approximate size, each capable of carrying 75 planes, Great Britain could build seven to our five. The totals would then be:

Great Britain: nine carriers, 669 planes, ratio 1.20.

US: seven carriers, 555 planes, ratio 1.00.

15. Thus in addition to be able to base on carriers one-fifth more planes than we [can], Great Britain would have the added great advantage of nine decks to our seven, giving greater mobility and flexibility. This constitutes a very real handicap in a dual sense, one we cannot hope to overcome under present Treaty limitations.

16. It is pertinent here to invite attention to the potential value of merchant vessels for conversion to carriers in time of war. It is entirely feasible and permissible after war has begun, to fit landing decks on top of merchantmen which will permit very effective operation of airplanes of great potential striking power and defensive ability. It is well known that Great Britain has an immense superiority in ships of this category.

17. In the light of the foregoing, it is of paramount importance that steps be taken in the forthcoming Armament Conference to remove this permanent handicap placed upon us and the only method of accomplishing this end seems to consist of finding some way of replacing the tonnage embodied in the *Lexington* and *Saratoga* by smaller units prior to the 20 year limit.

18. A practical method of accomplishing the above would be to have these two vessels placed in the experimental category. Such line of thought

is based on a very reasonable premise because, in fact, these ships were, on 12 November 1921, much more experimental than those of Great Britain. They were of an experimental nature even as battlecruisers; they were doubly so as converted carriers.

19. The support of Japan in such a step, could in all probability be obtained. Two of her carriers, the *Kaga* and *Akagi*, were converted to carriers under similar conditions to our *Lexington* and *Saratoga* and although the tonnage as carriers, is not so great, it is possible that that they would desire it in smaller units and would look on such a proposition with favour.[1]

…

21. Great Britain has in carrier based planes a potential superiority of 152 planes over us. While true that she has not had this superiority of planes actually assigned to carriers at present, the carrier decks necessary to support [it] do exist and the planes could be so based at very short notice. To obtain parity, we must have permission to replace the *Lexington* and *Saratoga* tonnage prior to the 20 years minimum now set.

98. *Minutes of the British Commonwealth Delegation*

3 January 1930

Cruisers

Admiral of the Fleet Earl Jellicoe: … Personally, I cannot agree that a total of 50 cruisers … is sufficient for the security of our sea communications, which, as everyone is well aware, are of vital importance to the *life* of the people in the British Isles and the prosperity of the people in the whole Empire. Only as recently as 1927 the British Admiralty stated that the *least* number of cruisers which could possibly meet our requirements was a total of 70. Nothing has occurred since that date to render our sea communications more secure, except the signing of the Pact of Paris. As to this in French opinion at any rate the Pact does not give that sense of security needed by France, because its rational application has not yet been organised, and it does not settle all the questions of peaceful procedure, and of mutual assistance against an aggressor.

Even in the US there are differences of opinion in regard to the Pact, and to the ordinary mind the insistence of the US on Parity with the British

[1]*Kaga*: 1928, 26,900t, 27.5k, 60 aircraft, 10×8in, 12×4.7in; sunk Midway 4 June 1942.
Akagi: 1927, 26,900t, 60 aircraft, 10×8in, 12×4.7in; sunk Midway 5 June 1942.
Both carriers were conversions from capital ships.

Empire can only be interpreted as due to a feeling of suspicion and distrust.

A glance, too, at the present international situation does not give a real sense of security or indicate that human nature has changed.

99. *General Board: Senior Member Present to Secretary of the Navy*[1]

3 January 1930

Parity in Naval Air Strength

2. In the basis letter the Chief of the Bureau of Aeronautics had expressed the following opinions:

(a) that two 18,500 ton carriers have several advantages over one 33,000 ton carrier,

(b) that the custom of measuring the striking power of ships in terms of tonnage when applied to carriers for the purpose of judging relative air strength is dangerously misleading,

(c) that for this purpose flight deck area is the most important factor,

(d) that comparison of the effective air strength on a basis of total carrier tonnage alone will lead to false conclusions unless numbers of flight decks be also considered.

(e) that it is of paramount importance in the forthcoming Reduction and Limitation of Armament Conference to remove the permanent handicap placed upon us due to the large size of the *Saratoga* and *Lexington* by transferring these carriers to the experimental class, thus permitting replacement of their aggregate tonnage by a greater number of carriers of smaller size prior to the expiration of the 20 year age limit.

…

6. The advantages of utilising part of our carrier tonnage in building carriers of medium or small size are evident. Some of the advantages are highly important especially the increase in number of units. On the other hand the great size and high speed of the *Saratoga* and *Lexington* possess distinct advantages which are essential. However, an adequate number of carriers must be built.

7. The terms of the Washington Treaty, Articles VIII and IX, are explicit and there does not appear any practical or logical way of placing the

[1]SMP: R Adm Andrew T. Long, US Navy (1866–1946): USNA 1887; Capt 1913; *Connecticut* 1916–18; *Nevada* 1918–19, S Ireland; Actg RA & NA, Paris 1919; RA & cdr, Bat Div 4, Atl F 1920; DNI 1920–1; CoS, Atl F 1921–2; Actg VA & Cdr, US N Forces, Eur 1922–3; chief, Bu Nav 1923–4; Gen Bd 1924–30; ret 1930.

Saratoga and *Lexington* in the experimental class unless that Treaty be specifically modified.
8. If at the forthcoming London Conference a proposal should be made to reduce the carrier limitation below 135,000 tons, the General Board is of the opinion that the US should insist that the *Saratoga* and *Lexington* be placed in the experimental class as a necessary provision for agreement. The *Saratoga* and *Lexington* were converted from battle cruisers under the terms of the Washington Treaty which left available tonnage for the construction of an adequate number of additional carriers. Any reduction of total carrier tonnage below 135,000 tons would be to the serious disadvantage of the US. The present handicap in numbers of carriers due to the large size of the *Saratoga* and *Lexington* would then be relatively increased.
9. Reduction of total carrier tonnage will operate to a disadvantage greater to the US than to any foreign country. The US must conduct any naval war at greater distance from home than would be the case of other Powers signatory to the Washington Treaty.

100. *General Board Memorandum*

6 January 1930

Battleships

1. If modification of the terms of the Washington Treaty relating to capital ships be undertaken, it appears highly desirable, from a standpoint of equity and economy, that the ultimate number of capital ships prescribed by the Treaty be arrived at immediately, namely, US – 15; Great Britain – 15; and Japan – 9.
2. This would require the US to scrap now three ships (*Florida, Utah* and *Wyoming*); Great Britain to scrap now five ships (*Iron Duke*, *Marlborough*, *Emperor of India*, *Benbow* and *Tiger*); and Japan now to scrap one ship (*Kongo*).[1] After scrapping the ships mentioned, the resulting capital ship tonnages would be:

US	462,500 tons.
Great Britain	474,750 tons
Japan	266,070 tons.

[1] *Florida, Utah, Wyoming*: 1909–11.
Iron Duke, Marlborough, Emperor of India, Benbow: 1911–12.
Tiger: 1913.
Kongo: 1912.

3. While the capital ship tonnages retained in 1931 are in approximate accord with the Washington Treaty ratios, both the US and Japan are at a disadvantage with regard to Great Britain, not only as regards actual tonnage but also because neither the US nor Japan possess a capital ship of post-Treaty design, whereas Great Britain has two ships (*Rodney* and *Nelson*) laid down and completed since the Washington Treaty was signed.
4. Therefore, to offset the *Rodney* and *Nelson*, it would appear just, fair and necessary that the US now lay down two ships and that Japan now lay down one ship, these three ships to be completed in 1934, at which time the US should scrap the *Arkansas* and *Texas*, and Japan should scrap the *Hiyei*.[1]

Results

5. On 31 December 1934 the capital ship tonnages in standard tons would thus be:

US	479,400 tons
Great Britain	474,750 tons
Japan	274,740 tons.

US reduces from	18	to	15 ships.
Great Britain	20	to	15 ships
Japan	10	to	9 ships,

thus saving the cost of maintenance.
6. Beginning with 1935, and until 1947, the US would replace one ship each year; Great Britain would replace one ship each year except for the year 1944, in which year Great Britain would replace two ships; Japan would replace one ship each year, except for the years 1938, 1940, 1942, 1944 and 1946, during which years no replacements would be made by Japan.
7. Any reduction in the size of battleships is not acceptable.
8. No battleship holiday is acceptable until approximate parity is attained by elimination of the handicap of the *Rodney* and *Nelson*, as outlined in paragraph 4.

[1]*Arkansas*, *Texas*: 1911–12.
Hiyei: 1912.

101. *First Lord: Speech at Sheffield*

10 January 1930

… After the Washington Conference, at which the question of cruiser strength was only to a limited extent touched upon, the Board of Admiralty advised the Government of the day of their view of the needs of the British Empire in cruiser strength. The number, which is based on the needs of the defence of our world-wide and vital sea communications, was fixed at 70. That was the number for which we held out at Geneva. That is the number which, had conditions remained the same, would be our requirement today. But today we have to take account of a new situation which has arisen through the signing of the Pact of Paris outlawing war by most of the nations of the world, including all the major Naval Powers – not only those who are members of the League of Nations, but also by the USA, who by their authorship of this pact took their second great step in the practical solution of the world's need for assured peace.

With such powerful support for peace we feel justified in looking forward to a period in which armed conflict need not be expected. The Board of Admiralty, therefore, having regard to all the circumstances of today, and especially the Pact of Paris, are prepared to agree to 50 cruisers as the minimum needs of the Empire up to the next date for conference and revision, which we expect will be near 1936. …

We hope that international peace may be permanent, and that a further agreement in 1936 will confirm and extend the present agreement, but if unhappily the international horizon should become in the future less unclouded than it is today it would be open to the Board of Admiralty to review their position and make further proposals to HMG.

102. *Memorandum by the Chief of Naval Staff*[1]

14 January 1930

The Basis of British Naval Strategy

…

2. Our special problems of defence arise from the unique British conditions of the British Empire: its world-wide distribution, the fact that all parts of it are to a greater or lesser extent dependent upon communications by sea for their well-being or in some instances for their very existence,

[1]Adm Madden.

and that in the last resort it is on the transport of adequate forces by sea that the Empire relies to resist aggression and ensure the security of our interests and integrity of our territory. Thus it is that the security of sea passage to and from all parts of the Empire forms the basis and foundation of our system of Imperial Defence, without which all other measures of defence can be of little avail.

...

38. The maximum figure of 10,000 tons with 8in guns was accepted at the Washington Conference and became the standard for further large cruiser construction. The USA wishes to build this type, though her previous type of cruiser was only of 7050 tons, with 6in guns. The reasons she gave at Geneva [1927] were that (i) the gun must be of the maximum size of 8in in order to meet a supposed menace from our greater merchant fleet, and in order that their cruisers might never be outgunned by an enemy cruiser, and (ii) the ship must be of the maximum size of 10,000 tons so that their cruisers can operate at great distances and in order to counterbalance their lack of overseas bases. The reply to (i) was that no merchantman could stand up to a modern 6in cruiser, and that, for the sake of reduction in the burden of armaments, we are willing to build smaller type cruisers and feel that the USA could do likewise, and as to (ii), that, if a 6in gun is agreed to, a similar (or greater) radius of action to the 10,000 ton type can be obtained on a smaller individual tonnage. Furthermore, there is a distinct tactical use for a smaller type with 6in guns operating with the Battle Fleet.

...

40. Repeated investigations carried out and laid before successive Governments and Imperial Conferences have established the number of 70 cruisers as the minimum necessary for our full defensive requirements. This number 70 is based on the necessity for defending our vital sea communications in all parts of the world, the USA not being taken into account as a possible enemy.

In general this number 70 for security in the East provides:

25 cruisers for work with the Battle Fleet, which is considered by the Admiralty a minimum for the necessary strategical and tactical functions.

25 cruisers are required on the vital lines of communication stretched across the Indian Ocean and including the Persian Gulf and the Western Pacific. The lessons of the late war show our vulnerability in this area even from a Power so badly situated geographically as Germany.

10 cruisers are allotted to prevent our Home and Mediterranean waters being entirely denuded.

10 cruisers remain to cover Australia, South Africa, New Zealand, Canada and the South Atlantic and the Eastern Pacific.

For security in the West, the distribution above has to be modified. When it is realised that the protection of British food supplies along the Atlantic routes, on the flank of a possible enemy, may involve on any one day over 30 convoys being at sea, not including arrangements for the Mediterranean and North Sea, and when it is remembered that at any one time about 25% of the 35 trade route cruisers will be refitting or refuelling, the number 70, after provision has been made for the Battle Fleet requirements, cannot be considered as anything but a minimum figure.

41. The Naval Staff do not recede from the position that 70 represent the minimum for our full defence requirements, without taking the USA into our calculations. Under international conditions today, however, a number of 50 cruisers has been accepted for a strictly limited period, provided adequate limitations of projected building programmes are made by other Powers, and provided that in our number there is a proper provision of new construction suitable for extended operations. That is, they must be comparable to the types being built by other Powers, they must be capable of defeating any armed merchantmen or raider, they must have sufficient radius of action to carry out their tasks and must be habitable in all climes.

The majority of British cruisers were built in the war specifically for North Sea work and have not the characteristics indicated above. Thirty-four of these will become obsolete and worn out during the course of the next 10 years, and a yearly building programme of approximately three each year will be necessary to make provision for a number of 50 at the end of the 10 year period.

...

45. Bricfly, an acccptancc of 325,000 tons of cruiser tonnage would result in our building an inferior type of 6in cruiser to those which are afloat and will be built by other Powers. Expenditure on such ships would be inefficient and entail an uneconomic use of our money.

Further, after 1936 the total tonnage available for replacements will be comparatively low, due to the small size of the old cruisers. Consequently, it will not be possible to build the larger type of 6in cruiser if the numbers are to be maintained. For this reason, a tonnage of 339,000, which will enable the British Empire to build the required number of larger 6in cruisers before the replacement programme of small cruisers after 1936 is commenced, is essential.

46. The Admiralty have accepted a grave responsibility in agreeing to a reduction in the number of cruisers from 70 to 50, and should not be pressed to accept so low a tonnage that these ships will be inefficient.

103. *Memorandum by Rear Admiral Hilary P. Jones*

London,
5 February 1930

As adviser to the American Delegation I feel compelled to express an opinion in opposition to the Tentative Plan of the American Delegation of 6 February 1930 in regard to the proper cruiser allotment for the US on p.1.[1] In my opinion such an allotment weakens us in Sea Power relatively to the allotment submitted by the General Board of the Navy, which was:

Total Tonnage	Type
210,000	10,000 ton cruisers carrying guns of 6in or above in caliber,
70,500	existing 'Omahas'
35,000	new cruisers carrying guns not exceeding 6in in caliber.

This allotment was the result of careful study and full consideration of the programs submitted by Great Britain as her minimum, now adhered to by Great Britain without change, and was agreed upon by the General Board as constituting a sufficiently close approach to parity as to warrant acceptance.

In view of the above, I am convinced the Tentative Plan of the American Delegation of 6 February 1930 weakens the relative naval strength of the US both as regards the original building program approved by the Congress, that is, of 23 10,000 ton, 8 in gun cruisers, and also the modified program approved by the General Board, given above, in that it decreases tonnage most suitable to the US and increases the tonnage less suitable to the needs of the US.

104. *Admiral William Veazie Pratt, US Navy, to Stimson*

13 February 1930

Memorandum prepared on 5 February 1930 by Rear Admiral Hilary P. Jones, US Navy

In view of the memorandum submitted on 5 February 1930 by Rear Admiral Jones, … I feel obliged, as an Advisor to the Delegation, to express my own view in the matter. … I do not agree …

[1]Unless Adm Jones got his dates wrong, he must have had a preview of the statement.

Therefore, as I see it, instead of sacrificing sea power, as is stated in the memorandum, I consider that I have gained fleet strength under the Delegates' Plan and, as I have said before, I consider a 'sound fleet' the goal to be aimed at under any scheme of limitation of naval armament. It might be noted here that under the Delegates' Plan the radius of action of the first of these new 6in, 8500 ton cruisers is only 2000 miles less than the radius given to the 8in, 10,000 ton type and the 10,000 ton 6in ship, if we choose to use it, has the same radius as the 8in gun ship.

If, however, there is one thing which this analysis tends to prove vital is, I believe, this – namely, that the discussion as to whether we have three more 8in, 10,000 ton cruisers or an adequate number of the 6in gun type to offset these three ships is not worthy of the discussion it has raised. I consider it a very minor detail in the whole scheme, and have no hesitation in saying so. Our sea power has not been jeopardised by the adjustments made.

105. *Meeting of the British Commonwealth Delegation*

10 Downing Street,
London,
9 February 1930

...

Mr Craigie ... understood their difficulties were with Admiral Jones, who had great influence with the Senate.[1] Colonel Stimson had told him that without Admiral Jones' support they could not get any proposal through the Senate. Admiral Jones wanted 21 [10,00ton, 8in gun] cruisers. It was with the greatest difficulty he had been brought to accept 18. Colonel Stimson's view was that in time the Americans might come as far as alternative 2 in their policy, namely, absolute parity. They expected to be attacked, as the British Government expect to be attacked, on the basis that their agreement was not real parity: but by putting this proposal as an alternative they proved that their aim was a real parity.

Mr Alexander said that Sir Charles Madden had reported to him that the American views were gradually approaching the British in regard to the value of the 6in cruiser, and eventually, therefore, they might come to their alternative proposal. He understood their Admirals were solid on the basis of 1.4 as a ratio figure for comparing 8in and 6in cruisers.

[1]Robert Leslie Craigie (1883–1959): FO 1907; Berlin, Bern, Sofia, Washington; head, American Dept, FO, & chief negotiator, arms limitation; Asst U Sec 1935; Amb, Japan 1937–41; ret 1944.

Sir Charles Madden said that Admiral Pratt, who said that he belonged to the younger school of thought, supported the British policy in regard to small cruisers.
Mr Craigie emphasised how far the Americans had come to meet the British view. They had brought their figure of 8in cruisers from 21 to 18, and had admitted our right to 50 [in total]. ... In reply to Sir Charles Madden he expressed the view that it would not be of any value to put forward the American alternative proposal of absolute parity as a basis. Colonel Stimson had made clear that they could not accept it at present. They might come to it one day when Admiral Jones's influence was reduced.
...
Mr Craigie said [absolute parity] was a bad proposition from the American point of view since it involved both sides, namely the 'Big Navy' people who wanted large ships, and the supporters of economy, who wanted few ships.
... In effect their point of view was that if we would help them with Senator Borah, and the like, in the Senate, by reducing our figures, they would also come down on their terms.
...
Sir Charles Madden described Admiral Pratt's attitude. The Admiral was willing to come down to Battleships of 27,000 tons, which probably meant that they would be armed with 14in guns, of which the Americans had large numbers in reserve.
The Prime Minister suggested that Sir Charles Madden should try and discuss these technical matters with Admiral Jones, but Sir Charles Madden said he had not found the Admiral very approachable.
Mr Craigie confirmed this.

106. *Memorandum for Mr Morrow by Captain van Keuren, US Navy*[1]

17 February 1930

Comparison of General Characteristics of Battleships

Displacement
The published tables of the Washington Treaty Standard Displacement are correct to best of my knowledge. It is fair to assume that 3000 tons

[1]Dwight L. Morrow (1873–1931): lawyer, banker; chm, President's Aircraft Bd 1925; Amb, Mexico 1927; Delegate 1930.
Capt A. H. van Keuren, CC, US Navy (b. 1881): USNA 1903; CC 1906; Capt 1925; London Conf 1930; RA & Chief, Bu Cnstrn & Repair 1939; ret 1945.

additional displacement will be required for each vessel to modernize the *Pennsylvania* and *Arizona*, now at New York being modernized, and the eight succeeding vessels.[1]

Protection

Captain Smyth has furnished information comparing ship for ship the first 10 British battleships with our first 10, the basis of comparison being gun power, side and deck protection. The zones of penetration and immunity given in his tables are undoubtedly as nearly correct as our best information can provide.

There is some uncertainty as to how much protection, especially deck protection, the British have installed during modernization. However, there are one or two points that would not appear in a comparison such as Captain Smyth gives, which have some influence on the programme as a whole.

Take deck protection on ships prior to the *Rodney* and *Nelson*, for instance. The British seem to attach much more importance, in a sense, to the attack of aerial bombs than do we, for their plans show thin deck protection on the forecastle deck, apparently for the purpose of bursting bombs on their first contact with the ship, whereas our real first deck protection is two decks lower, where it prevents as effectively as the British, the penetration of bombs to magazines, but does not explode them at the same vertical level. The difference lies in favor of the British; their non-vital living spaces may suffer less from bomb attack than ours. On the other hand, our more concentrated protection at a lower level should be better against shell fire than theirs.

Next, take side protection. There are differences here also between British and American practice. Their heavy belt apparently does not extend as far as ours below water, so that we should have some advantages under certain conditions of roll of ship and of shell hitting close alongside and running submerged for a short distance. On the other hand their belt is higher out of water and surmounted by another later belt of, say, 6in thickness on vessels prior to *Rodney* and *Nelson*. This advantage in height of armor belt results in virtually reducing the area of the armor decks in wake of the side belt, since to be fully effective on the deck, a shell would have to pass over the top of the side belt.

Lastly, take the turrets and barbettes of ships prior *to Rodney* and *Nelson*. Our turret front plates and barbettes are consistently heavier than theirs.

[1]*Pennsylvania, Arizona*: 1915.

On the whole, as regards these secondary matters of protection, we have the advantage in barbettes, while as to decks and side protection, the advantages and disadvantages perhaps offset each other.

Speed
In all case the British have greater speed than our corresponding vessels, from one knot in the 'Royal Sovereign' class, to close to three or four knots in the 'Queen Elizabeth' class. Their battlecruisers are of course of greatly superior speed to our battleships.[1]

Battlecruisers
It is believed important to realise that the *Hood*, while probably out of the picture of direct comparison with battleships, is itself a high speed, fairly well armed battleship, better protected on the whole than the battleships prior to the *Rodney* and *Nelson*. We have full information, secured during the war, on this ship. She is the newest vessel in the British Navy, outside of *Rodney* and *Nelson*. The *Repulse*, *Renown* and *Tiger* are scantily protected to lie in line of battle.

107. *Rear Admiral H. I. Cone, US Navy, to Admiral Pratt, US Navy*[2]

22 May 1930

I have been thinking of you a lot of late, and while it may not make much difference to you, I want you to know how much I admire your stand in the present controversy over the Naval Treaty. It looks as though the General Board and the conservative element in the Navy are practically unanimous against your views, but I hope you will not be discouraged and believe this is the universal opinion of the Navy, for it is not.

You, of course, are in closer touch with the officer personnel than I am, and know that there is a large element of sound and solid naval opinion back of you. I have certain contacts which plainly show me that the younger and aggressive element in the Navy are looking forward with much optimism to the approval of this treaty as a solution of their difficulties if for no other reason than the fact that it gives us a definite naval policy to aim for.

[1]Speed of British capital ships: 'Royal Sovereign' class: 21k; 'Queen Elizabeth' class: 24k; *Rodney*, *Nelson*: 23k; *Hood*: 31k; *Renown*, *Repulse*: 29k. American capital ships: 21k.

[2]R Adm H. I. Cone, US Navy (1871–1941): USNA 1894; Manila Bay 1898; Capt & CO, N Aviation Forces, Eur 1917–19; Asiatic F 1919–21; R Adm & ret 1922; V Pres & Gen Mgr, US Shipping Bd 1924–33; Chm, Moore-McCormack Lines, 1937.

108. *Memorandum by Captain A. H. Van Keuren, Constructor Corps, US Navy*

15 April 1930

The 8in and 6in gun Light Cruiser compared

VII. *General Conclusions*

1. That the 8in gun cruiser is superior to the 6in type both because of its superior range and the superior ability to control the fire of its guns by splash observation.

2. That partially offsetting the advantages of the 8in gun type at long ranges should be considered:

(a) The comparatively small percentage of weather and light conditions during which the visibility will be good enough to permit of long range firing.

(b) The use of airplanes for spotting, tending to equalize fire control as between 8in and 6in fire.

(c) The small percentage of hits at long ranges possible with either caliber of gun, hence the tendency to close the range in order to increase the effectiveness of fire.

(d) The doubtful possibility of circumstances arising, even in favorable conditions of visibility, which would permit the 8in gun type to utilise its potential advantages in long-range firing. Most of the duties and functions of a light cruiser would either require closing the range or permit of opening it beyond the danger zone. Scouting and detached duty where a superior force might be encountered suddenly are the principal functions that would render a superiority in range desirable. Standing off a flank attack or smaller cruisers would be made easier by such a superiority, but even here the deciding factor might conceivably be the number of the opposing cruisers and their ability to close into a range where their gunfire would be effective.

(e) The vulnerability of the 8in gun type due to defective protection. This is a distinct disadvantage inherent in the 8in gun type of limited displacement, especially since the vulnerable spots – the turrets – are among the most dangerous of the whole suit of armor, vulnerable not only to shells of 8in caliber but even to 6in shell.

(f) That the 6in gun cruiser is superior to the 8in gun type in volume of fire at close and probably at medium ranges.

(g) That the duties of a light cruiser can, in many, perhaps most, instances be preformed efficiently by the 6in gun type.

(h) That the 6in gun type is not only a balanced design on 10,000 tons or slightly less, possessing protection against its own guns, but that it has superior protection to the 8in gun type and can take punishment from 8in shells better than the 8in type.

109. *Naval Attaché, London, to the Chief of Naval Operations*[1]

n.d. *c.*1930

…

22. The British have never regarded disarmament as a British problem. The upper classes in England, who are also largely the ruling classes, believe in imperial destiny, and that the Navy, Army and Air Force are really smaller than they should be. Any reduction in British arms would be welcomed only on grounds of economy. The subject of disarmament in general awakens little popular interest. The views of educated men as expressed in the papers are vague and divergent. There is a certain popular sentiment for it among the labouring classes, prompted by the belief that it might help British markets by improving economic and industrial conditions on the Continent. The War Office, the Admiralty and the Air Ministry all maintain that they are already cut to the bone. There is ever the feeling that the Locarno Treaties, by increasing England's responsibility on the Continent, have created a justification for increasing British armaments. England has given guarantees of assistance in the Locarno Treaties, but has got nothing similar in return. Air power has taken from her the advantages of an island position, and the submarine has added to its disadvantages. England would give much to see both of these weapons abolished but she realizes the futility at present of making such a proposition. In addition there is a general feeling that there can be no real disarmament or real peace until the Russian problem is solved.[2]

…

24. In general it is believed that the attitude of Great Britain on any question arising in the Conference will be governed by the following political and naval objectives:

British Political Objectives

(a) To draw together in close union politically, economically and industrially all parts of the Empire.

[1]NA, London: Capt William W. Galbraith, US Navy.
CNO: Adm Charles F. Hughes.

[2]The 'Russia problem' was lack of meaningful diplomatic engagement with USSR for all nations, till USSR joined League 1935, alarmed by Hitler.

(b) To preserve predominant influence in Europe by supporting a policy of opposition to the strongest power on the Continent.
(c) To preserve predominant influence in the League of Nations and to take practical measures to see that the execution of its decrees is never unfavorable to British interests.
(d) To control all methods of world communications and thereby insure the safety of British trade in peace and in war.
(e) To be the leading world power morally, financially and industrially.
(f) To utilize the friendship of the US to forward British policies.

British Naval Objectives
(a) Abolition or restriction of submarines.
(b) Abolition of battleships (only as a concession to disarmament).
(c) Restriction of aircraft to use against military objectives.
(d) Recognition of Britain's right to larger cruiser and auxiliary forces than those of other nations.
(e) Right of merchant marine to arm in time of war.
(f) Ultimate naval supremacy. …

110. *Memorandum by Rear Admiral William A. Moffett, US Navy*

n.d. *c.*1930

Comment on British Navy Proposal in Regard to Aircraft Carriers

1. 'Tonnage and gun caliber to be limited.'
There would be no objection to reducing the maximum tonnage from 27,000 tons, Washington Treaty, to 25,000 tons.
2. 'Age increased from 20 to 26 years.'
This would extend the handicap which the US now labours under, the British having potentially nine carriers to the US's seven.
3. 'Reduction of total tonnage for aircraft carriers for the British and the US from 135,000 tons to, say, 100,000 tons.'
This would be a calamity for the US. Every ton taken off the 135,000 tons is a detriment. With 135,000 tons, the British can, as stated, build nine carriers to our seven; with 100,000 tons, they would have available 55,000 tons in aircraft carriers, whereas the US would have only 34,000 tons. The British could build four efficient carriers, when at most the US could build three comparatively inefficient carriers, and unquestionably would only build two more efficient carriers. The ratio of carriers would therefore be six for the British and four for the US. Four carriers would be inadequate

for what is necessary for Fleet training in time of peace. We have been and now are severely handicapped in this respect owing to the fact that the British have six aircraft carriers to our three. A reduction to 100,000 tons would be detrimental to the interests and security of the US. Japan will probably be in favor of reducing to 100,000 tons because they now have an aircraft carrier tonnage of 61,276, which is a little more than the 5: 3 ratio, and it is to their interests to keep our aircraft carrier tonnage as low as possible, just as it is to the best interests of Great Britain.

The aircraft carrier is still in the experimental stage, especially in our Navy. We do not yet know from experience what is the most efficient size, whereas the British have had long experience in sizes from 11,000 tons to 23,000 tons. We do not know the most efficient unit for service under all conditions. We need at least 10 carriers for a balanced fleet and for necessary training in time of peace. Under 135,000 tons at most we can only have seven aircraft carriers. Therefore, no reduction in the 135,000 tons allowed by the Washington Treaty should be made at this time.

111. *International Treaty for the Limitation and Reduction of Naval Armament*

22 April 1930

Part I

1. The High Contracting Parties agree not to exercise their rights to lay down the keels of capital ship replacement tonnage during the years 1931 to 1936. …
2. The US, UK and Japan shall dispose of the following capital ships as provided in this Article:

US:
Florida, Utah, Arkansas or *Wyoming.*

UK:
Benbow, Iron Duke, Marlborough, Emperor of India, Tiger.

Japan:
Hiyei.

…

Part II

7. No submarine the displacement of which exceeds 2000 tons or with a gun above 5in calibre shall be acquired by or for any of the HCP.

…

Part III

15 For the purpose of this Part III the definition of cruiser and destroyer categories shall be as follows:

Cruisers

Surface vessels of war, other than capital ships or aircraft carriers, the standard displacement of which exceeds 1850 tons or with a gun above 5.1in.

The cruiser category is divided into two sub-categories, as follows:

(a) cruisers carrying a gun above 6.1in in calibre.

(b) cruisers carrying a gun not above 6.1in in calibre.

Destroyers

Surface vessels of war the standard displacement of which does not exceed 1850 tons and with a gun not above 5.1in

16. (1) The complete tonnage in the cruiser, destroyer and submarine categories which is not to be exceeded on 31 December 1936, is given in the following table:

	US	British Commonwealth	Japan
Cruisers (a)	180,000	146,800	108,400
Cruisers (b)	143,500	192,200	100,450
Destroyers	150,000	150,000	105,500
Submarines	52,700	52,700	52,700

…

(3) The maximum numbers of cruisers of sub-category (a) shall be as follows:

For the US, 18; for the British Commonwealth of Nations, 15; for Japan, 12.

…

Part IV

22. The following are accepted as established rules of International Law:

(1) In their action with regard to merchant ships, submarines must conform to the rules of International Law to which surface vessels are subject.

(2) … a warship, whether surface vessel or submarine, may not sink or render incapable of navigation a merchant vessel without first having placed passengers, crew and ship's papers in a place of safety. …

112. *Rear Admiral Hilary P. Jones, to Senator Hiram Johnson*[1]

13 June 1930

Admiral Yarnell's view that war between us and Great Britain is a remote possibility should be accepted without question.[2] Indeed, it is earnestly hoped that it is so remote as to render such a tragedy unthinkable. However, it should be recognised that attempted dictation on one side and complete acceptance of such dictation on the other will not tend in the long run to foster that mutual regard and good feeling so necessary to peace. …

A careful analysis of the features of a war between us and Great Britain, … conclusively indicates the type of cruisers best suited to our conditions. The more we depart from that type and accept the British demand for a smaller gun type, the more we weaken our ability to fulfil our own requirements. … the necessity for widely dispersed unit operations and convoy protection is proved beyond question. For these purposes the type of cruiser best suited to our needs is that in which the maximum power of survival in combat, i.e., offensive and defensive strength, is combined with the maximum speed and sea endurance that can be incorporated in the unit within the limits of size and gun caliber permitted by the Washington Treaty, namely, the 10,000 ton, 8in gun type. On the other hand, due to her possession of well located bases and fuelling ports and preponderant readily convertible merchant tonnage, Great Britain would be in far better case with numbers of units of a smaller gun type. Therefore, her persistent demand for as drastic restriction as possible in the larger type and greater liberty in the smaller type is natural.

The preponderance of two knots in favour of the British [battleship] fleet makes it possible for that fleet to control somewhat that range at which an action shall be fought. According to the best evidence we have, two of the British ships, the *Nelson* and the *Rodney*, are impenetrable by virtue of their deck and side protection by any guns in our Fleet between ranges of 21,000 and 30,000 yards, whereas all of our ships are penetrable by their guns. However, modernisation of certain of our ships as allowed under the terms of the Washington Treaty probably will correct that dangerous condition.

… The division of the cruiser category into two sub-categories is a distinct repudiation of the consistent and strong attitude of the former

[1]H. Johnson (1866–1945): Calif Repub progm; Govr 1911–17; Sen 1917–45. Voted against US mem League and UN.

[2]Adm Harry E. Yarnell, US Navy (1875–1959): USNA 1897; NWC 1915; Gibraltar & London 1917; advisor, London N Conf 1930; cdr, Air Sqdns, Battle F 1931–3; Cdt, Pearl Harbor 1933–6; CinC, Asiatic F 1936–9; ret 1939; Adm 1942.

administration maintained at all disarmament conferences; a violation of all the conclusions and recommendations of the General Board of the Navy arrived at as the result of long and careful study; distinctly contrary to the teachings and experience of the Naval War College arrived at by careful and exhaustive studies and war games, as given in the testimony of the President and students of the College; and in the well considered opinions of the vast majority of experienced naval officers who have given serious thought to our naval situation.

113. *Chief of Naval Operations to the Secretary of the Navy*[1]

30 July 1931

Plan to maintain and operate the Treaty Navy

1. Reference (a) presents a normal peacetime operating plan based upon the assumption that Navy has been built up to the full strength permitted by existing treaties. The essential features are:
(a) It affords adequate training of the personnel of the US Fleet.
(b) It maintains the fleet combatant vessels in a satisfactory material condition.
(c) It provides adequate forces to protect American interests in unsettled localities.
(d) It provides sufficient auxiliaries to furnish logistic support to the forces afloat and at outlying stations.
(e) It maintains out of commission certain auxiliary vessels and certain vessels not of the fleet combatant type.
(f) It makes provision for the training of the reserves.
2. Under this plan the Navy will not attain as high a state of efficiency and readiness as if all vessels were maintained in full commission. Consideration of economy will always preclude this, except when a national emergency exists or is foreseen.
3. The proposed plan does, however (in addition to providing for normal peacetime operation), place the Navy in position to handle minor peacetime situations of an emergency nature while possessing flexibility which will permit transition to an augmented strength capable of meeting major exigencies in time of peace subject only to the necessary peacetime procurement of funds and personnel. This increase in operating strength, which world conditions might force upon us, should be understood as neither partaking of the flavour of preparation for war nor as a preliminary

[1]Still Pratt and Adams, respectively.

to mobilization. On the contrary, if assumed at the proper moment, it should prove an effective step toward preventing us being drawn into war.

4. The plan proposed herein maintains the selected number of each fleet combatant type in active operation by providing for rotation with ships of the same type in reserve commission. During the reserve commission period the Navy Yard overhauls are accomplished. A comparison between this plan and the one where the same selected operating strength is maintained by keeping additional ships in full commission to provide for Navy Yard overhauls, indicates that the plan proposed will cost about $1,000,000 less per annum.

5. Preliminary estimates indicate that 92,693 enlisted men and 6402 line, 2013 staff and 1600 warrant officers will be required to carry out the plan proposed. This on a basis of supplying ships in full commission with an allowance of enlisted personnel equivalent to 90% of complement. To meet a major exigency in time of peace will require additional personnel strength and, if all ships of the Treaty Navy were in commission with full complements, a minimum of approximately 135,000 enlisted men and 8699 line, 2441 staff and 1923 warrant officers will be necessary. A maximum war effort will require in excess of 409,000 men and 35,000 officers of all corps.

6. The details of the plan, which the CNO now recommends for approval, are fully covered in reference (a).

PART IV

THE SECOND LONDON NAVAL CONFERENCE
1930–1936

In the summer of 1934, Leslie Craigie, the British Government's chief diplomatic advisor on arms limitation, wrote to Ray Atherton, the long-serving Counselor at the American Embassy, 'It is unfortunately the case that since the London Naval Treaty was concluded in 1930 a very serious deterioration in the international and political outlook has occurred.'[1] Craigie wrote in the midst of lengthy preliminary negotiations between the British and the Americans (led by President Franklin D. Roosevelt's confidant, Norman H. Davis) held in advance of a projected naval arms limitation conference scheduled for 1935 and intended to carry forward the Treaties of Washington (1922) and London (1930) for another six to ten years [120–27, 130–41, 143–6].[2] They were conducted amid war and rumours of war and thus had an unpromising backcloth. Since the 1930 conference, Japan had witnessed two Prime Ministers assassinated, other civilian leaders cowed into silence and several senior naval officers who had supported the Treaty system forced into early retirement. Worse still, a rogue element in the Japanese Army, supposedly guarding a railway concession in Manchuria, had provoked the 'Mukden Incident' with Chinese troops in September 1931. This was a major step on the road to Pearl Harbor, one compounded by the abjectly weak response of the League of Nations and the United States to an event of militaristic opportunism, if not of outright aggression. It was followed in January 1932 by a Sino-Japanese clash in Shanghai, occasioned by local patriotism but leading to the use of overwhelming force by the Japanese and much suffering for the local population; the western powers helped to stitch up a shaky peace. It was no longer clear who really spoke for Japan.[3] A few months later Adolf Hitler came to power in Germany and quickly made his intentions clear internally and

[1]Craigie to Atherton, 26 July 1934, in W. N. Medlicott et al. (eds), *DBFP*, series 2, vol. XIII (London, 1973), p. 10 (henceforth *DBFP*, s. 2, XIII).

[2]Franklin D. Roosevelt (1882–1945): Dem, NY State Senate, 1911–13; Asst Sec of Navy, 1913–20; V Pres cand, 1920; Govr, NY 1929–33; Pres, 1933–45.

Norman H. Davis (1878–1944): banker, Wilsonian internationalist.

[3]D. Borg and S. Okamoto (eds), *Pearl Harbor as History: Japanese-American Relations, 1931–1941* (New York, 1973), *passim.*

on the European stage.[1] In Italy, Mussolini, dormant for a decade, was moving towards a seizure of Abyssinia, accomplished in 1935 [125, 132, 134, 141, 145, 146].[2]

The London Naval Treaty of 1930 was due to terminate on 31 December 1936, at the same time as the landmark Washington Naval Treaty of 1922, and there was provision for another conference in 1935, with London again nominated as the venue. It remained to be seen whether France and Italy, who had not signed the 1930 Treaty, could be persuaded back into the system. They were not, however, the major concern of its main sponsors, Britain and America. Japan was less amenable to compromise than in 1930. She had successes in China behind her, unhindered by international action, and her politics was dominated increasingly by hawkish officers of both services, backed by middle-ranking fanatics, whose answer to even mild or suspected criticism of their preferred seniors was a knife between the ribs. Out of this ugly picture there emerged a Japanese demand, fuelled by hubris and national pride, of parity in warships of all classes, a claim underlined by a threat that otherwise she would withdraw from the Treaty system at the earliest opportunity. The British and Americans stood firm and united against parity with Japan, arguing that Japan had both security and local dominance in her quarter of Asia and had only her home seas to defend, whereas America had two long coastlines and widely-scattered dependencies like Alaska, the Philippines, Samoa, Hawaii and other Pacific islands, while Britain was the centre of a world-wide and very scattered empire. The British, beset by the rise of Hitler and German re-armament, and without reliable allies in Europe, toyed with the idea of making an accommodation with Japan but the Americans pointedly rejected any such notion, in effect telling the British that they must choose between Tokyo and Washington. As they well knew, faced with such a stark choice, Britain, as in 1921, had no option but to bed down with Roosevelt [143, 144]. The President and most of his advisors did not realise that their refusal to give Britain the practical support of an ally forced her to consider a deal with Japan; had the United States been mature enough in world affairs to offer Britain a firm alliance or even an entente, the latter would not have felt compelled to delete a potential enemy. As it was, Britain argued for doors to be left open in the subsequent Treaty of London, signed on 25 March 1936, for Japan

[1] Adolf Hitler (1889–1945): corporal, 1914–18; leader, Nat Soc party; failed coup 1923; Chllr 1933; Pres 1934.

[2] Benito Mussolini (1883–1945): tchr, jnlst, socialist; soldier 1914–18; leader, Fascist party 1919; PM 1922; dictator 1925; dismissed by king, July 1943; rescued by Germans, Sept 1943; puppet ruler, N Italy; capt & shot by partisans, April 1945.

to re-enter the limitation system without loss of face when she had recovered her senses, perhaps after two years (the Admiralty – and the Americans – remained sceptical about this happening) [120, 122–5, 129, 133, 135, 139, 145, 146, 148, 149].[1]

From March 1934, Davis conducted talks in London with a variety of British politicians, diplomats and naval officers, assisted from time to time by the chairman of the US Navy's General Board, Rear Admiral Richard H. Leigh and later by the Chief of Naval Operations, Admiral William H. Standley, with occasional input from Roosevelt's ambassador in London, Robert W. Bingham, and Atherton.[2] The preliminary discussions ambled on through 1934 but 1935 was occupied mainly by British talks with the French and the Germans. Many on both sides of the Atlantic wondered whether it was worth holding a formal conference, not because the British and Americans were at loggerheads but because of the uncompromising attitude of the Japanese. In October 1934, the Japanese Government had indicated an intention to quit the Treaty system and gave formal notice on 30 December 1935 to leave it with the expiry of the Washington and London [1930] agreements on 31 December 1936.[3] Even in this sombre setting, however, MacDonald, a man sincerely dedicated to peace, thought it worthwhile to send out on 24 October 1934 formal invitations to a second London conference, convening a meeting on 9 December 1935. A Japanese Delegation, led by Admiral Nagami Osami, the Navy Minister, attended the talks but finding the Anglo-American line implacably firm and allowing no alteration of the 5: 5: 3 ratios agreed at Washington, walked out on 15 January 1936.[4] The British and Americans salvaged what they could from the Treaty system. France came back on board and was one of the signatories on 25 March 1936 and the Treaty came into force on 29 July 1937. Italy, the Soviet Union and the Scandinavian

[1]FO/Admiralty Joint Memo, 11 Oct 1935, *DBFP*, s. 2, XIII, p. 668.

See C. Hall, *Britain, America and Arms Control, 1921–1937* (London:Macmillan, 1987), pp. 193–218.

[2]RAdm Richard H. Leigh, US Navy: Cdr, Asst Chief, Bur Steam Engrg; cond trials of submarine listening devices; Sims' staff, Dec 1917; Capt & CO, destroyers and sub chasers, Plymouth, Feb 1918; RA & Chm, Gen Bd 1931–4.

Adm William H. Standley, US Navy (1872–1963): USNA 1895; Capt, battleship 1919; NWC 1920–1; RA 1927; VA 1832; Adm & Cdr, Battle Force June 1933; CNO 1 July 1933–1 Jan 1937; war production appts; Amb to USSR April 1942–March 1943; Planning Group, OSS, March 1944–Aug 1945.

Robert W. Bingham (1871–1937): judge; newspaper magnate, Louisville, Ky; Amb to UK 1933–7.

[3]In Oct 1934, VAdm Yamamoto Isokuru, V Minr & chief of N Affs Bur, arrived to join in prelim talks with Amb to UK, Matsudaira Tsuneo; both were realists & moderates but had to obey the hard line imposed by Tokyo. Yamamoto later masterminded the attack on Pearl Harbor.

[4]Adm Nagami Osami: N Minr 1936–7; Chief, N Gen Staff, 1941.

countries were persuaded to sign it later, and the British made a separate naval limitation Agreement with Germany on 18 June 1935. On the face of it, the Treaty seems a major triumph for Anglo-American diplomacy, but it had serious flaws. It was deliberated as the storm clouds of war gathered and by the time it came into operation Japan and China were engaged in a full-scale conflict; Germany, Italy and the Soviet Union were supporting rival sides in the Spanish Civil War (which had broken out in August 1936); and Italy had swallowed Abyssinia. When analysed, the long-drawn out and complex negotiations and the eventual Treaty form an essentially Anglo-American compact [152]. 'The main success of the Conference', said Anthony Clayton, 'was the continuing improvement in Anglo-American naval relations.'[1] In the absence, however, of tangible American guarantees to support Britain's world position – and global peace – the British had no choice but to prepare for war on two fronts – and in 1935 Italy's attack on Abyssinia turned her into a third potential enemy. Their 'default setting' thus was:

> We should be able to send to the Far East a fleet sufficient to provide 'cover' against the Japanese Fleet; we should have sufficient additional forces behind this shield for the protection of our territories and merchant marine against Japanese attack; at the same time we should be able to retain in European waters a force sufficient to act as a deterrent to prevent the strongest European power … from obtaining control of our vital home terminal areas while we can make the necessary re-dispositions. [126]

There was precious little disagreement between the British and the Americans, in contrast to previous negotiations [116–17, 140]. Even the earlier rows about parity were muted [133, 134, 140, 151]. The British, led by the First Sea Lord, Admiral of the Fleet Sir Ernle Chatfield, insisted on reinstating their claim for 70 cruisers (60 under-age and 10 over-age). They argued also for phasing out 8in, 10,000 ton cruisers, effectively ending new construction in that category [114, 117, 130, 140, 152]. While conceding that America and Britain could both build a class of 9,000–10,000 ton 6in cruisers, they managed to stipulate that light 6in cruisers in general should be limited to 8,000 tons [117, 122, 126, 130, 137–40, 148, 150, 152, 153].[2] They were unsuccessful in reducing capital ships to

[1]A. Clayton, *The British Empire as a Superpower, 1919–1939* (Athens, Ga, 1986), p. 265

[2]'M' or 'Southampton' class: 8 ships, 1937–8, 9,100–9,400t, 32k, 12×6in, 8×4in, 6×21in tt; there were also *Edinburgh* and *Belfast*: 1939, 10,550t, 32.5k, 12×6in, 12×4in, 6×21in tt.

'Brooklyn' class: 7 ships, 1938–9, 10,000t, 32.5k, 15×6in, 8×5in.

25,000 tons and 12in guns, the Americans insisting on 14in guns and proving reluctant to give up a 35,000 ton displacement [114, 126, 130, 134, 136, 137, 140, 148, 152]. Aircraft carriers were to be limited to 23,000 tons and 6in guns [114, 126, 130, 140, 152]. Once again, Britain proposed the abolition of submarines and, failing that, a severe restriction in size to coastal defence units only, and a reduction in total tonnage, with somewhat ambivalent support from the Americans, but little change occurred [114–17, 127, 130, 140, 152]. By a series of separate Protocols, the 'Root Resolutions' of 1922 on submarine warfare were extended to 40 nations. More interesting than the detailed 'dos-and-don'ts' of the Treaty was the incorporation of several 'escape' clauses [152, 153]. These could be activated if a signatory's national security was as stake, and new battleships, limited to 14in guns under the Treaty, could be re-armed with 16in guns if the Japanese remained outside the system. To allay American domestic suspicions that the American delegates had 'sold out' on parity to the crafty British, Davis and Eden exchanged cordial notes, confirming parity once and for all [151].[1]

Why were the British and Americans able to come to an agreement so easily? In part, they had much experience of each other's positions, especially on the cruiser problem and there were no new arguments at London in 1934–36. Secondly, the personnel on both sides was amenable and flexible. For Britain, the lead was taken by MacDonald, Prime Minister until 1935, still an ardent disarmer but less ready to tinker with the Empire's security than in 1929–30. Sir John Simon, Sir Samuel Hoare and Anthony Eden, successive Foreign Secretaries, presided over day-to-day contacts with the Americans, while the First Lord of the Admiralty, Sir Bolton Eyres-Monsell, assisted by the Earl of Stanhope (later First Lord himself), were on the British Delegation.[2] All were concerned with maintaining good relations with the Americans, now imperative as threats to Imperial security grew. Most of the preliminary talks were handled by

[1]Anthony Eden (1897–1977): Brig Maj, 1914–18; Con MP, Warwick & Leamington, 1923–57; M for League Affs 1935; FS 1935–8; SSt for Doms 1939; SSt for War, May 1940; FS 1940–5, 1951–5; PM 1955–7; Earl of Avon.

[2]Sir John Simon (1873–1954): Lib MP; Atty-Gen 1913–15; HS 1915–16; FS 1931–5; HS 1935–7; CEx 1937–40; Ld Chllr 1940–5.

Sir Samuel Hoare (1880–1959): Con MP; SSt for Air 1922–4, 1924–9, 1940; SSt for India 1931–5; FS 1935; FL 1936–7; HS 1937–9; LPS & WC 1939–40; Amb to Spain 1940–4; Visct Templewood.

Bolton M. Eyres-Monsell (1881–1969): RN 1894; tpdo spist; MP 1910–35; Egypt 1914–18; Cdr 1917; Civ Ld, Admy 1921; Fin Sec, Admy 1922–3; Parl Sec, Treasy 1923–9; FL 1931–6; Visct.

Earl Stanhope (1880–1967): Con; S Af war 1902; major, 1908–20; W Frt 1914–18; Parl Sec, WO 1918; Civ Ld, Admy 1924–9; Parl & Fin Sec, Admy 1931; U SSt, WO 1931–3; Parl U Sec, FO 1934–6; 1st Cmnr of Works 1936–7; Pres, Bd of Educ 1937–8; FL 1938–9; LPC 1939–40; Ldr, HL 1938–40; Pres, Navy Records Soc, 1948– 58.

Craigie, an American specialist at the Foreign Office, a diplomat of resource, clarity and stamina, and a man thoroughly versed in disarmament matters, together with several naval officers of high calibre. Foremost among them was Ernle Chatfield, formerly Beatty's Flag Captain and, like him, able to deliberate with civilians on level terms. Chatfield was lucid, far-sighted, had a clear vision for the Royal Navy, a wide strategic perception and proved a tireless and commanding presence throughout the two years of talks. The Deputy Chief of Naval Staff, Vice Admiral Sir Charles Little, was no less able, nor was the Director of Naval Operations, Captain Victor Danckwerts.[1] All were concerned to strike a firm understanding with the United States, notably on the Far East. There, Britain had large and vulnerable Imperial and commercial interests, while she recognised that, as a result of the Washington Treaty, only a combined Anglo-American naval presence off Japan could match Japan's local superiority. For the Americans, the Delegates were Norman H. Davis, an international financier and one of the few Americans of those days who thought in terms of world politics, and Admiral Standley. Standley was there effectively in place of the sick Secretary of the Navy, Claude A. Swanson, whose frequent absences augmented the power of successive Chiefs of Naval Operations.[2] Roosevelt himself, a former Assistant Secretary of the Navy, acted as his own Secretary anyway but though he corresponded frequently with Davis, like the politician he was, he blew hot and cold between American naval expansion and a world-wide cut of 20%. Like his predecessor Pratt and his successors Leahy, Stark and King, Standley was a naval officer of some substance, with a clear idea of a balanced 'Treaty' fleet, a keen appreciation of Japan's threat in the Pacific, and a broad sympathy with the Royal Navy's obligations; he, too, was concerned to develop as firm an Anglo-American understanding, especially in the Pacific, as was compatible with America's stifled internationalism.[3] Rear Admiral Richard H. Leigh, an early negotiator,

[1]Capt Victor H. Danckwerts: Capt 1930; Asst DP 1934; DP 1938–Jan 1940; Admy 1940–1; ret June 1941; CoS (Shore), EF March 1942; d 1944.

[2]Claude A. Swanson (1862–1939): Dem, Va; HR 1893–1906; Govr 1906–10; Sen 1910–33; Chm, Sen N Affs Cttee: Sec N 1933–9.

[3]FAdm William D. Leahy, US Navy (1875–1959): RA 1927; CNO 1937–9; Govr, Puerto Rico; Amb to Vichy France 1941–2; Pres's CoS & Chm, JCS, July 1942; F Adm 1944; ret 1949.

Adm Harold R. Stark, US Navy (1880–1972): destroyers & staff, Med & UK 1917–18; NWC; ND; battleship cmd; Chief, Bu Ord; cruiser cmd; CNO 1 Aug 1939–26 March 1942; CinC, US N Fcs in Eur Waters 1942–5; ret 1946.

FAdm Ernest J. King, US Navy (1877–1956): USNA 1901; instr, staff & engrg appts; staff of Adm Mayo, CinC, Atl F 1915–19; Cdr, Sub Div 11, 1922–6; Capt *Wright* 1926; pilot 1927; Bu Aer & other aviation cmds; *Lexington* 1930–2; NWC 1932; RA & Chief, Bu Aer 1933–6; further air cmds; Cdr, Patrol Force, Atl, Dec 1940; Adm & CinC, Atl F Feb 1941; CinC, Dec 1941; CNO 27 March 1942–31 Dec 1945.

was less hidebound and narrowly nationalistic than previous General Board chairmen (and the Board, a tunnel-visioned and suspicious organisation, occupied a less influential role in the Pratt and Standley eras). The American officers 'hit it off' with their British counterparts. Thus it came to pass that familiarity with one another's arguments, the common threat of Japan and personal compatibility served both countries well at this time [120–23, 125, 129, 132, 146, 151].

As with the negotiations of 1926–27 and 1929–30, those of 1934–36 were concerned principally with the cruiser question. The American position remained one of faith in the 10,000 ton, 8in gun cruiser ('sub-category (a)' in the 1936 Treaty). Because of America's perceived lack of bases, they had to be powerful, sturdy ships of great radius of action. Britain, though she built similar ships, would not have done so if Japan had not led the way, and preferred a multitude of light cruisers ('sub-category (b)' in the Treaty) to guard the sea lanes, with 6in guns and 'short-legged' as they would operate from a network of bases throughout the world. The snag was that, while the Royal Navy had a host of small cruisers, they were First World War designs and would be 'over-age' between 1936 and 1940. Moreover, they were built for the narrow, shallow, choppy North Sea and were thus unsuited to the defence of trade on ocean routes. Furthermore, they were in general small vessels of inadequate armament when compared with cruisers designed after the war by all powers (particularly France and Italy) and Chatfield wished to replace them with 6in gun cruisers of 7,000–8,000 tons. This scheme came as an uncomfortable surprise to the Americans, who were prepared to concede Britain a total of 70 cruisers but balked at the total tonnage requested by Britain, pitched initially at 541,800 tons against the 339,000 tons allowed at London in 1930, though the amount was quickly scaled down to 491,800 tons and eventually to 408,800 tons.[1] Even that represented an increase of more than 50,000 tons on the 1930 figure and the American Delegates were perturbed about its probable hostile reception in Congress, the popular press, and public opinion if they accepted it without question [114, 117–19, 122, 126, 130, 134, 137–40, 150, 152, 153].

Thus ended the era of naval limitation, which had lasted from 1919 to 1936. Was it 'cost-effective'? One has to consider it in relation to world

[1]British First World War-design light cruisers were the small 'C' and 'D' classes, *c.* 5000t; *Emerald*, *Enterprise*, 7,550t; 'Hawkins' class, 9,800t, armed with 7.5in guns, later re-armed with 6in. Modern ships were 'Leander' class: 8 ships (3 RAN), 1933–6, 7,000t, 32.5k, 8×6in, 4×4in, 8×21in tt; 'Arethusa' class: 4 ships, 5,250t, 32k, 6×6in, 4×4in, 6×21in tt.; and the 'M' or 'Southampton' class, plus *Edinburgh*, *Belfast*.

R. L. Craigie, note, 11 Jan 1935; Admy memo, 4 Dec 1935, pp. 713–20, in *DBFP*, s. 2, XIII, pp. 164–5.

conditions and other international measures. In the years after 1919, people in all lands hoped that the mightiest war in history, in the end a truly global conflict, was indeed 'the war to end all wars'. Parallel to this was the belief that a major cause of this enormously destructive conflict had been an arms race, especially between Britain and Germany. The cure for the conditions which were said to have led to the First World War was the League of Nations, sponsored by Woodrow Wilson but which his own country refused to join. The League was, however, an untried device and it was, therefore, supplemented by all sorts of regional and global agreements. The United States, moreover, wished to do its own bit for world peace, as well as to buttress its own security and, using its own overwhelming might at Washington, caused the leading naval nations to halt a burgeoning naval race and apportion strengths on a scale reflecting, more or less, their responsibilities. This was extended, after a stiff-collared fiasco at Geneva, in two conferences at London. Washington, though too imprecise on non-capital ship vessels, was, in hindsight, the pinnacle of the endeavour. Geneva was a flop because it was insufficiently well-monitored by statesmen of standing, had a narrow and essentially nationalistic agenda, and was handled by men with inadequate diplomatic skills. The first London conference of 1930 owed much to two men of impeccable pacific intentions, good preparation, the primacy of political rather than diplomatic or naval figures, and rather more flexibility than had been displayed at Geneva. The writing was nevertheless on the wall, for France and Italy could not be kept in the limitation envelope and the Japanese Premier, who had sanctioned his nation's adherence, paid for his temerity with his life, shortly after its adoption. That and other internal events in Japan led to Japanese intransigence ahead of the next conference and, although the 1936 London Naval Treaty looked good on paper, it was in reality as flimsy as the printed copy itself. 'The whole proceedings', wrote Roskill, 'were a colossal waste of time and effort.'[1] Looking back after 1945, so they were, but given the momentum of limitation talks and the historic impulse behind them, together with the uncertain situation of the mid-1930s – neither peace nor war, with the omens unclear to all statesmen – it was not hard to see why MacDonald, Davis and other men of goodwill felt they had to try. In sum, limitation treaties probably prevented Japan from building as large a navy as she would have done otherwise, while, at the last, allowing the democracies just enough scope and time to construct barely enough ships to save the day come Armageddon. The United States and the United Kingdom and, from time

[1] S. W. Roskill, *Naval Policy between the Wars*, II, *The Period of Reluctant Re- armament, 1930–1939* (London, 1976), p. 320.

to time, other nations, flew the flag of peace from the yardarm; their efforts remain proud in principle if honestly flawed in practice. In the end, all compacts, whether with teeth or without, rely on all nations (signatories or not) complying with them out of consent; should rogue elements flout them, never mind the fangs they may or may not contain, the guardians (often self-appointed) of the international order must have the collective will to quarantine effectively the law-breakers. In the inter-war years, the keepers of the peace were unwilling to risk another mauling to hold the wild men in check. The men in pinstripes and wing collars were perplexed when Hitler, Mussolini and the Japanese militarists did not play the game by established rules.

As the world voyaged toward the war already looming on the horizon, the trail of scraps of paper of all kinds but with the same olive branch message, tossed in its wake. Talking of limitation and disarmament before security was assured to all by diplomatic and political agreements of some concreteness was like putting the horse before the cart. The ever-wise Chatfield, a monumental figure in naval statesmanship, should have the last word: 'The one thing that causes all the trouble is the endeavour to make military agreements to limit arms. That is why I should like to see the attempt to make Naval agreements abandoned and substitute for them political understandings, leaving each Nation free to build what she wants.' [129].

114. *Admiral Pratt to the Secretary of the Navy*

12 October 1931

Naval Holiday

...

... any sane man knows that it is not a practical plan for us to build up to a full Treaty Navy between now and the time of the next Conference in 1935. ...

1. Regardless of what many think I maintain that this Country does need battleships. I won't go into the discussion here, [but] I'm willing to compromise in the future on a smaller ship of 27,500 tons. I have gone thoroughly into the matter and while at odds with most naval men, who want a larger ship, I think the reasons for 27,500 tons and 12in guns are sound. But whatever the size, they must be kept up to date and it is [sound] economy to do it, because modernization can prolong the life of a battleship from 20 to 30 years.
2. Let us consider the next in the group of the big three (battleships, aircraft carriers and 8in cruisers), *viz.*, the aircraft carrier. We need something badly to replace the *Lexington* and *Saratoga* in operation, something more economical to run, but which will give us the same training facilities. Then we need something to replace the *Langley* which is getting old. In addition to the Fleet we must look towards the Far East. If we save $1m a year on each new carrier over the *Saratoga* and *Lexington*, that is almost the cost of a *Saratoga* in the present lifetime of that ship.
3. Take the cruiser question. I don't see how we can afford not to build the 8in cruisers we are allowed to lay down in 1933, 1934, [and] 1935. They will assure us of proper ratio strength in the big three [ships]. Their completion gives us 180,000 tons of 8in cruisers, which with 70,500 tons of 6in cruisers is a total of 250,000 tons. This seems a minimum. Even with the completion of five more 10,000 ton 6in [8in?] cruisers which were authorized by Congress in the 1923 cruiser programme, this is only 300,500 tons which is some 32,000 tons short of the [1930 London] Treaty Strength. However there would be no particular use in building, or maintaining the right to build over the amount authorized now, during the period of the holiday, since in 1935, I cannot see how England can avoid coming down to 300,000 tons of cruiser tonnage.[1]

[1]Pratt's idea was swiftly disabused, as Chatfield's plan for 70 cruisers would take the RN's cruiser fleet to over 400,000 tons. The five (later seven) 10,000 ton, 6in gun cruisers became the 'Brooklyn' class.

4. Let us consider the destroyer type. We have too many now, but they all go out by 1936. I would not recommend creating another hiccup by excessive building now, nor would it be wise to refrain from all building. I would prefer to see building go on at the steady rate of six or seven a year which is the normal rate of building and replacement per year, with a 150,000 tonnage limit and 1500 tons displacement of ship.[1]
5. The next consideration is the submarine. We are on record as favoring its abolition, but so long as they exist, they must be reckoned with and it would seem to me that the same policy in building in this type, as was proposed in the destroyer type, would be sound.[2]
6. Last we have aircraft themselves. They are perishable. They should be replaced when over-age if for no other reason than hazard to the life of the flyer. Although new tonnage in ships will require their complement of planes, just as they do their complement of guns, for under the present naval policy, aircraft rise and fall in numbers according to the mobile units they serve.

Finally, summing up all the considerations above mentioned I believe that – A truce or limitation of naval construction extending over a period of time not greater than from the present time to the date of the next Naval Conference in 1935, could be entered into by us as one of the contracting parties, provided all other naval powers were participants, and the naval position of this Country would not be jeopardized materially from the fact of participating in this truce, provided the following policy were adhered to and reservations were secured which would authorize our right to:

(a) Continue building on all ships which have been authorized, or are under construction, or for which the contracts have been let.
(b) Continue the modernization of battleships, a thing not in the nature of new construction but which if done well will prolong the usefulness of this type.
(c) Lay down three new aircraft carriers, intended to replace in operation the *Lexington* and *Saratoga* which are now operated at a very high cost, and the *Langley* which is experimental and will soon be obsolete.

[1]Most US destroyers were 1917–22 vessels of around 1,100t, the 'flush-deckers', totalling 267. New vessels began to appear in 1934 and 23 of about 1,500t, 36k, 5×5in, & 8–16×21in tt, were launched, together with eight 'Porter' class of 1,950t, 37k, 8×5in, 8×21in tt.
[2]US submarines built from 1924 were mainly large ocean-going patrol vessels for Pacific duty. A dozen were built by 1935, varying from 1,120/1,650t to 3,000/4,045t.

(d) Lay down each year not more than seven new destroyers to replace in some measure a type all of which are due for scrapping by the date of the next Naval Conference in 1935.
(e) Lay down each year not more than three submarines, to prevent us from getting into a position of too great inferiority in case this type is not outlawed at the next Naval Conference, where there is little prospect of doing so as long as France and Japan favor this type.
(f) To lay down in the exempt tonnage class as many ships or gunboats as we deem necessary to safeguard our police interests throughout the world in time of peace.
(g) Build aircraft as replacements for aircraft becoming obsolete, and as may be necessary to complete the air equipment of the ships laid down under clauses (a) and (c).
(h) Be free to consider, without prejudice, any reservations accorded other naval powers, and to act as best suits the interests of the US, provided however that no act of ours shall violate any previous Treaty agreements.[1]

115. *Memorandum by Captain J. H. D. Cunningham*[2]

6 February 1932

Cruisers

...

5. The 'Ten Year Rule' is in process of being proved so utterly inadequate an instrument by which to measure our security as to call for no comment.[3]

116. *Chairman of the General Board to the Secretary of the Navy*

After 30 September 1932

...

41. The British Delegation in the early days of the Conference was most active in trying to adjust differences and effect an agreement among the

[1]Pratt's programme was largely carried out in the next decade.

[2]AoF Sir John H. D. Cunningham (1885–1962): ent RN 1900; navig spist; Med F & Grand F 1914–18; Cdr, Navig Sch 1922–3; Mr of F 1923; Capt 1925; staff cmds; NWC; DP; *Adventure*; *Resolution*; RA & ACNS 1936; ACNS (Air) & 5SL 1937–9; RA, 1CS, Med F 1939; VA & 1CS, Home F 1939–40; N cmdr, 'Menace', Dakar, 1940; 4SL 1941–3; Adm & CinC Levant & then Med 1943–6; FSL 1946–8; AoF 1948; Chm, Iraq Pet Co 1948–58.

[3]10 Year Rule: rolling guideline of 'no major war for 10 years', 1919–32.

various powers. Their relations with members of our own Delegation were particularly friendly. Although Great Britain advocated reduction in the displacement and gun caliber of battleships and cruisers, these questions at first were not emphasised because of our unyielding position with respect to them. The British strongly believed in maintaining intact the Washington and London Treaties until [31] December 1936. Perhaps somewhat inconsistently, they also advocated the total abolition of the submarine. They stated frankly that, when the London Treaty was revised in 1935, Great Britain would have to have more cruisers. When President Hoover's proposals were made on 22 June [1932] the British attitude towards us changed instantly to one of intense opposition. The friendly cooperation disappeared. The British counter-proposal, which will be discussed later, contained all of the old points of controversy. A rapprochement of the British and French Delegations developed, and indications pointed to cooperation of Great Britain and Japan in opposition to the proposals of the US. Great Britain is directly interested in and has taken part in the Franco-Italian naval negotiation because of the 'two power standard' which Great Britain is endeavoring to maintain in naval strength. The recent British proposal indicates no fundamental change in her attitude except in regard to Germany.

117. *Chairman of the General Board to the Secretary of the Navy*

18 January 1933

Memorandum on Naval Disarmament

B. *Indirect Purpose of Limitation of Armament*

...

5 (a). The direct purposes of the Washington Treaty are stated in the preamble in the following words:

> 'Desiring to contribute to the maintenance of general peace, and to reduce the burdens of competition in armament.'

It is a matter of record in the files of the General Board that even during the Peace Conference at Paris representatives of the British cabinet were seriously concerned at the growth of the US Navy and of the US merchant marine. At the end of the World War it was apparent that Great Britain was losing her traditional supremacy at sea. The large British tonnage included many obsolete or obsolescent ships. Great Britain was financially unable to undertake a large replacement program. The US had under construction the most powerful force of capital ships yet projected. Many of these ships were far along towards completion and funds for their completion were available. Being unable to follow the practice of outbuilding a rival, Great Britain employed other means of safeguarding her sea power. Hence the Washington Conference. Great Britain's agreement to parity in capital ships resulted in the scrapping by the US of 11 powerful capital ships, and the conversion of two others to airplane carriers, all of which were under construction and some of which were nearing completion. Great Britain had no capital ships under construction at that time but gained the right to lay down two which were subsequently completed. Both powers scrapped a number of obsolete vessels. Having obtained this agreement regarding capital ships by 9 January [1922], Great Britain's main purpose at the conference was attained and the British delegates prepared to return home and engaged passage for 14 January [1922]. Their departure was reported to have been prevented only by strong representations by the President of the US.

(b) Again at the Geneva Conference in 1927, self-interest was manifested by the British in regard to the cruiser category. No tonnage limit having been placed on cruisers by the Washington Treaty, the US for a time stopped building cruisers while Great Britain and other powers speeded up their cruiser construction programs. The result was that the US had a weak hand in playing for reduction, while Great Britain had a strong hand to maintain her existing cruiser strength. The conference failed. The US then passed the 15-cruiser bill, whereupon Great Britain suspended work on several cruisers and became eager for a conference. When the US thus gave evidence that it seriously intended to build, Great Britain consented at London to a smaller maximum than she had demanded at Geneva.

...

55. In cruisers, our proposal to reduce total tonnage without changing the characteristics of individual ships is strongly opposed by Great Britain, in spite of the concessions made by the US to equalise the number of cruisers allowed the US and Great Britain. The British are insistent on a reduction in displacement and gun caliber in cruisers and have failed to mention a figure for total tonnage limitation. They have stated that when the London Treaty is revised in 1935 Great Britain would have to have a larger number of cruisers than at present obtainable under treaty limitations. In her latest proposals Japan suggested reduction in displacement of both 8in and 6in cruisers, a large increase in her ratio in these vessels, and the prohibition of the flying-deck cruiser type.

...

57. The proposals respecting submarines met with opposition from many quarters. Great Britain strongly advocated abolition of the submarine. So, also, did the US up to the time of making these proposals

which were regarded as a compromise with many nations who opposed abolition of submarines. The British, however, seemed to feel that the US had failed to keep faith and had let them down. If submarines are not abolished, Great Britain advocates a reduction in displacement to 250 tons. Japan is opposed to reduction in the [total] tonnage or displacement of submarines. Italy would abolish submarines and capital ships together, but not one or the other. France and many other nations oppose abolition of submarines but might accept a reduction in size.

...

K. *British Counter-Proposals*

...

66. Again, if the limit for cruisers were reduced to 7,000 tons and 6.1in guns, the replacement of existing 8in cruisers would not take place for many years. Our oldest modern 8in cruiser does not become over-age until 1949 and we have six building but as yet uncompleted. The British are required to scrap four of the 'Hawkins' class by the London Treaty [1930] and their first replacement of 8in cruisers would take place in 1948. Japan has her full allotment built and could make her first replacement of 8in cruisers in 1946. Because of the numerous British naval bases and of the numbers of large merchant ships, the 7,000 ton, 6in cruiser serves the British interests markedly better than the interests of the US.

118. *Draft Memorandum by Rear Admiral Bellairs*

7 September 1933

US Naval Construction, 1934

...

'He [Secretary of State Henry L. Stimson] thought, however, that it was very unlikely that the US would actually build a 6in gun 10,000 ton cruiser.'

Unfortunately, however, circumstances have arisen which have now led to the decision by the USA under their programme framed within the provisions of the National [Industrial] Recovery Act to proceed with the laying down of four cruisers each of 10,000 tons and carrying 15 6in guns.

There can be little doubt that this decision has been reached in answer to the building programme of Japan.

In 1931 Japan launched a first 'replenishment' programme to give effect to terms of the London Treaty [1930], and in October 1931 two ships were laid down, each designed to displace 8,500 tons and to carry 15 6in guns. ...

The second instalment of the Japanese 'replenishment' programme was known unofficially by us to be in the course of preparation early in 1933 and it was understood to include two more cruisers of 8,500 tons with 15 6in guns. Money was voted in April 1933 for the commencement of this programme but details of the ships were not published.

It may be supposed, therefore, that when the USA Recovery Act was introduced in June 1933, Japanese intentions in respect to building for completion before the end of 1936 under the London Treaty [1930] were known. The Act gave the US Navy Board the opportunity for pressing their claim to meet the Japanese Navy's construction. The result is that in answer to the four Japanese 8,500 ton cruisers mounting 15 6in guns the USA now propose to build four ships of 10,000 tons each carrying the same armament as the Japanese ships.

...

We are now witnessing the first steps in competitive building in a new type. We shall have to follow suit. And it is probable that if the USA proceeds with her programme Japan will reply by increasing the size of ships which she can lay down in 1934, 1935 and 1936. She would be able to build two ships of over 9,000 tons. In the same years the US would be entitled to lay down three more ships of 10,000 tons each.

All this will make the problem of fixing a lower quantitative limit for the 6in cruiser in 1935 more difficult, a new expensive type of cruiser having been established. Failure to fix a lower quantitative limit will mean that the problem of quantitative limitation already difficult will become insoluble.

...

We might then suggest without prejudice to their future attitude both the USA and Japan should agree not to lay down these ships pending a full and frank discussion between ourselves, the USA and Japan on the situation as it affects naval limitation in the future.[1]

[1]The Japanese ships were the 'Mogami' class: 4 ships, 1935–7, 8,500t, 37k, 15×6in, 8×5in, 12×24in tt. Re-armed with 10×8in in 1939–40.

The British ships were the 'M' or 'Southampton' class and the American ships the 'Brooklyn' class.

119. *Chairman, General Board to the Secretary of the Navy*

16 September 1933

Replacement of 6in gun Cruisers

...

3. The determination of the type of 6in gun cruisers to be built by the US was made by the Navy Department upon the recommendation of the General Board of 21 January 1931 [not reproduced]. The displacement of 10,000 tons recommended by the General Board was based upon the strategic and tactical requirements to be fulfilled by a vessel of the cruiser type in such US naval operations as might be foreseen. The determination of this 10,000 ton type of cruiser was not influenced by the Japanese 8,500 ton type of cruiser, the first of which were not laid down until, respectively, October and December 1931.[1]

...

5. The Board recognises that the British Government for some years has desired to reduce, by international agreement, as now by 'quantitative limitation', the maximum displacement of ships, particularly of battleships and category (b) cruisers.

The General Board has however consistently recommended characteristics for vessels to fit the needs of the US Navy. The Board believe it would be detrimental to the interests of the US to agree to the reduction in size of the cruisers under discussion. It considers that the exploration of quantitative limitation with respect to the cruiser type will not be fruitful, and, consequently, that cruiser construction should not be suspended on account of awaiting such exploration.

6. With respect to the status of construction of the four 10,000 ton cruisers, the Board understands that contracts for two of these vessels have been concluded at private shipyards and two have been allocated to US Navy Yards, with consequent commitments for labor and material. The suspension of work on these four vessels would cause a material reduction in the number of men re-employed in the shipbuilding industry.

7. The Board considers that the suspension of the construction of the recently ordered 6in gun 10,000 ton cruisers, with a view to their abandonment on subsequent international agreement, would represent a distinct loss to the offensive and defensive value of the US Fleet and would materially delay the US Navy, already far below treaty ratios with respect to other nations, in building up to treaty tonnage.

[1]This appears to give the lie to the common myth that the 'Brooklyn' class was a response to the 'Mogami' class.

8. The Board notes that the British proposal makes no reference to the disposition of the two 8,500 ton Japanese cruisers, reported as carrying 15 6in guns, now nearing completion after two years' building. So far as the General Board is informed, no objection has heretofore been made to this type of vessel.
9. In view of the foregoing, the General Board recommends that the US decline the suggestion of the British Government that it consider the suspension of the laying down of cruisers of the 6in gun 10,000 type.

120. *Memorandum of conversation between Prime Minister MacDonald and Norman H. Davis*

London,
2 March 1934

…

He [MacDonald] then said that Great Britain would not agree to parity with Japan. He had thought the first step would be to inform the Japanese Ambassador and to tell him that Great Britain was disturbed by the Japanese talk about an increase in their naval ratio, which was unjustifiable because Great Britain is entitled to a larger ratio than Japan since her fleet has to cover two oceans, whereas Japan has only a limited area to cover. He said he would like to feel that US felt the same way about it. Furthermore, he thought he ought to advise the Japanese Ambassador that Great Britain is quite disturbed by their fortifying the mandated islands, which they had no right to do. He said that before having such a talk he thought it well for us to be in accord in refusing to accord parity to Japan, to iron out any difficulties as regards the future make up of our respective navies and also to decide what we would do with regard to a naval agreement as between ourselves in case Japan refused to renew the present Treaty.

I told him that the US was also definitely opposed to parity for Japan but that, as regards the proposed talk with the Japanese Ambassador, I thought it would be wiser and more effective for the US and England to speak separately to the Japanese, rather than for the one to speak for the other.

…

Mr MacDonald manifested considerable anxiety and concern about the attitudes and activities of Japan and said, in effect, that he not only considered it of the greatest importance that the US and England reconcile any differences in the point of view as to their respective navies but, for the promotion of world peace and stability, it was vitally important that they cooperate most closely. I told him that I had always favored the most friendly cooperation between our two countries and was satisfied that President Roosevelt feels the same way.

121. *Davis to President Roosevelt*

London,
6 March 1934

… The British are unquestionably disturbed as to the far-reaching effect which the present Japanese activities may have, and they are most desirous of reaching an agreement with us, if possible, because of the salutary effect which it might have on Japan. … their policy will, in my judgment, be to iron out their differences with us with regard to maintenance of naval parity, to reach a common understanding as to the Japanese demands for an increased ratio and even to go further, if we are disposed to do so, for the maintenance of peace and the protection of our respective rights and interests.

122. *Ambassador Bingham to Roosevelt*

American Embassy,
London,
8 March 1934

Since writing to you this morning [not reproduced], I attended a lunch given by our retiring Naval Attaché, Captain Arthur L. Bristol, and was seated next to the First Lord of the Admiralty, Sir Bolton Eyres-Monsell.[1] Almost immediately he said to me that he thought our general situation, particularly our Japanese situation, made it highly desirable for both countries to cooperate in dealing with the whole naval situation, and that we could handle the Japanese situation satisfactorily if we handled it together. I told him that I agreed with him and thought there was every reason why we should act together in our common interest. He said that their situation required a number of fast, light cruisers in order to protect their commerce, and I told him that I quite understood that, and, furthermore, that our situation required ships large enough to make long journeys and come home, because we did not have the facilities for re-fitting and re-fuelling which the British had, and he said that he understood

[1]Capt Arthur L. Bristol, Jr., US Navy: Capt & NA, London, 1932–4; Hawaii 1941; VA & Cdr, Support Force, Atl F., & CinC, US Forces, Argentia & Iceland & UK, & Cdr, TF24.

that perfectly. At the end of the conversation I told him that we ought to be able to carry out our naval programs along the lines best suited to our own countries, without suspicion, competition or hostility, with which he expressed himself as heartily agreeing.

123. *William Phillips to Roosevelt*[1]

State Department,
Washington, DC,
21 March 1934

…

Mr Bingham confirms our guess, that while the British are disturbed over the naval situation and are eager to cooperate with us, they prefer to cooperate 'on their own terms', and that 'we are to seek their cooperation as a favor to us'. However that may be, I am confident that the British are slowly moving towards the realization of the need of a change of front.

124. *Memorandum of a Conversation between R. L. Craigie, Vice Admiral C. J. C. Little, Ambassador Bingham and Norman H. Davis*

Claridge's,
London,
12 April 1934

…

With regard to the Japanese claim for parity or an increased ratio, Admiral Little said that, from the naval standpoint, they would be opposed to any increase in the Japanese ratio, that he did not see how Japan could justify such a claim, that the Washington Treaties were negotiated on the basis of security and that since the navies of England and the US have much more territory to protect in a defensive way, whereas Japan has only a very limited area, from a defensive standpoint the Japanese were already on a parity.

[1]William Phillips (1878–1968): diplomat; Peking; Chief, Div of FE Affs; London; Sec, Harvard 1912; 1st Asst Sec St 1917; Minr to Netherlands 1920–2; U SSt 1922–4; Amb to Belgium 1924–7; Minr to Canada 1927–9; U SSt 1933–6; Amb to Italy 1936–41; Dir, OSS, London 1942; India; Amb to SHAPE 1943–4; Anglo-US Cttee on Palestine 1946; Thailand-French Indo-China Bdr Cmn 1947.

125. *Bingham to Roosevelt*

London,
23 April 1934

. . .

The British are deeply concerned over the situation, both in Europe and in the Far East. They realize they are in no position to repel an attack from the air. They believe all hope for disarmament is gone, and I am convinced that all thoughtful people here believe that the only hope for peace in the world lies in cooperation between the British and ourselves, and that they eagerly desire it. They want peace as earnestly and sincerely as we want it, and we are in a better position to deal with them now than in all the long period since I have known them. We are in a good position to treat with them, so far as it may be advantageous to us. …

126. *Admiralty: Naval Staff Appreciation*

April 1934

Requirements for the 1935 Naval Conference

I. General Strategic Requirements

Naval Strategy

1. Our naval strategy is based on the principle that a fleet of adequate strength, suitably disposed geographically and concentrated against the enemy's fleet, provides the 'cover' under which security is given to widely dispersed territories and our mercantile marine on the trade routes. … Whilst, however, the main fleet is the basis upon which our naval strategy rests, naval requirements are not satisfied solely by its provision. The 'cover' it can provide is rarely complete, and instances have occurred in all wars of units detached by the enemy evading the main fleet and carrying out attacks of a sporadic nature on territories and trade. To deal with these sporadic attacks, cruiser squadrons are required above and beyond those forming part of the main fleet. It may be sufficient to maintain these squadrons cruising within various areas liable to attack, but if this system fails, or, after experience, is thought likely to fail, it will be necessary to resort to the Convoy system to provide adequate security.

2. The Convoy system to be efficient depends on sufficient escorts being available. The normal form of attack being by enemy cruisers, supplemented

by armed merchant cruisers, it follows that vessels of these types are required as escorts. It is thus seen with our numerous and essential merchant shipping, numbers of cruisers and armed merchant cruisers are necessary. Whereas the latter ships are in existence and can be fitted out in an emergency, cruisers must be provided in peace.

3. Without escort the grouping of merchant ships in convoy becomes a source of danger rather than a safeguard. The alternative method of defence for merchant ships in areas where the enemy is active is by independent routed sailings, which is a less efficacious method. If this fails, shipping must be held up till adequate escorts are available. This delay can only be acceptable for brief periods.[1]

…

Requirements for Full Security

…

7. A proper naval defence policy is that we should be able to provide in the Far East a naval force of sufficient strength to secure the Empire and our supplies against any Japanese encroachment, and at the same time insure ourselves in Europe against interference by the strongest European Naval Power – at present France. …

…

9. In the last 12 years our naval security has been seriously jeopardised, so that the despatch to the East of a fleet sufficient to meet that of Japan, combined with a distribution of cruisers to ensure the security of our sea communications against Japanese attack, would leave us with a strength in European and Home Waters definitely inferior to that of the strongest European Naval Power. …

Minimum Requirement

…

14. It has been assumed in this paper then that our minimum strategical requirement for security can be stated as follows:

> We should be able to send to the Far East a fleet sufficient to provide 'cover' against the Japanese Fleet; we should have sufficient additional forces behind this shield for the protection of our territories and mercantile marine against Japanese attack; at the same time we should be able to retain in European waters a force sufficient

[1]It is arguable, geometrically, that even unescorted convoys are safer than independent sailings, as a given number of ships in convoy occupies a smaller area of sea and gives fewer opportunities of attack than the same number sailing independently.

to act as a deterrent to prevent the strongest European Power (at present France) from obtaining control of our vital home terminal areas while we can make the necessary re-dispositions.

It is on this strategical requirement that these proposals are based.

Summary of Capital Ship Proposals

...

45. The Naval Staff's proposals for capital ship limitation may be summarised as follows:

(a) We should seek a qualitative limitation of 25,000 tons with 12in guns but can accept a figure as high as 28,000 tons with 12in guns.
(b) We should seek to maintain the Washington ratio of 15:9:1.75 for ourselves, Japan and the strongest European navy.
...
(f) It is essential to begin replacement of capital ships in 1937, and we should seek an agreed replacement programme for the principal naval Powers at the rate of three ships in two years for ourselves and the US and a corresponding rate for Japan.[1]

Strategical Requirements

...

47. Our cruiser requirements may be considered to be made up of three parts –

First, the cruisers required for working with the Main Fleet and the smaller fleet in Home Waters. This [is] governed by the size of the fleets in question, and thus the capital ship ratio can be accepted for this part of our cruiser requirement.
Second, those required for distribution in squadrons in various parts of the world for protecting our merchant ships from attacks by enemy cruisers and for exercising control over the enemy sea communications. This part of the requirement is governed principally by the world wide distribution of our territories and the great number of merchant ships on which we rely for vital supplies, and partly by the strength of the attacking forces that may evade our covering force.
Third, cruisers required as convoy escorts in any part of the world in which risks to our trade are deemed to be sufficiently serious to require imposition of the convoy system. The magnitude of this

[1]The five ships of the 'King George V' class were laid down in 1937 and completed in 1940–2: 35,000t, 28k, 10×14in, 16×5.25in.

requirement is governed by the number of merchant ships in the area in which convoy is to be instituted.

48. In an Eastern War for the first requirement we need 25 cruisers for work with the Main Fleet, and as a bare minimum 4 for the Fleet in Home Waters, a total of 29.

For the second requirement we need 73 cruisers or AMCs, and for the third requirement 46 more, sufficient to provide escorts in the Indian Ocean and Western Pacific only. This gives a total of 148 cruisers or AMCs as security requirement for a Far Eastern War.

49. For a war against the strongest European Power – France – … It is calculated that in such a war we require 40 cruisers in Home Waters and the Mediterranean with the Main Fleets, and 30 for cruiser squadrons in other parts of the world. These figures make no allowance for convoy escorts. A system designed to counter submarine attack visualises the possibility of placing the North and South Atlantic [trades] in convoy, and would require about 110 ocean escort vessels, on the basis of one per convoy. …

…

52. Nevertheless, the total required by the calculation in paragraph 48 above is now far beyond the financial capacity of the country in time of peace. The ideal would be to provide a cruiser escort with each convoy. This is not practicable, but on ocean passages the vastness of the area compared with the number of merchant ships renders enemy attack so unfruitful that they would probably employ only AMCs in these areas, and consequently an AMC might be sufficient. A compromise, therefore, has been adopted by stipulating a minimum of 70 cruisers, of which 10 may be over-age, as the number necessary for peacetime security, and making arrangements to provide rapidly the balance of 78 required for a Far Eastern War in the form of AMCs to be taken up on the outbreak of war. …

…

66. As regards large 6in cruisers, Japan is building six of 8,500 tons each, the USA are building four, and a further three are projected, of 10,000 tons each. Our own 'M' class will be about 9,000 tons. Like the 8in gun cruiser, these powerful ships would be such a threat to our other 6in cruisers, which are necessarily dispersed for trade protection, that we must have an ample margin in the type, and the least that is acceptable is the Washington ratio [of] 5:3 *vis-à-vis* Japan. We should, therefore, have 10 ships against the Japanese six, and the USA will presumably require parity. With these exceptions no more ships of the type should be built if we can secure agreement to a lower qualitative limit for 6in cruisers in future.

Tonnage Requirements

...

69. The cruiser requirements of the British Empire then are –

15 8in gun cruisers	146,800 tons
10 'M' class	95,000 tons
37 6in gun cruisers at 7,000 tons	260,000 tons
8 6in gun cruisers at 5,000 tons	40,000 tons
70	541,800 tons.[1]

70. ... To limit ourselves to a point on the upward curve of increasing cruiser tonnage, as was done in the London Naval Treaty [1930] for the sake of acceding to the US desire for parity on a low level, is too rigid and hampering for a treaty which, as proposed earlier in this paper, may last for 10 years.

...

72. The corresponding tonnage of the USA is principally of importance to us as it affects Japan's demands. We can not accept for the latter any figure for 6in cruiser [total] tonnage that would give Japan more than 60% of our total cruiser tonnage.

Aircraft Carriers

Quantitative Limitation

...

85. The air requirements of the Fleet necessitate the provision of five ships of 22,000 tons, of which four should always be with the Main Fleet. ...[2]

Duration of the Treaty

...

155. It is proposed that the Treaty should remain in force for a period of about 10 years.

[1]11 (+2 RAN) 'County' of 10,000t, 8×8in; *York*, *Exeter*, of 8,400t, 6×8in; 8 'M' or 'Southampton 9,100–9,400t, 12×6in; *Edinburgh*, *Belfast*, of 10,550t, 12×6in; 8 'Leander' of 7,000t, 8×6in; 4 'Arethusa', 5,250t, 6×6in. It is not clear what other ships are included.

[2]As it was, Britain built only *Ark Royal*: 1938, 22,000t, 31k, 16×4.5in, 60 aircraft. She retained *Eagle*, *Hermes*, *Argus*, *Courageous*, *Glorious*, *Furious*.

127. *Memorandum by Chatfield in Preparation for the 1935 Naval Conference*

April 1934

X. Summary of Proposals

Duration of the Treaty

95. (a) We should repeat our conviction that the total abolition of submarines is desirable and that failing total abolition they should be limited to a unit size of 250 tons.
(b) Failing (a), we should retain the existing qualitative limitation of 2000 tons standard displacement and 5.1in guns.
We should propose an ultimate reduction to a total submarine tonnage of 40,000 tons and a limitation of not more than 45 units.

128. *Memorandum by General Board*

9 May 1934

Building Program, Fiscal Year 1935

2. In the Estimate of the Situation, in discussing new construction the CNO states:
'Appropriations for 1936 should, therefore, include laying down of one carrier [of] 15,000 tons, two 1,850-ton destroyers, 12 1,500-ton destroyers, and six submarines of about 1,300 tons. Furthermore, it is believed that the plans for Fiscal Year 1936 should also provide for the laying down of replacements for the light cruisers *Omaha* and *Milwaukee*. These replacements cannot be laid down before 1 January 1936.'[1]

The General Board considers that this statement by the CNO is in effect his part of the joint action of the General Board and the CNO directed by the Secretary of the Navy in reference (a) [not reproduced].

. . .

4. In its recommendations for Building Programs in recent years the General Board has emphasised the importance of rapidly building the US Navy to Treaty strength. In its letter, GB 420-2 (serial no. 1578) of 16 September 1932 [not reproduced], it stated:

[1]Adm Standley's proposals led to the carrier *Wasp*: 1940, 14,700t, 29.5k, 8×5in, 76 aircraft. There were also several 1,500t destroyers, plus more 'Porter' class of 1,850t, six 'Perch' class submarines: 1936–7, 1,330/1,997t, 19.25/8k, 1×3in, 6×21in tt.

> '10. The consideration of national security warrants extraordinary effort in the existing situation. For reasons already indicated, the Board considers the period in the immediate future a critical one from an international naval standpoint. The Board accordingly recommends such action as may be necessary to ensure the laying down at the earliest possible date of all vessels needed to supply the deficiencies noted herein.'

(Prior tables showed deficiencies below treaty limits in underage ships in the several categories).

Again, in its letter GB 420-2 (1619) of 10 May 1933 [not reproduced], it stated:

> '3. World conditions have not improved since August 1932. Due to the continuance of building in the interval by the other Powers the relative naval inferiority of the US has increased rather than decreased. …
>
> …
>
> 5. The commencement at once of a large building program is necessary to correct the US naval inferiority. Because of the time necessary to fabricate naval vessels, this correction can only be partly accomplished before the expiration of the London Treaty on 31 December 1936. Without such a program actively under way it will be difficult if not impossible to secure in the forthcoming 1935 Conference the maintenance of the present Treaty ratios.'

The Board then recommended building programs for 1934 (additional to the vessels in the 1934 Appropriation Act), for 1935, and for 1936. These three programs as recommended provided for laying down all vessels permitted by the Treaties by the end of the FY 1936.

5. Since the submission of these letters, the President has authorised the construction of a number of vessels under the National Industrial Recovery Act, and the 1935 Appropriation Act has provided for the building of the last 8in gun cruiser permitted by the London Treaty [1930], and of three 6in gun cruisers which will utilise, except for 3000 tons, all cruiser tonnage available at present under the Treaty. Thus by the action of President and Congress a material change in the naval situation outlined by the Board has been made and a substantial beginning of the attainment of Treaty strength has been accomplished.

6. Further the act of 27 March 1934 (the Vinson bill[1]) has established 'the composition of the US Navy with respect to the categories of vessels

[1]Carl Vinson (1883–1981): Dem, Ga; HR 1914–65; Chm, HR N Aff Cttee 1932–47; Chm, Armed Forces Cttee, 1949–65; sponsored several important naval bills.

limited by the Treaties [of Washington and London] ... at the limit prescribed by these Treaties, and has authorised the President

(a) to undertake the construction, prior to 31 December 1936, or thereafter, of the remaining available tonnage in the carrier, destroyer and submarine categories.

(b) to accomplish replacements when permitted by treaty, and

(c) ... 'to procure the necessary naval aircraft for vessels and other naval purposes in numbers consistent with a treaty navy.'

6. It is understood that the President intends to request an additional appropriation for Public Works, under which, if enacted, are to be laid down in the FY 1935 two 1,850-ton destroyers and 12 1,500-ton destroyers, and six submarines. Adding these to the vessels carried in the 1935 Appropriation Act, the construction begun in that FY will then be:

One 8in gun cruiser, three 6in gun cruisers, two 1,850-ton destroyers, 12 1,500-ton destroyers, and six submarines.[1]

7. It therefore appears

(a) that the construction of a Treaty Navy, including the replacements for ships becoming over-age, is fully authorised, and

(b) that the actual laying down of vessels has been ordered, or is intended, in such degree as to leave by the end of the FY 1936 the following tonnages necessary to complete the treaty navy for the US, in under-age vessels:

Category	*Tonnage*
Carriers	15,200 (+ app. 500 tons saved in construction of CV5 and CV6)[2]
Cruisers (a)	0 (full, permitted no new construction, although some margin in tonnage will remain)
Cruisers (b)	17,100 (3,000 remaining, + 14,100 in replacement of *Omaha* and *Milwaukee*)
Destroyers (1,850 tons)	5,500 (three vessels)
Destroyers (1,500 tons)	72,000 (48 vessels)[3]
Submarines	27,550 (20 vessels – includes 15,100 for replacement of vessels becoming over-age in 1937–39).[4]

[1]The last 8in gun cruiser the US was permitted was *Wichita*: 1939, 10,589t, 33k, 9×8in, 8×5in. There were probably three 'Brooklyns'; two 'Porter' class & 12 'Mahan' class destroyers; and perhaps the six 'Salmon' class submarines.

[2]CV5 = *Yorktown*; CV6 = *Enterprise*: 1937–8, 19,875t, 32.5k, 8×5in, 96 aircraft.

[3]Likely to be three 'Porter' class and probably vessels of 'Mahan', 'Gridley' and 'Bagley' classes, and perhaps ships of 'Sims' and 'Benham' classes.

[4]Perhaps 'Tarbor' class.

129. *Chatfield to Sir Warren Fisher*[1]

4 June 1934

...

I agree with Vansittart to the extent that we do not want to prompt Japan at the expense of a hostile and jealous US.[2] At the same time I am entirely with you that we do not want to tie ourselves as we have done in the past to the US, because she is unreliable and does not know her own mind and her statesmen do not know the mind of their own country.

Nothing that is said by the President or any of their Statesmen can ever be accepted at more than its face value, as we all know. Whether our diplomacy can steer so difficult a course as seems to be necessary between the USA and Japan I do not know, but if our recent example of trying to steer a course between France and Germany is to be trusted, it does not seem very hopeful, excepting that of course the type of antagonism between the USA and Japan is a very different type of antagonism than that between France and Germany.

The one thing that causes all the trouble is the endeavour to make military agreements to limit arms. That is why I should like to see the attempt to make Naval agreements abandoned and substitute for them political understandings, leaving each Nation free to build what she wants.

...

There are inherent differences between us and the US over Naval matters and I do not see how we can get agreement with them unless we are willing to sacrifice our security, or they are willing to sacrifice their pride.

130. *Experts' Meeting*

21 June 1934

At 1100, 21 June, experts met in Mr Craigie's office at the Foreign Office.

Present:

British: Mr Craigie, Counsellor at the Foreign Office; Vice Admiral Little, DCNS; Captain Danckwerts, Assistant Chief of Plans Division; Commander Clark (Secretary).[3]

[1]Sir Warren Fisher (1879–1948): CS 1903; Pmnt Sec, Treasy 1919–39.

[2]Sir Robert Vansittart (1881–1957): diplomat; Paris, Tehran, Cairo, Stockholm; Personal Pte Sec to PM 1928–30; Pmnt U Sec, FO 1930–8; Chief Dip Advsr to FS 1938–41; Baron 1941.

[3]Cdr A. W. Clarke: Capt, Admy 1939; Asst NA, Washington, July 1940; *Sheffield* Aug 1941; CoS to CinC Med, Jan 1943; Cdre & CoS, BAD, Jan 1944.

American: Mr Atherton; Rear Admiral Leigh; Commander Wilkinson; Mr Field.[1]

...

Vice Admiral Little then proceeded to supply details concerning the British Empire. He stated that the underlying reason for the figures to be given was to get what they (the British) wanted as cheaply as possible. He discussed the several categories in succession as follows:

Battleships

For reasons of economy it was desired to reduce the maximum size of battleships to 25,000 tons and 12in guns, but maintain the present treaty number of 15 ships. The characteristics which they believed attainable in such a ship, ...

8×12in guns – 50 calibre.

Speed 23 knots.

Radius 10,000 knots at economical speed.

Protection against 12in gunfire, against 750lb underwater charge, and against 1000lb bomb (structural hit, not underwater).

...

Dimensions: 610ft × 100ft × 26ft (standard displacement).

Regarding the drop from 16in to 12in guns, he admitted that some risk was involved during the transition period, but that this risk must be accepted for economy's sake. It would not seem serious because, at Jutland, for instance, three calibres of guns were mounted – 12in, 13.5in, and 15in. The separate calibres could be organised by divisions and any tactical advantage gained by opposing strong ships to weak might be balanced by the exposure of one's own weak ships to the enemy's strong. The risk could, of course, be reduced, or at least equalized by proper replacement tables.

...

Captain Danckwerts added that a new 12in ship would be preferable to an older ship even with heavier guns.

Admiral Little stated that 15 battleships were necessary in order to have two squadrons, roughly of 11 and four ships, in order to produce equality at the point of contact with the larger squadron, to be able to leave some ships at home, and to provide for the unavoidable absence of ships under repair. He stated that in regard to replacement, it should start in January 1937, and the rate of replacement was, of course, a question for decision,

[1]VAdm Theodore S. Wilkinson, US Navy (b. 1888): NA 1907; Vera Cruz 1914; Bu Ord 1917–18; gun spist; destroyers 1920–6; Bu Nav 1926–9; FGO, Scoutg Force 1930–1; Sec, GB 1931–4; Bu Nav 1939; CSO, Scoutg Force 1939–41; *Mississippi*; DNI 1941–2; Bat Div 2, 1942–3; Dep Hd, COMPAC; Cdr, III Amph Force 1943; Jt Strat Survey Cttee 1946.

Mr Field: unidentified.

but he doubted if discussion of that rate was profitable at the moment. Mr Atherton agreed that at present it was not profitable.

Aircraft Carriers

Admiral Little stated the British proposal as the reduction of maximum size to 22,000 tons, and of total tonnage allowance to 110,000, which would allow five maximum ships (or more smaller ships), permitting freedom of characteristics. He recognised the large absorption of tonnage by the *Lexington* and *Saratoga*, but stated that a reduction to the new maximum tonnage need be made only on the replacement of these vessels. He proposed a reduction of aircraft carrier guns to 4.7in, but admitted that 5in appeared suitable. This reduction in guns seemed logical since the aircraft carrier would normally avoid action, and guns for anti-aircraft defense or counter-destroyer fire would only be needed.

…

Cruisers

Admiral Little stated the following as the British position:

No more 8in gun cruisers to be constructed; the question of the replacement of existing cruisers (except for the 'Hawkins' class, which would be scrapped without replacement) would presumably not arise during the length of the Treaty, particularly if [it was] only for 10 years, because of the newness of these vessels. At the expiration of the Treaty the question as to this type of cruiser would be reopened.

Large (10,000 tons or thereabouts) 6in gun cruisers should be limited in the same ratio as 8in, and should be fixed in number, as 10, 10 and six for England, the US, and Japan respectively.

The remaining 6in cruiser tonnage should be allocated to vessels of not over 7000 tons.

On the above assumption the tonnage for Great Britain would be

Type	*Number*	*Tonnage*
8in gun	15	146,800
6in gun (large)	10	95,000
6in gun (small)	35	250,000
Total	60	491,800

He stated that 70 cruisers were considered necessary for the double purpose of protecting merchantmen and augmenting the fleet. The exact assignment of a given number to each purpose would depend on the enemy distribution of his cruiser force, whether in commerce raiding or with his fleet. He dwelt at some length on the necessity of having escort vessels with convoys not inferior in type to prospective enemy attackers, and emphasized, first, the desirability of avoiding the convoy system where possible, and second, the difference in any future conflict from the last war wherein the usual threat to a convoy was only from submarines. He noted, however, the two unfortunate instances where superior surface vessels had destroyed North Sea convoys after outclassing and defeating their escorts.

The table he gave showed 60 cruisers only; they would reach 70 by keeping 10 overage cruisers additional to these 60; these overage ships to be replaced successively by others becoming overage, while these last were also replaced by new building. He admitted that a modification of the London Treaty [1930] provisions would be necessary in order to preserve sufficient overage tonnage instead of scrapping down by 31 December 1936 to the Treaty limits.

...

Destroyers

Admiral Little said that the destroyer tonnages were necessarily dependent on submarine tonnage allowances, rather than on merchant shipping. If submarines could be abolished the British would fix the destroyer allowance at 100,000 tons. The present number of 150,000 related to the 40,000 ton submarine allowance striven for at London [1930].[1]

When, however, on account of Japanese objections, to avoid scrapping their underage submarines, the submarine allowance was fixed at 52,700 tons, the agreement of destroyer tonnage had proceeded too far to permit ready change, and the 150,000 figure was accepted. The British now, however, if submarines were not reduced to 40,000 tons or less, would retain 50,000 tons of overage destroyers, approximately four flotillas.

In size the British would retain the present figures of 1,500 and 1,850 tons, but would increase the 16% allowance of the latter sufficiently to obtain temporary parity with the large Japanese allowance of these heavy vessels, which allowance, however, disappears eventually under the terms of the present London Treaty [1930], if such terms are to be continued.[2]

Submarines

Admiral Little stated that the British thought the total abolition of this category desirable or, if not abolished, the greatest reduction practicable in submarine allowances. They would prefer a reduction in size to 250 tons, which would render these ships suitable only for coast defense work, but if this were not practicable would be satisfied to leave submarine size

[1]Essentially the ‘V’ & ‘W’ classes of 1917–20: 1,500t, 34k, 3–4×4in, 6×21in tt; modified for A/S & AA escort duties.

[2]These were the ‘Tribal’ class: 16 ships, 1938–9, 1,959t, 36k, 8×4.7in, 4×21in tt. RAN & RCN also built vessels of this type.

as at present. They desired a reduction at least to 40,000 tons maximum allowance, and the number to not more than 45 ships. If the French or Italians, for instance, wanted 70–80,000 tons they [the British] might take 40,000 and retain the overage destroyer tonnage as stated above. All Powers should, however, be granted parity in principle in submarines, as the grant of such parity to Great Britain for instance might help to pull down the demands for submarine tonnage of other Powers. …

General Discussion

…

… Upon Mr Atherton's noting that a 40% increase in cruiser tonnage would be difficult to explain, Admiral Little stated that the 339,000 tons of the London Treaty [1930] represented 50 ships, but that now with the larger ships built by other nations 408,000 tons would be necessary for 50 ships, and that therefore the actual increase asked was only 83,000 tons.

131. *Roosevelt to Davis*

26 June 1934

Tell the Prime Minister confidentially from me that it is still my thought that the difficult situation of modern civilization throughout the world demands for the social and economic good of human beings a reduction in armaments and not an increase; that I am well aware of the pressures exercised by Navy Departments and Admiralties; that, nevertheless, I hope those in high authority in government will work with me for a new naval treaty calling for a reduction in navies and that to that end I have suggested a renewal of the Washington and London Treaties for at least 10 years on a basis of a 20% reduction to be accomplished during that 10 year period.

I am not going into technicalities of tonnage or classes and guns at this time, because these can be solved if the naval nations agree on the big basic principle.

132. *Davis to Roosevelt and Hull*[1]

London,
27 June 1934

...

... In substance they [the British] tell us that in 1930 England and America faced a single problem, namely, the Japanese; whereas today America still faces only this single problem, England now also faces the acute problem of Europe which is relatively academic to the US. Although they believe that real understanding between the US [and] Great Britain is developing in spite of many differences, which in the long run will grow and improve, they feel that our policy in the Pacific is an uncertain factor, increasingly so on account of our withdrawal from the Philippines, and that, therefore, they must, themselves, be prepared for all eventualities. This opinion is predominant in the Baldwin group which is the dominant factor in British politics. They are thus confronted with the problem of dealing with the Japanese problem alone, for which they want to be prepared but which they do not wish to tackle until the European situation is eased. While they do not definitely say so they intimate that if they cannot count upon our cooperation in the Pacific they must be prepared to deal with it alone but that if we could agree upon a policy of cooperation in the Far East – which they would like very much to do – our differences on technical naval questions would automatically solve themselves. They intimate however that public opinion here would not approve of any understanding with us as to such a policy unless it were embroiled in an agreement ratified by the Senate. ...

133. *Memorandum by R. L. Craigie*

Foreign Office,
27 June 1934

Note with reference to the records of the Anglo-American naval discussions, copies of which have been circulated to members of the Cabinet Naval Committee.

In the case of the first and second meetings with the US representatives two points were mentioned which, owing to their secrecy, it was agreed by both sides not to include in the official record.

[1]Cordell Hull (1871–1955): Dem, Tenn; HR 1903–21, 1923–31; Sen 1931–3; Sec St 1933–44.

At the first meeting on 18 June Mr Norman Davis suggested that both sides should undertake that in no circumstances would either country agree to any increase in the Japanese ratio of naval strength. The Prime Minister pointed out that it might be a mistake to lay down a hard and fast rule of this character but, as a compromise, it was agreed neither side would depart from its attitude of opposition to any increase in the Japanese ratio in any category without previous conversation with the other. It was agreed by both sides that it would be both risky and unnecessary to incorporate such an understanding in the official record, particularly when it was remembered that throughout the preparations for the London Naval Conference [1930] during that Conference there was the fullest consultation between the two delegations on all points without there having been any written undertaking to this effect.

The second point (which it was decided to record in the minutes) was raised by the US representatives at the second meeting and related to the position which would arise if, as a result of the Conference, it was found that agreement in regard to future construction could be reached between the UK and the US but with no other important naval Power. It was felt that in this case it would be most unfortunate if a race in naval construction were to ensue between the two countries and that accordingly our objective should be to reach a naval agreement between the two countries to regulate their respective naval construction, it being understood that the level agreed upon would be liable to modification, either upwards or downwards in accordance with the rate of building activity undertaken by other powers.

134. *Memorandum by the DCNS*

28 June 1934

Preliminary discussion with US representatives

I think it would not be without use to endeavour to summarise the position at which we have arrived in our preliminary Naval talks with the Americans.

2. At the meeting in the Prime Minister's room at the House of Commons yesterday Mr Norman Davis made one or two definite statements and proposals.

3. First, the Americans are surprised and alarmed at the proposed increase in cruiser strength which we have put forward.

4. Secondly, they do not criticise the necessity for the maintenance of an increased Fleet by the UK, in fact Mr Davis stated quite explicitly that they agree with our proposed increases.

5. Thirdly, the Americans agree that [the] political situation is not what it was in 1930 when the strength set out in the London Naval Treaty was agreed to.
6. In spite of the above Mr Davis said that his Government would like to see us make a 20% reduction on the London Naval Treaty [1930] tonnages. He did, I think, qualify this by saying that they would agree to continue the London Naval Treaty as it stands.
7. The position therefore *vis-à-vis* the Americans is once more evidently illogical. They agree that we require a greater Fleet but at the same time want parity at their own figure, that is the lowest they can get us down to.
8. Mr Davis admitted that the Americans had no figures and that their idea was to model their Fleet after ours.
9. He then went on to make the proposal that we should, at this stage, have no further discussions with the American representatives but that we should sound out the other Powers because it may be, as a result of these talks, presuming them to be favourable, we might be able to reduce our requirements.
10. There can be no doubt that the great surprise which the American representatives have shown at our increased cruiser requirements must be artificial.
11. In the first place, a close study of the problem which undoubtedly must be made in the Navy Department at Washington shows that with the increased qualitative limit of cruisers there is an automatic and unavoidable increase in the London Naval Treaty [1930] tonnages from this reason alone.
12. Secondly, our minimum requirements were explained to the Americans in 1927 and subsequent to the 1930 Conference the Prime Minister and the First Lord of the Admiralty stated in the House of Commons that these were still our requirements although we had agreed in the London Naval Treaty to reduce tonnage for a short period on account of the political situation. Since then the number of 70 cruisers has been frequently mentioned in this country and the American Press and Mr Davis himself admitted that he had heard of this number.
13. In the conversation between Admiral Field, the First Sea Lord, and Admiral Hepburn [US Navy] on 13 October 1932 [not reproduced], it was made clear to Admiral Hepburn that our requirement in cruisers was 70 but that we were ready to accept that 10 of these should be over 20 years of age.
14. We have been very frank with the Americans but in view of Mr Davis's suggestion that we may be able to reduce our requirements after discussion with the other Powers it seems that he had not understood that the figures we have put forward for cruisers are a minimum based on an

absolute requirement, in spite of the very full explanation of this problem given at the meeting with the technical experts.

15. I think, therefore, that we should now go further and emphasise this point with Mr Davis and point out that the only possible basis of agreement lies with the US agreeing to forego parity with us in cruiser strength and that they should adjust their own requirements after we have heard the Japanese proposals.

16. I would suggest that I should convey this idea to Mr Davis as being purely my own, pointing out to him the historical fact that, in the assessment of naval strength in the past, cruiser strength has always been omitted for the obvious reason that every Naval Power has their own particular requirements and that it is impossible to reconcile these on the basis of a ratio.

17. Mr Davis stated at the meeting yesterday that there was no possibility of the Senate ratifying a treaty which showed such an increase as we propose in cruiser strength.

18. I would like to ask Mr Davis whether he thinks there is any possibility of the Senate ratifying a Treaty which allowed the UK a greater cruiser strength than that of the US. I would also like to confirm from Mr Davis that he is going to tell us what the reactions of the Navy Department are to our battleship proposals and what basis they are working on.

135. *Davis to Roosevelt*

London,
28 June 1934

... While insisting that ... Anglo-American cooperation was more important than anything else, they [the British] did not recede from their position but did urge us to have patience and continue our efforts in a friendly and accommodating spirit to reach a treaty agreement ultimately. My personal opinion is that their strategy is directed in the last analysis towards either having a navy that will enable them independently to take care of themselves in the various eventualities they envisage or to say at a given time that if we can agree upon a common policy in contractual form in the Far East which would give them advance assurance that they would not have to deal with Japan single-handed, then they would not need so large a navy.

While the British feel that the possibility of a conflict with us is too remote to be taken into their calculations and while the Admiralty is, I am persuaded, in favor of the closest possible friendship with our navy and opposed to making concessions to Japan, they are nevertheless concerned over our superiority in large cruisers and likewise over those of the Japanese.

…

I am hoping Baldwin will realise that if the US and England should both propose to Japan a renewal of the London Treaty [1930] with such modifications as will result in a net total tonnage reduction, we would be on better ground to refuse a change in ratio. …

136. *Memorandum of Admiral Leigh's Interview with Vice Admiral Little, DCNS*

4 July 1934

…

After a friendly greeting Admiral Little went directly to the point, asking me if it were not possible for me to give the Admiralty some better idea of our program for the 1935 Conference than had yet been given. He stated that without talking figures we could, in a way, discuss ships, characteristics, sizes needed, capabilities, etc.

At the outset I told him that we did very much wish to come to a friendly understanding with them, that their figures for increased tonnage were much higher than we had any idea they would be, that we earnestly wanted a reduction in total tonnage of approximately 20%, that this was the wish of our President and we had hoped they would agree if all other countries involved did so. The situation would change if all agreed to a reduction since our respective needs would change.

I told him that we had made special effort to meet their views in regard to the size, 25,000 tons, of the battleships which they want; that our constructors could not meet our desire for protection, armament, speed, etc., in a 25,000-ton battleship; that we were not willing to go below a 14in gun and that we wanted more than eight guns to the ship. We felt so large and expensive a gun platform should have at least 12 × 14in guns and that we were evidently requiring more protection all around than they were getting in the 25,000-ton, eight gun, 12in gun battleship.

I said it was essential for our battleships to have what we called power of survival, ability to go long distances, fight it out with an enemy and be able to return a long distance to a base. This meant the protection must be such that the ship would not be so badly damaged that she would sink en route to a base miles away. Our constructors had been informed what we wanted and they had made very long and careful study and found that what we required was very close to 35,000 tons – in fact it really ought to be 35,000 tons.

I told him that what I said about power of survival applied also to our cruisers. Because of our limited numbers we had to have what might be called an all purpose cruiser – one that could work not only with the fleet but one that could be sent out on independent hazardous duties, with expectation of success, and with strong offensive powers. For while the ships were built for our defense in actual war we all know that the best defense is a strong, energetic offense.

Admiral Little said that they had made very careful study and said they were satisfied with what they could get in a 25,000-ton battleship with 12in guns. He repeated much of what he had said at the experts' meeting on 21 June [130].

He said he believed that the US and England could come to a general understanding about this conference which would be agreeable to each other. He said we must hold together as later some country might put forward figures or a program that would be impossible.

137. *Rear Admiral Richard H. Leigh, US Navy: Conversation with Admiral Little*

13 July 1934

In a previous conversation Admiral Leigh had told Admiral Little that we were asking the Navy Department to give us data on our battleship designs in a form similar to that of the British, i.e., protection, allocation of weight, etc. ...

At 1500 Admiral Leigh and [Commander] Wilkinson met with Admiral Little and Captain Danckwerts in Admiral Little's office, and gave them copies of data on [a] 35,000 ton and [a] 32,000 ton 14in gun battleship, and of a sheet of comparative data of these designs and of the British 25,000 ton 12in gun design, with percentages of weight allocation noted. The variation in allocation of weight to hull and armor, respectively, in which a much greater percentage was allotted to armor in the American designs, was mentioned, and Captain Danckwerts stated that the British armor weight had been pared down very fine to get within the 25,000 ton displacement limit. Admiral Little said that they did not really expect to find agreement on a 25,000 ton limitation but he thought that if agreement could be reached on 30,000 tons a fine 12in gun ship, amply protected, could be achieved. (Later, in Admiral Leigh's temporary absence calling on Admiral Chatfield, he stated that the Navy would really like to have a 35,000 ton type, but they couldn't afford it.)

Admiral Leigh showed them the US blue-print listing various possible battleship designs, but did not leave a copy with them.

Admiral Little then reverted to the cruiser subject and stated he hoped they had made their position clear as to their need for cruisers, even though we might not agree to the increased tonnage, and showed a station chart of the world, with the present assignment of cruisers thereon, noting particularly the Australian and New Zealand cruisers on duty in [their] home waters, from which they could not readily be removed. These assignments totalled approximately 45, including some few in reserve. He stated that they were now too few. In reply to a question as to the maintenance of the 50 cruisers contemplated at the time of the London Treaty [1930] running eventually on replacement to a figure of 408,000 tons, as cited by Mr Craigie, Captain Danckwerts showed a table in substance as follows:

15 8in gun cruisers	142,800 tons
10 6in gun large cruisers	95,000 tons
10 'Leanders'	71,000 tons
10 new 6in gun ships	72,000 tons
4 'Arethusas'	21,000 tons
1 ?	7,000 tons
50	408,800 tons

At this point Admiral Leigh went in to see Admiral Chatfield. During his absence Admiral Little remarked as quoted above, on their battleship size, and said he hoped [he] had made their cruiser position clear. [Commander] Wilkinson agreed that they had explained fully and hoped Admiral Leigh had likewise made clear to them our battleship position, with particular reference to the necessity of 'power of survival', which latter feature also applied to our cruiser designs and involved the requirement of large cruisers. Admiral Little stated that he had not talked with Admiral Leigh on cruiser displacements.

138. *Interview between Admiral Chatfield and Admiral Leigh*

13 July 1934

...

Vice Admiral Little told me that the First Sea Lord would like to see me around 1530. At about this time I went into the First Sea Lord's office, where he talked mostly about their cruiser figures. He gave me the Admiralty's view of the need for 70 cruisers. He stated that their War Plans Division had made a careful and thorough study of their cruiser needs with a view to reaching *minimum* figures which would meet their needs. That the figures presented to him showing 70 cruisers, as the minimum, were very convincing. That he had gone thoroughly into the matter personally and that holding the position he does and realizing his responsibility he could do nothing less than urge the 70 cruiser program. He went quite into details as to the stations of the cruisers, and said he hoped our Navy would understand their position. He stated that this program of their needs was without any thought of defense against the US. That the War Plans Division had no plans for war with the US; that such a thing did not enter into their calculations. He was very anxious that we should understand their position.

139. *Leigh and General Board to CNO and Secretary of the Navy*

30 July 1934

[Part of preliminary conference with MacDonald, Monsell, Little, Craigie, with Cdr T. S. Wilkinson, US Navy, Ambassador Bingham, Davis and Atherton]

…

3. Summarising the course of the conversations, …

(a) The British officials were most cordial and friendly and on every occasion evidenced their desire for cooperation with the US, both in matters affecting the 1935 Conference and, as far as might be practicable, in general political affairs, such as a common understanding with reference to the Orient.

(b) The British stated very definitely their fleet needs, especially as to more cruisers, and no indication was apparent, up to the time of discontinuing the conversations, that later on or at the actual Conference, they would moderate their proposals as to cruisers. They did indicate, however, that they would not force the issue of the 25,000 ton battleship, and in fact would be satisfied with 30,000 tons or even more.

(c) The British emphasised the fleet needs were not concerned directly with our navy, but occasioned by the French and Japanese construction. They were affected indirectly however by the size of our ships, in that it furnishes precedent and occasion for similar construction by the Japanese. There was never any open reluctance to accord parity to the US. There was, on the other hand, an agreement at the first meeting to sustain the British-US-Japanese ratios.

(d) In view of the British figures, which showed an inevitable large increase in combat Treaty tonnage, unless compensating decreases were gained by reduction in battleship size and carrier tonnage which were unacceptable to us, no concrete American figures were given, save for a statement that in general a renewal of the existing Treaty terms was desired, with such reductions within a maximum of 20% as could be agreed upon. This policy was adopted to avoid striking a compromise between the two stated programs, British and American, which might ensue if our desires were given in detail.

(e) The discussions were left open, for resumption when the Japanese delegation arrived in October, without any tentative agreements as the renewal of the Treaties. Mr Davis assumed that the US would be represented at that time.

(f) The British are, I believe, anxious for a continuation of the Treaties in some form, rather than the return to a status of no limitations whatever. They desire, however, that such continuation does not prevent their having a fleet satisfactory for their needs. The Admiralty views, overridden in 1930, are again in the ascendant and it appears probable that England would let the Treaties lapse before consenting to an unsatisfactory renewal.

4. Despite the British assertion of unconcern at our construction, I cannot but feel that, while honestly setting forth the type of Navy, and of individual ships, they require, they are at the same time determined to deter us acquiring vessels individually superior to theirs. Further, I believe that they are anxious, in the renewal of the Treaties, to establish a condition wherein the achievement of parity, not accomplished in 1930 under the London Treaty but only to be reached by 1937, is again deferred, possibly to the end of a subsequent Treaty. …

5. With respect to the US participating in a renewal of the conversations on the Japanese arrival in October, I do not now feel that any retrogression of the British from their present position can be expected so soon. On the other hand it may be unwise to abstain from those conversations both

(1) because an apparent mutual support between British and American representatives may subdue Japanese aspirations and

(2) because the British in our absence might be more inclined to 'trade' with the Japanese, particularly in view of our obviously cold reception of their own figures. The developments in Europe since our departure from London may, however, preclude or postpone any October meeting.

6. The British views do not, of course, supply a reasonable basis for discussion. Unless they are modified there appears little utility in calling the 1935 Conference. Such modification may however be forced either before or at the Conference by the Government overriding the Admiralty. At any rate, it would appear advisable for the US to continue preparation for the Conference, in order that we may avoid the charge, nationally and internationally, of prematurely scuttling it.

140. *Chairman, General Board to Secretary of the Navy*[1]

1 October 1934

1936 Conference for the Limitation of Naval Armaments

Part III

International Naval Status

27. Estimate of Situation, 31 December 1936.

Table C-3
Total built over-age and under-age 31 December 1936

	US		Britain		Japan		France		Italy	
	No.	Tons	No.	Tons	No.	Tons	No.	Tons	No.	Tons
Capital Ships	15	455,400	15	474,750	9	272,070	9	185,925	4	86,532
Aircraft Carriers	5	112,000	6	115,350	4	68,370	1	22,146	0	0
Cruisers (a)	16	152,550	15	144,260	12	107,800	10	105,923	11	103,641
Cruisers (b)	14	110,500	34	191,350	18	100,450	14	95,814	19	91,556
Destroyers	120	150,000	120	150,000	78	105,500	83	129,788	90	92,718
Submarines	49	52,700	44	52,700	35	52,700	109	94,496	75	52,807
Total [tons]		1,033,150		1,128,410		706,890		636,092		427,254

[The tonnages for destroyers and submarines for the US, UK and Japan are approximate.]

Part IV

6. Considering the ratios which should be established at the Conference:

As regards Britain and the US: The continuance of equality, parity, seems indicated. The necessity of trans-oceanic communication with outlying possessions and vital interests exists for both countries. Although Great Britain as an island empire is dependent upon the sea-lanes for its support, so too is the economic welfare of the US dependent upon its commerce and upon certain essential materials which must be obtained from overseas. The protection of territory and commerce dictates equal fleets between the two; similarly the possession of an equal fleet by either would prevent the development of any confidence by the other in a

[1]RAdm Frank H. Clark, US Navy (1871–1947): USNA 1903; Capt *Vermont* 1918–19; CoS, Bat Sqdns, Pac F 1919–20; NWC 1920–1; ONO 1921–3; *Maryland* 1923–5; ND 1925–7; RA & Cdr, Destroyer Sqdns, Scouting F 1927–9; cdr, LC Divs 1929–30; Dir, F Trng, ONO 1930–2; VA & Cdr, Scouting Force 1932–3; Gen Bd 1933–6; ret 1936.

successful outcome of an aggressive policy. (As a matter of fact this parity in combatant vessels does not represent a true parity of naval *strength*, because the larger merchant fleet and the far greater number of naval bases of Great Britain than those of the US throws the balance of naval power, when combatant fleets are equal, strongly in favour of Great Britain.)

...

11. With regard to natural resources, the US and Great Britain are both more capable of large increases of their naval armament than is Japan; between the two the US because of greater national wealth is probably capable of constructing and maintaining a larger naval armament than Great Britain, although the shipbuilding facilities of the latter are at present of greater capacity.

12. The factor of governmental and national temperament is difficult to project into the future. At present Japan is keenly interested in naval armaments and probably will continue so; Great Britain may be expected from her long tradition of seapower to continue naval construction at such rate as may be necessary to maintain her position on the sea. The US is now desirous of maintaining and increasing its fleet but no prediction can safely be made as to what the temper of the people and of the government on this point will be in the future.

13. ... The national resources would permit the construction of naval armaments by the US superior to that of Great Britain and greater than the 5:3 ratio of Japan. The governmental and popular interest in all three nations in naval construction would at present authorize the maintenance of fleets up to the present treaty limits. In the future, national interest in Great Britain and Japan would probably support maintenance up to treaty limits, and beyond if the Conference should fail or should produce wider limitations. In the US the lack of direct interest in the Navy by a large proportion of the population and the history of intermittent naval construction in recent years render it uncertain whether naval building would be regularly continued beyond the present treaty limits, unless the President himself strongly favors such action.

...

15. With respect to the ratios of France and Italy, the Board has considered in Part I of this series [not reproduced] that the naval armaments of these nations are of no direct concern to US. They are of concern to Great Britain. A common understanding with Great Britain with regard to naval armament is important to the US. The Board, therefore, believes that the US should take no direct stand with regard to the ratios of France and Italy, but that it should in general defer to the views of Great Britain with regard to the naval armaments of those two countries.

...

Part VI

Qualitative Reduction

...

4. Before discussing the characteristics of each respective category, it may be well to examine briefly the needs of the US in naval vessels. Naval strength is essentially a composite of fleets and bases. The US has few bases throughout the world and no secure base in the Western Pacific. With respect to the British Empire throughout the world, and to Japan in the Western Pacific, the US Fleet must operate with far less opportunity of recourse to a base. In order that this handicap may be minimized, the US needs vessels of the greatest practicable *power of survival* which can be produced within the characteristics of the respective types. This term includes not only ability to reach, operate in, and return in possibly wounded condition from distant area[s], but also the ability to give and take punishment with a fair chance against the preponderant numbers of attacking craft of all types that may be brought into action by an enemy from his nearby bases or home ports. The indispensable elements of survival are striking power (guns, torpedoes, airplanes, etc.); defensive power (deck and side armor, underwater protection by compartmentation); radius of action (fuel and stores of all kinds necessary for maintenance); speed; habitability (for protracted cruises).

...

Capital Ships

9. Any reduction of characteristics is disadvantageous. Considering the maximum reduction in size which has been seriously proposed, to 25,000 tons, this reduction cannot be accomplished without decreasing, to a vital degree, the power of survival of the individual ship in the essential elements of defensive power (against other weapons as well as against guns), radius of action, and speed. Such a decrease in size of our capital ships would render them less than capable of prolonged operation away from bases and more vulnerable to attack from light craft operating from enemy bases, thereby increasing the advantage due to British and Japanese bases (in operations in the Western Pacific), and of the British system of bases throughout the world. It would lessen the superiority of the capital ship to the cruiser forces. It would, in other words, reduce the present relative naval strength of the US with respect to that of the British Empire and Japan.

...

Cruisers

24. For the same reason that power of survival is essential to the US's capital ships, so it is necessary for cruisers. The essential elements of power of survival for the cruiser type cannot be supplied within a limiting displacement materially less than 10,000 tons. The cruiser must, in addition to service with the Fleet, operate against enemy commerce and in protection of our own commerce. A reduction in maximum permitted displacement would reduce the protection which could be afforded the cruiser, thus decreasing its power of survival and rendering it more *vulnerable* to the attack of cruisers and auxiliary types.

. . .

Submarines

31. Of the 15 submarines laid down or appropriated by the British Empire since 1 January 1930, six are from 1,500 to 1,850 tons, and nine are from 640 to 670 tons; however, the British Empire had previously laid down 15 boats of 1,475 tons.[1] Of the eight submarines laid down by Japan since 1 January 1930, six are from 1,400 to 1,900 tons and two are of 700 tons; Japan had previously laid down and completed 20 submarines of 1,635 to 1,955 tons displacement.[2] After the London Conference [1930] the US reduced the size of its submarines from the previous 'V' boats, which were of from 1,540 to 2,730 tons, to the 1,130 ton *Cachalot*. This reduction in size was due to the desire to increase the number which might be built within the total allowed tonnage. Later experience showed that 1,130 tons was insufficient to incorporate the characteristics desired by the US and the boats now building are from 1,300 to 1,400 tons displacement.[3] France and Italy, like Great Britain and Japan, are building two types of submarines, the large ocean-going submarines and the smaller coastal type. The smaller type submarine is more suited to the needs of these nations than it is to the needs of the US. For example, in operations by France, and Great Britain in the English Channel, by France and Italy in the Mediterranean, and by Japan in the restricted waters surrounding Japan, a number of these smaller types can be usefully

[1]British submarines, post-1918 types: *Oberon, Oxley, Otway*: 1927, 1,350/1,850t, 14/8k, 1×4in, 8×21in tt; 'O', 'P', 'R' classes: 16 ships, 1929–31, 1,475/1,780t, 17.5/8k, 1×4in, 8×21in tt; *Thames, Severn, Clyde*: 1933–4, 1,850/2,206t, 22/10k, 1×4in, 6×21in tt; 'S' class: 4 ships, 1931–3, 640/730t, 13.75/10k, 1×3in, 6×21in tt.

[2]Japanese submarines, 41 of them, built 1924–35, varied from 1,142/1,383t to 2,080/2,921t, with 1–2×3in, 3.9in, 4.7in or 5.5in guns, 6–8×21in tt.

[3]US submarines: 13 ships, 1925–36, 1,120/1,650t to 2,878/4,045t, 13.5–19.5/7.5–10k, with 1–2 3in, 4in, 5in, 6in, 4–6×21in tt.

employed.[1] However, it has been the policy of the US to build only general purpose submarines which can fulfil any duty which they may be called upon to perform.

. . .

Summary of Recommendations

34. For convenience, the recommendations developed above with respect to reduction of characteristics of vessels of the several categories are summarized as follows:
(a) *Capital Ships*: Present characteristics should be maintained, except the allowed caliber of gun may be reduced to 14in.
(b) *Aircraft Carriers*: Reduction of the present maximum characteristics to 22,000 tons and 5in guns is acceptable if urged by other powers, but should not be proposed by the US.
(c) *Cruisers*: No reduction of the maximum permitted displacement should be considered. No reduction of the gun caliber permitted to cruisers (a) or cruisers (b) should be considered.
(d) *Destroyers*: No reduction of the present characteristics should be considered. Increase of the percentage allowance of heavy destroyers, if proposed, may be accepted.
(e) *Submarines*: No reduction of present characteristics should be considered.
(f) *Aircraft*: No limitation of airplane characteristics should be considered.

Part VII

Quantitative Reductions

. . .

Capital Ships

12. The capital ship force is the backbone of a modern navy. The command of the sea can be exerted only by surface vessels which can occupy the sea areas as the infantry occupies the land; air or submarine craft may threaten this occupancy by capital ships but cannot of themselves occupy and control such areas. The basic strength of the

[1]French submarines, of which about 80 were built 1925–36: *Surcouf*: 2,880/3,250t, 18.5/10k, 2×8in, 8×21.7in tt, 4×15.7in tt; otherwise, largely 558–947/787–1,441t, 12–15/7.5–9k, 1×3in or 3.9in, 3–10×21.7in tt, or 32 mines; 'Redoutable' class: 31 ships, 1,384/2,084t, 17–20/10k, 1×3.9in, 9×21.7in tt, 2×15.7in tt.

Italian boats: 15 ships, 1928–36, 970–1,545/1,239–1,940t, 15–17/8–8.5k, 1–2×3in or 3.9in, 6–8×21in tt, or 20–36 mines.

surface fleet is in its heaviest vessels, under the protection of which its lighter craft may operate.

13. A large reduction in capital ship strength will weaken the staying power of the US Fleet, - its ability to operate in distant waters. Some reduction may be made, necessarily accompanied by compensating reduction in the fleets of Great Britain and Japan, without, however, too greatly reducing this staying power. …

…

Aircraft Carriers

16. The treaty allowances for the three major powers in the aircraft category are, respectively, 135,000, 135,000 and 81,000 tons. These allowances were fixed in the Washington Treaty. With the *Lexington* and *Saratoga* of 33,000 tons each, 135,000 tons permits the US to have, in addition to these two vessels, two 20,000 ton ships and two of 14,500 tons.[1] In the ultimate replacement of the *Lexington* and *Saratoga*, the US may construct three additional 22,000 ton carriers, making a total of seven. Similarly Great Britain which now has six carriers of a total tonnage of 115,350, may by the construction of another ship possess seven. Japan's allowed tonnage will permit five.

17. In view of the need for aircraft with the Fleet and of the large wastage factor which, due to the vulnerability of their decks, may be expected of carriers in an active campaign, these numbers should not be reduced. With respect to the US, particularly, the present treaty tonnage of aircraft carriers is required for operation in areas where no other facilities exist for the maintenance of aircraft.

…

Cruisers

19. The present total cruiser tonnage permitted the three major naval powers is: for Great Britain 339,000, for the US 323,500, for Japan 208,850; the disparity between the US and Great Britain is due to a differential introduced in the London Treaty [1930]. Great Britain has stated in the London naval conversations of 1934 a desire for 491,800 tons of under-age vessels, *plus* the retention of 10 over-age vessels, in order to furnish her with a total of 70 cruisers. Japan at Geneva in 1932 proposed an increase of her allotment to 230,000 tons, accompanied by reductions for the US and Great Britain. It is apparent that no serious proposals will be made in the 1935 Conference by Great Britain or Japan for a reduction of cruiser tonnage.

[1]Apart from *Lexington* and *Saratoga*, these included *Wasp*, *Yorktown*, *Enterprise* & *Ranger*: 1934, 14,575t, 29k, 8×5in, 76 aircraft.

20. From the point of view of the US, a reduction of its cruiser tonnage would be disadvantageous. Under the present allowance a total of 25 10,000 ton cruisers and 10 7000 ton cruisers, 35 in all, may be maintained. All estimates, based upon differing employments which may be required of cruisers, establish the requisite number for the US as greater than 35. As noted in the preceding chapter [Part VI, above], any decrease in the size of cruisers, by which the number could be increased without exceeding the limited tonnage, would be undesirable for the US. The role of the cruiser is so varied and the need for these vessels so widespread that any decrease in the number available, resulting necessarily from a decrease in the allowed tonnage, would seriously hamper the efficiency of the Fleet. Furthermore, the 18 cruisers (a) of the US, built and building, are all relatively new vessels, and of the 17 cruisers (b) built and building, only two (14,100 tons), will be over-age by 1943; a reduction of cruiser tonnage in any marked degree would require the scrapping of new and valuable vessels. No reduction should therefore be considered in the cruiser category, except that in connection with a reduction program to be outlined later a cut of up to 10% of category (b) cruiser tonnage may be accepted. No reduction of category (a) cruisers is acceptable.

141. *Memorandum by General Board*

1 October 1934

Summary of Recommendations

IX

1. …

(a) Since the Washington Conference, Internationalism, which was then at its peak, has been superseded in all countries by a strong feeling of Nationalism. Parliamentary government in many countries has been superseded by dictators, or by the rule of powerful, autocratic, radical or militaristic groups.

(b) The faith of the world in Treaties in general and of disarmament Treaties in particular has wavered due to Japan's actions in China, the failure of the General Disarmament Conference in Geneva to accomplish any concrete results, the large increase in the German military budget, the realignment of the World Powers in seeming preparation for eventualities, the unwillingness of France to state the terms of a security pact which she would consider acceptable, etc.

(c) The history of limitation of naval armaments has been marked by the efforts of the British Empire and Japan to limit and restrain the

US in every category the latter deems essential, and in the development of which the US may appear to excel. These efforts were successful at the Washington Conference in limiting the size and number of capital ships, and the then but partially developed airplane carrier. At the London Conference [1930] the 8in gun cruiser program of the US was successfully curtailed. In the development and operation of carriers, the US now leads the world; the latest US 8in gun cruisers are superior to those of other nations. Proposals to further curtail capital ships, carriers and 8in gun cruisers may be expected at the forthcoming Conference, and have already been suggested in the London conversations of last June.

(d) The attitude of the people of the US toward national interests, national policies, especially those which do not seem to be directly menaced, and toward national defense in particular has been listless and with little understanding.

These conditions make it imperative that no sacrifice be made in the present naval strength of the US relative to Japan and the British Commonwealth of Nations.

142. *Chatfield to Beatty*

10 October 1934

...

The second point that you might ram home is that meanwhile we should make the utmost endeavour to put the Fleet in a more satisfactory position in other types of vessel, particularly carriers and defence vessels of the anti-submarine type. Here you might refer to the new American programme launched by President Roosevelt last June, which included two 20,000 ton carriers and four 10,000 ton cruisers, not to speak of a host of other vessels. The US is helping to solve her labour difficulties by using her unemployed forces and men in what they call ‘rounding off the Navy’, an example which might well have been followed by our own Government in the past.

143. *Davis to Roosevelt*

London,
6 November 1934

…

When we got here there was a sentiment in certain quarters in favor of making some kind of a deal with Japan as the best means of keeping Japan in bounds, and also a feeling that Great Britain might, at any rate, play the role of mediator. However, the Japanese proposals, made public by Yamamoto, have been looked upon as so unreasonable and unjustifiable as to force the British Government to take a definite stand and to realize that it could not honestly or usefully act as a mediator. …

While the British still wish to be as conciliatory as possible with Japan, and avoid an absolute impasse, it is still my belief that, whenever they feel the situation demands the choice between standing with us on basic principles or of trying to conciliate Japan in such a way as to alienate us, they will choose the former.

144. *Roosevelt to Davis*

9 November 1934

…

I hope you will keep two definite considerations always in mind. First that Simon and a few other Tories must be constantly impressed with the simple fact that if Great Britain is even suspected of preferring to play with Japan to playing with us, I shall be compelled, in the interest of American security, to approach public sentiment in Canada, Australia, New Zealand and South Africa in a definite effort to make these Dominions understand clearly that their future security is linked with us in the US. You will know best how to inject this thought into the minds of Simon, Chamberlain, Baldwin and MacDonald in the most diplomatic way.[1]

…

If the worst comes to the worst and Japan in effect walks out on the three party conference, I am inclined to go along with your thought …, that England and the US should join in a statement. As a matter of practical fact, in such a case we could easily agree with the British by

[1]Simon was a National Liberal. Neville Chamberlain (1869–1940): dir of natnl svc 1917; Post Mr Gen 1922–3; Pay Mr Gen 1923; Minr of Health 1923, 1924–9, 1931; CEx 1923–4, 1931–7; PM 1937–40; LPC 1940.

some form of dovetailing categories so that they would have more light cruisers and we more battleship strength or something along that line.

It is unthinkable that the British would go along with even a slight Japanese increase. It would mean a further increase five years from now. You will remember that 1930 did give Japan an increase over 1922.

145. *Davis to Roosevelt*

London,
27 November 1934

…

… Chamberlain told Lord Lothian[1] that he was now convinced that Japan could not be trusted. He thought that she was perhaps bluffing and that England and the US must at the proper time take a common stand and call this bluff. He thought, however, that it was better to avoid a rupture just now for fear that we would drive Japan in desperation to make an alliance with Germany, which he was satisfied was under consideration.

146. *Davis to Roosevelt*

London,
14 December 1934

…, the Government leaders insist that they want cooperation with us more than anything else, but that cooperation, in order to be successful requires day-to-day, close and friendly contact and consultation on matters of common interest.

…

…, the British are most eager to avoid a naval race which they feel they cannot afford and which they feel will be inevitable if the Japanese get away without some arrangement for returning later.

… MacDonald particularly is obsessed with the fear that if the door is now shut tight on Japan and it is not made known to her that she may, if she wishes, re-enter negotiations, not by another door but by the same one, it will be politically impossible to knock and ask for re-entrance, and naval limitation will be over. …

…, the British are also becoming more fearful of a German-Japanese alliance and point to the fact that there is an increasing amount of

[1]Philip Kerr, Marquis of Lothian (1882–1940): col civ svc; Lib MP; Chllr, D of Lancr 1931; USSt for India 1931–2; ed, *Round Table* 1933; Amb to US 1939–40.

propaganda in the Japanese press in favor of this, with the added suggestion that Germany should be brought into any Naval Conference. They insist, therefore, that if Yamamoto gets away from here without being tied up in some way to return at a fixed date, Japan will inevitably get together with Germany.

To sum up, since the British cannot get a binding agreement from us for cooperation such as they would like, they do not feel like casting Japan entirely aside. Their policy is, first and foremost, to cooperate with us in any event, but, second, to induce Japan as far as possible to cooperate with us both, which they are hopeful of achieving by making Japan realize that, while there is not today a common Anglo-American front, there is a common point of view on fundamentals from which we will not depart.

In my talk with MacDonald yesterday, … he impressed me definitely as being suspicious of Japan but, at the same time, most fearful of getting into trouble with Japan. He sang his old song about being fearful of inciting the Japanese jingoes and thus placing the British interests in the Far East under the possibility of attack. He said, for instance, that if the Japanese should try to take Hong Kong there was no guaranty of our aid since we could not enter into an alliance which, of course, he understood. I replied that what we should have was a broad basis for cooperation and nothing in the way of a political alliance to which the American government and people would never agree. …

147. *Meeting of the British and American Delegations*

17 December 1935

The First Sea Lord briefly outlined the UK bilateral interviews with the Japanese. The UK had gained the general impression that the Japanese have some scheme at the back of their minds for adjusting the common upper limit for some Powers either above or below the general level. The Japanese idea is not at all clear. The UK representatives had finally stated that further clarity was necessary. …

2. *Mr Norman Davis* then gave a general account of the meeting between the USA and Japanese Delegations on the morning of 17 [December 1935]. The Japanese had reiterated their statement about the removal of menace and aggression and said that public opinion demanded that they should have parity with America. The USA repeated their argument that the Washington Treaty gave equal security and Admiral Kato had at that time said that he did not want equality with the USA. An attack on Japan with existing ratios was not a possibility. On the other hand, the USA had the Philippines and Alaska to protect, both of which

were nearer to Japan than America, and the Japanese proposal would make it impossible for the USA to defend these places if Japan attacked them. The US representatives said that if there was anything they could do to remove Japanese suspicion of the menace from the USA they would do it, provided that thereby they did not jeopardise their whole position. Finally, they said that they could not accept the common upper limit and Japan could not accept the ratios. The world position at present is very disturbed – with the war in Abyssinia and the Japanese armies on the march in China. The USA could not understand what Japan's policy was or what it might develop into. Consequently, the political foundation of the past treaties is now defective, and we could not erect another building on this faulty foundation.

…

9. *Mr Norman Davis* said that we must definitely state to Japan some time before the Conference breaks up, that if Japan does anything to disturb the present relative strengths, this action will be countered by the USA and Great Britain who will outbuild her whatever she does. He also thought the time will come when we must definitely say that we will not accept the common upper limit, but admitted that this had been practically said already.

10. *Admiral Chatfield* asked what would be the American view if Japan agreed to the building programme idea provided that it was accompanied by acceptance of the right to parity. *Mr Norman Davis* and *Admiral Standley* replied very definitely, 'No, we could not accept that'.

11. … *Admiral Standley* was understood to say that they were prepared to build 70,000 tons of cruisers if necessary. *Admiral Chatfield* pointed out that on the same naval income Japan could do much better than we could. She has cheap labour and no large pensions bill to absorb a portion of her Estimates. Nevertheless, *Admiral Standley* felt confident that either the USA or the UK could easily outbuild Japan. …

148. *Meeting of British and American Naval Representatives*

23 January 1936

Admiral Chatfield … said we should have to build some 25 to 30 cruisers in the next five or six years. Consequently the limiting of the size of cruisers was very important to us, they had to be large enough to do their work and keep the sea, but they must not be so large that the British Cruiser Force would bear the appearance of being a threat to the entire world. We concluded that the best size was from 7–8000 tons.

…

… *Admiral Standley* [said] The overriding object of the US Delegation was to foster a closer Anglo-American understanding, but in so doing it was all-important that it should not be possible for them to be accused, on return, of having 'sold out to the British'. They had come to this country prepared to give a six-year building programme. They were ready to refrain from 8in gun cruiser building and to agree, for a period of years, not to build any more 6in gun cruisers of 10,000 tons. …

… *Commander Schuirmann* suggested that the UK should build only nine of the 'Southampton' class. *Admiral Chatfield* pointed out that nine cruisers of 10,000 tons for the US corresponded to 10 cruisers of 9,000 tons for the UK.[1]

The meeting then turned to the discussion of capital ships. … We were agreed upon the facts, *viz.,* that if everybody came into the Treaty the gun calibre limit should be 14in, whereas if the Japanese or any other country was out of the Treaty the limit should be 16in.

It was important to maintain the Anglo-American accord, but at the same time to meet criticism in the US. …

149. *Davis to Roosevelt*

London,
20 December 1935

…

In the first place, there is every indication that the pro-Japanese group here, who were routed last year, have been unable to mobilize their forces again, and there seems to be no tendency in that direction. On the contrary British cooperation has so far been 100%. Instead of trying to put the onus of disagreement with Japan upon us, they have been taking a positive stand against Japanese contentions, and the Admiralty tells us that they are convinced that, while it is important to be patient and tactful with Japan in order to try not to give them an occasion to run out, it would be a mistake even to flirt with the idea of making any concessions as to principle. The Japanese apparently had the idea that they might tempt the British by taking the position that, because of their far flung Empire, they were justified in having the largest navy but that did not apply as between Japan and the US. The British did not take the bait. My contention has been that the question of parity between the British Empire and the US

[1]Cdr Roscoe E. Schuirmann, US Navy (b. 1890): USNA 1912; Sec, Gen Bd 1933–5; Tec Advsr, London N Conf 1935–6; Admin Aide to CNO 1936–7; destroyers 1937–9; Dir, Central Div, ONO 1939–42; RA 1942; ACoS (Intelligence) to CinC, 1943–4; Dep Cdr, US N Forces Eur 1944–5.

has already been settled, that each one feels that this gives it equal security, and that each one of us is convinced that with a ratio of 3 to 5 Japan unquestionably has equal security and an equal power of defense. The British have definitely committed themselves to this thesis.

150. *Davis to Hull*

London,
3 February 1936

. . .

Chatfield stated today that although he could not commit the British Government, the present intention of the Admiralty is to have 60 underage cruisers as soon as possible after 1942. The last of the cruisers necessary to attain 60 underage would be laid down in 1940 and completed in 1943. In addition they intend to retain 10 overage cruisers so that in 1943 they would have 60 underage and 10 overage cruisers. The majority but not all of the cruisers laid down would be of 8,000 tons, the remainder would be somewhere around 5,000 tons displacement. We estimate that the resultant increase in British underage cruiser tonnage will be between 125,000 and 150,000 tons and in addition 10 overage cruisers of about 50,000 tons will be retained, so that the total increase over the cruiser tonnage allowed by present treaties will be between 175,000 and 200,000 tons. The British intend to maintain 150,000 of underage and 40,000 tons of overage destroyers, a total of 190,000 tons.

In this connection, it should be borne in mind that even on the basis of the 50 cruisers which the British were able to retain under the London Naval Treaty [1930] they would have to increase their total tonnage beyond the 339,000 [tons] provided by that treaty, because the replacement of their small wartime cruisers by larger units would add approximately 70,000 tons to their present treaty strength. The large increase in underage tonnage now forecast by the British is, therefore, not entirely due to an increase in numbers but is in part accounted for by the replacement of small cruisers built for special service in [the] World War.

151. *Exchange of Notes between the Foreign Secretary and the Head of the American Delegation*

London,
24 March 1936

Note from Mr Davis

The US Delegation wish to record that it has been recognised and accepted as a policy as between the Government of the UK and the Government of the US that competitive building as between the countries should end, and that the principle of parity should apply to all classes of vessel. Notwithstanding the fact that it has not been possible to negotiate a general agreement designed to continue the system of limitation of naval armaments by total tonnage in categories, the Government of the USA desire to preserve the benefits resulting from the existing system and to avoid the dangers and expense attendant upon unrestricted competition in naval construction. They would be glad to learn the views of the Government of the UK upon the matter.

Note from the Foreign Secretary

The Foreign Office,
London,
25 March 1936

...

I can assure you that the friendly relations which have prevailed between the US and UK Delegations have been a source of pleasure to all of us, and we are greatly indebted to yourself, Admiral Standley and the other members of your Delegation for your wholehearted co-operation throughout the difficult period of negotiation which now lies behind us.

I am glad, furthermore, to be able to confirm the correctness of your understanding in regard to the maintenance of the principle of parity. We are in full agreement that there should be no competitive building between our countries and that neither country should question the right of the other to maintain parity in any category of ship. I can go further than this and say that, in estimating our requirements, we have never taken the strength of the US navy into account.

152. *The Treaty of London for the Limitation of Naval Armament*

25 March 1936

…

3. No vessel which at the date of the coming into force of the present Treaty carries guns with a calibre exceeding the limits prescribed by this Part of the present Treaty shall, if reconstructed or modified, be re-armed with guns of a greater calibre than those previously carried by her.

4. (1) No capital ship shall exceed 35,000 tons standard displacement.

(2) No capital ship shall carry a gun with a calibre exceeding 14in; provided however that if any of the present Parties to the Treaty for the Limitation of Naval Armament signed at Washington on 6 February 1922, should fail to enter into an agreement to conform to this provision prior to the date of the coming into force of the present Treaty, but in any case not later than 1 April 1937, the maximum calibre of gun carried by capital ships shall be 16in.

5. No aircraft carrier shall exceed 23,000 tons or carry a gun with a calibre exceeding 6.1in.

6. (1) No light surface vessel of sub-category (b) exceeding 8000 tons, and no light surface vessel of sub-category (a) shall be laid down or acquired prior to 1 January 1943.

(2) Notwithstanding the statement in paragraph (1) above, if the requirements of the national security of any High Contracting Parties are, in His opinion, materially affected by the actual or authorised amount of construction by any Power of light surface vessels of sub-category (b), or of vessels not conforming to the restriction of paragraph (1) above, such High Contracting Parties shall … have the right to lay down or acquire light surface vessels of sub-categories (a) and (b) of any standard displacement up to 10,000 tons. …

Part III

11. (1) Each of the High Contracting Parties shall communicate every year to each of the other High Contracting Parties information … regarding His annual programme for the construction and acquisition of all vessels. …

Part IV

24. If any High Contracting Party should become engaged in war, such High Contracting Party may, if He considers the naval requirements of

his defence are materially affected, suspend … any or all of the obligations of the present Treaty. …

…

26. (1) If the present requirements of the national security of any of the High Contracting Parties should, in His opinion, be materially affected by any changing circumstances … such High Contracting Party shall have the right to depart for the current year from His Annual Programmes of construction and declaration of acquisition. …

Part V

27. The present Treaty shall remain in force until 31 December 1942.

153. *Standley to Hull*

27 May 1936

…

It appears that the British Government

(a) Intends to convert three 'Hawkins' class cruisers from sub-category (a) to sub-category (b).

(b) Desires to convert the fourth vessel of this class to a training ship and asks whether the US Government objects to such a conversion.

(c) Intends to increase her destroyer tonnage by retaining 40,000 tons of older destroyers, desires to arrange this increase by 'friendly negotiation' rather than by invocation of Article 21 (the escape clause), and desires the views of the US on the subject.

The Navy Department is of the opinion that the proposed action by the British Government as to the four vessels of the 'Hawkins' class is not in accord with the terms of the Treaty. Although this proposed action would impair the integrity of the Treaty as a whole, the Navy Department is of the opinion that it would not otherwise be detrimental to the naval interests of the US … The Navy Department therefore recommends that, while no specific objection be made to the proposed action, approval be not given in any form.

The Navy Department is of the opinion that the retention of excess destroyer tonnage should not be made the subject of 'friendly negotiation' and recommends that the US Government take the position that action by Great Britain other than as provided by Article 21, Part III, of the London Treaty of 1930 is not acceptable.

If Great Britain retains an excess of 40,000 tons of destroyers by invoking Article 21, the Navy Department recommends that the US exercise its right to retain an equal amount of destroyer tonnage.

PART V

THE SAILORS MEET
1919–1939

It might be thought that some of the pieces in this Part are rather humdrum but in their ordinariness lies their interest. Two items chronicle the formality and protocol of meeting between American and British ships [159, 160]. Their stiffness is relieved by reports of lavish dinners, entertainments and hospitality [159, 160, 162, 165]. Despite obvious nationalistic rivalries, relations between the men were extremely cordial [167, 170]. There were amusing tales of how Prohibition was circumvented [162, 165].[1] By tacit consent, wrangles over limitation at Geneva and London [1930] did not carry over into meetings between the sailors afloat [162, 163, 165] and there was a notable absence of the suspicion and distrust which is the repeated theme of other Parts.

The British marvelled at American technical expertise and productive capacity, and even more at the largesse apparently available to the US Navy [154, 167, 170, 178, 179]. It was undeniable that the Americans were more advanced in a material sense, their ships equipped with facilities and comforts the cause of admiring remarks by British officers. In part the comparative lack of modern equipment in British ships was the result of financial stringency but it was also a cultural decision – what had been good enough for Nelson appeared to be good enough for a much later Georgian navy. The US Navy, though founded in the time of Nelson, was much more up to date, reflecting the expectations of American society; and, as there were problems at times with recruitment and retention of enlisted men, it was also incumbent on the Navy Department to ensure that the gap between civilian life and that on the ocean waves was closed, not only with home comforts but also with a more relaxed code of discipline [154, 167]. The enlisted men were well educated and their life afloat was relieved not only by comforts but also by labour-saving machinery [154, 167, 170].

Nowhere was the American identification with the leading edge of technology more apparent than in naval aviation. Senior American officers were concerned to retain control of their service's air power and believed

[1]Prohibition of the manufacture and sale of alcoholic beverages was imposed by the 18th Amendment to the US Constitution (operable from Jan 1920) and enforced by the Volstead Act (1919).

it to be superior to the British system, where the RAF managed all aviation under the Trenchard doctrine of the indivisibility of air power.[1] American officers hoped fervently that Chatfield, First Sea Lord between 1933 and 1938, would win his fight to regain control of the FAA for the Royal Navy, as their own air wing would then be safe from the fate that befell the RNAS in 1918. Several attempts to create a separate American Air Force had been fought off in the decade following the Armistice [154, 164, 170]. American developments were followed keenly in the Admiralty, though there was a measure of complacency about British attitudes to air attack [177, 178]. American sailors of all ranks were air-minded and well-versed in naval aviation; the deck had been laid for the Pacific naval air war, ultimately a colossal triumph for the US Navy.[2] The Royal Navy's loss of its First World War lead in naval aviation was in part due to the disastrous hiving-off of the RNAS to the newly formed RAF, in which the FAA became a Cinderella, and in part due to the equally damaging lack of finance. There was also, however, the fact that British naval leaders were much less air-minded than their American confrères [164, 169, 170]. It is interesting to note also that there was talk of glider bombs and autogyros in naval air affairs; both became practical military equipment by 1945 [177, 179].[3]

Royal Navy observations on the American naval officer corps and its routine were unflattering: the senior officers as a whole seemed mediocre and beset by too much bureaucracy, while the ward rooms of American ships appeared to be peopled by strangers. Promotion was slow in the US Navy, and mostly by seniority, resulting in the average age of officers in senior ranks being rather higher than in the Royal Navy, a by-product of the tight civilian control over the fighting services traditionally exercised in America. Although the naval college at Annapolis merited high praise, it is noteworthy that most of its graduates did not take up naval commissions [163]. A handful of the most senior officers – Pratt, Hepburn, Standley and Leahy – drew approval, but Coontz was not highly thought of, though Secretaries of the Navy prior to Charles Francis Adams were averse to appointing men of superior ability to the Navy's top job – Chief

[1]Marshal of the RAF Viscount Trenchard (1873–1956): Army 1893; RFC 1912; Brig-Gen & cdr RFC, France 1915–17; CAS Jan–April 1918; W Frt bombers 1918; CAS Feb 1919–29; Marshal of RAF 1927. Single-minded believer in deterrent, war-winning bombing & indivisibility of air power; the RN's nightmare domestic opponent.

[2]Most US officers and many enlisted men learned to fly in the inter-war period and Captains commanding carriers were always qualified pilots, while experienced naval aviators headed the Bureau of Aeronautics at the Navy Dept.

[3]The autogyro, although practicable, was quickly replaced by the helicopter, under testing in America late in WWII. The glider bomb was successfully launched by the Germans in 1943; among its great naval successes were the sinking of the new Italian battleship *Roma* and heavy damage to the *Warspite*.

of Naval Operations [154, 163, 165, 168, 170].[1] It was evident from the meetings of the sailors at all levels that actual contact between the two Navies brought about not only cordiality but frankness [156, 157, 159–60, 162, 164, 167–71, 179]. Conversely, the brooding suspicion and malevolent distrust evident among some American flag officers – and portrayed in earlier Parts – was ascribed to lack of friendly and informal contact [166].

The British favoured close and frequent contact – increasingly so as the war clouds gathered – for they were keen on American support in future crises [158]. This desire for American backing in a second world war, nevertheless, should not hide a strong sense of competitiveness all across the world. While Americans felt that the British Empire sought to hold on to its territories, sea lanes, influence, markets and superior sea power, the British were uncomfortably aware of a young pretender's hot breath on their necks.[2] The Ambassador to Argentina, for example, bemoaned the decline of British prestige and presence in Latin America in the post-war era, again the product of financial stringency [161]. In the late 1930s it was evident that the United States was empire-building in remote, uninhabited Pacific islands, seeing them as staging posts for new air routes; disputes over landing grounds and rights simmered on throughout the Second World War.[3] There was a covert struggle over these more-or-less barren rocks, with the British occasionally asserting Imperial sovereignty and the Americans refusing to acknowledge it [172–6].

Since the British were increasingly desperate to secure practical American help in the darkening international situation of the 1930s, it is surprising that the Americans should make the running on the 'special relationship'. On several occasions, British Admirals on the North America Station were compelled to hear speeches by dignitaries (some highly placed) on an Anglo-American partnership to advance and ensure world peace, underwritten by joint action by their respective navies [155, 159, 162, 163, 168]. The Americans were, however, 'warm water' friends and envisaged merely a balmy world scene requiring only police measures to maintain an Anglo-American imposed peace. 'The public opinion cry is – at all costs keep out of everything European', said one British Admiral; another felt that the two might make common cause in the Pacific, against an expansionist Japan, but that Britain could not anticipate help in the Atlantic [168, 171]. While Britannia remained unconquered

[1]Adm Arthur J. Hepburn, US Navy (1877–1944): C-in-C, US Fleet; Chm, Base Constrn Bd 1938; reports on Pac fighting 1942–3.

[2]See *Anglo-American Naval Relations, 1917–1919*, pp. 477–614.

[3]A. P. Dobson, *Peaceful Air Warfare: The USA, Britain and the Politics of International Aviation* (Oxford, 1991).

and ruled the Atlantic waves, the United States and its Navy did not need to worry about its Eastern Seaboard and concentrated its focus – and its forces – on the great wastes of the Pacific. Standley and Leahy might have gone further in cementing a naval entente but the President, Franklin D. Roosevelt, though a realist, yielded to a public opinion, a press and a Congress generally hostile to an active role in world affairs, and preferred patiently to educate the nation in the frank realities of the world scene, pointing out international events unfavourable to American interests. The United States believed that the modern world could be divided safely into two Hemispheres; by the 1930s that was no longer possible, as Chatfield made clear [168, 171].[1]

By the end of Chatfield's term as First Sea Lord in 1938, Standley, Leahy and other senior American officers were coming round to the view that the 'special relationship' had to have more force than mere rhetoric.

[1]For Chatfield's views on the world situation, see Simpson, *Admiral Sir Andrew Cunningham* (London, 2004), pp. 32–4.

154. *Visit of Admiral of the Fleet Lord Jellicoe to the USA*

20 January 1920

…

7. Mr Schwab told me that he had built and was building 150 destroyers, all large modern vessels of 1200–1400 tons displacement, and that he has completed two in 40 days.[1]

9. …

A large number of the leading officers of the US Navy were met, including Admiral Coontz, at present Director of Operations, and Rear Admirals Benson and Mayo.[2] Admiral Coontz did not impress me as being an officer of much capacity.

…

14. I am greatly impressed by the vast preparations which are being made by the people in the US to strengthen and increase their navy, …

Although it is true that we have little, if anything, to learn from them on the subject of fleet work at sea, no one can visit the Navy Yards and the new vessels without being convinced that that in matters relating to material we can learn much from the US Navy, and full information on technical and scientific developments will be of the greatest possible assistance to us in the future. US naval officers have assimilated much information from us, and they are putting it to good use in their new vessels. Scientific appliances are used to a much greater extent than in our Service, though some of them are in the nature of luxuries.

…

16. At present the US Naval Authorities are having great difficulties in the provision and retention of their personnel, but if they can overcome these there is little doubt that their Navy will become a formidable force in the future.

Enclosure I

…

5. The US naval officers state that attempts are being made to form an Air Force independent of the Army and Navy. In the judgment of US naval officers, this is a very mistaken policy, the opinion being that there should

[1]Charles M. Schwab (1862–1939): Pres, US Steel Corp 1901–3; Pres, Bethlehem Steel 1904–18; Pres, Emergency Fleet Corp 1918.

[2]RAdm William S. Benson, US Navy.

RAdm Henry T. Mayo, US Navy (1856–1937): USNA 1876; hydrographic spist; Capt 1908; *California* 1909–10; Cdt, Mare Is NY, San Francisco 1911–13; Aide for Pers 1913; RA 1913; cdr, Bat Div 4, 1913; Tampico, Mexico 1914; VA & 2 i/c, Atl F 1915; C in C, Atl F 1916–19; ret 1920.

be a naval air force. The policy of a separate Air Force is being strongly opposed by the Navy.

...

42. The plant [at the Washington Navy Yard] has, however, convinced me that the US Navy is very earnestly pressing on with the perfection of most of its material, and is also completing a very large plant, which should enable them to carry out enormous naval programmes in the future.[1]

[Comment by an unknown staff officer:] This report emphasises the fact that the US intends to have 'the largest navy in the world.'

155. *Vice Admiral H. P. Huse, US Navy, to Daniels*[2]

Chatham,
21 October 1920

Report of Force Activities

...

4. If the Department considers it inadvisable to permanently assign battleships to the European station, I suggest a temporary assignment for about six months of a division of battleships which could be relieved at the expiration of this tour by another division from home waters. These ships should of course be temporarily merged in the forces in European waters and should operate under the orders of the Force Commander. The announced purpose of this policy should be to promote the morale and improve the education of our personnel, but the actual effect on world politics in the maintenance of peace would unquestionably be very great. It is difficult to realise the great power for good that rests in the battleships of the US. America's altruistic policy in the Philippines, in Cuba, and in the settlement of the World War has given us a position absolutely unique in history. Such a position, however, brings with it responsibilities as well as respect and power, and I believe that this responsibility would be met, in part at least, by the mere presence of our battleships in the troubled waters of Europe.

...

[1]The Washington NY produced ordnance.

[2]Vadm H. P. Huse, Cmdg, US N Forces in Eur Waters, 1920–21.

11. The time has passed when the US can withdraw inside the limits of its own territory and take no part in the affairs of European nations. The expansion of the British Empire and its success as a commercial power are clearly traceable to the fact that its navy has always been present in remote parts of the world gathering information, surveying possible localities of commercial opportunities, advertising England, protecting its citizens, and lending assistance in times of instability and stress. Such activities if carried on by the American navy would have the effect of a propaganda which would not only benefit American trade relations but would unquestionably make for a policy of justice and altruism in the world.

156. *Vice Admiral Mark Kerr to Sims*[1]

14 October 1921

… there is not a grain of imagination in either Admiralty or Air Ministry.

…

You are far ahead of our people in experimenting with aircraft in naval warfare. It is partly owing to shortage of money over here, but principally for want of imagination in controlling bodies.

157. *Rear Admiral Philip M. Andrews, US Navy, to Sims*[2]

Force Commander,
US Naval Forces in European Waters,
30 June 1924

…

The British Navy is top notch. When I visited last Fall at Greenwich [Naval] War College … they had about 300 officers taking different courses – War College, Anti-Submarine, Communications, Navigation, planning, etc. That's a thousand a year – four months' course for most of them. Where do we do that in practical things? And the Petty Officers and men get the same careful training. And their fleet is *doing* things. They are way ahead of us. Twelve years enlistment, better training. Then when

[1]Adm Mark Kerr (1864–1944): N Atl, E. Med 1903–4; head, British N Mission, Greece, 1913–15; 1st FO to qualify as pilot 1914; C in C, British Adriatic Sqdn 1916–17; Dep Chf, Air Staff & Maj Gen, RAF, 1918; Cdr, SW Area, RAF; ret 1918.

[2]RAdm Philip M. Andrews, US Navy (1866–1930): USNA 1886; Capt *Montana, Maryland* 1913; Cdt, N Trng Sta, San Francisco 1915–16; NWC 1916; *Mississippi* 1918–19; RA 1919, Baltic, E Med, Adriatic; Cdt, Norfolk NY & 5th N Dist 1921–3; Cdr, (tempy) VA, US N Forces, Eur, 1923–5; Cdt, 1st N Dist & NY, Boston 1925–30; ret 1930

they reduced heavily they threw out the poor ones and now they let few in, and only the best. It will never be 5: 5: 3. …

158. *Andrews to Sims*

Le Havre,
28 August 1924

The British are so keen on our friendship. They want, but know they can't have, an alliance or understanding with us. They can't understand the hostility still shown them. I think it is due mainly to Irish-American or German-American sentiment in our Navy and Navy Department. I believe that the future peace of the world depends on the US and Great Britain. There is a League of Nations! And that does not mean that both countries will not need rapping now and then. We both have politicians! And commercial rivalry will always cause dissensions, but they must be adjusted between us. Great Britain is *sick*. I have had them tell me Great Britain is near *ruin*. British Admiral told me that. ...

159. *Report of Proceedings of the Commander-in-Chief, North America and West Indies Station*[1]

January 1925

General Letter 7.

…

2. I left Nassau, Bahamas, in *Calcutta* on 2 January with *Capetown* in company, and arrived off the mouth of the Mississippi river at daylight on 5 January. The Division proceeded up the river to New Orleans and there found the *Richmond* flying the flag of Rear Admiral T. P. Magruder, US Navy, and the *Cincinnati* anchored in the stream. The USA was saluted with 21 guns, and the salute was returned by the *Richmond*. The latter then saluted my Flag with 15 guns, which salute was returned by *Calcutta*.[2]

[1]VAdm J. A. Fergusson (1871–1942): S Af War; 2LCS, 1914–18; 1LCS, 1920–2; C in C, NAWI 1924–6; Adm 1926; ret 1928.

[2]*Calcutta*, *Capetown*: 1918–22, 4200t, 29k, 5×6in, 2×3in, 8×21in tt.

Richmond, *Cincinnati*: 1921, 7050t, 34k, 10×6in, 8×3in, 6×21in tt.

RAdm T. P. Magruder, US Navy (1867–1938): USNA 1889; Capt & Cdr, Patrol Force 4, Lorient, France 1917–19; *Nevada* 1919; RA & NA, Paris 1919–21; Cdt, 8th N Dist & New Orleans n base 1921–3; Cdr, LC Divs, Scouting F 1924–6; Cdt, 4th N Dist & Philadelphia NY 1926–8; Cdr, F Base Force 1929–30; Cdt, 8th N Dist & New Orleans N Opg Base 1930–1; ret 1931.

Calcutta came to anchor between *Richmond* and *Cincinnati*, *Capetown* passing ahead and anchoring above the *Cincinnati*.

Rear Admiral Magruder called on me after anchoring.

The Coastguard, Mr Vuckin, also called on me.[1]

The following day I returned Rear Admiral Magruder's call.

The usual salutes were fired on these occasions.

3. During our stay at New Orleans great hospitality was shown towards both Officers and Men, and many entertainments were arranged for their benefit.

As is usual in the US most of the dinners, etc., were accompanied by speechmaking to a very tedious extent, the general trend of the speeches being in the key of the necessity of the 'English-speaking races' controlling the earth.

Calcutta and *Capetown* went alongside on 7 January, and an 'At Home' was given on board both ships that afternoon.

4. I left New Orleans in *Calcutta* on 10 January with *Capetown* in company. *Constance* and *Curlew* left Key West the same day. …[2]

160. *Report of Proceedings of the Commander-in-Chief, North America and West Indies Station*[3]

September 1925

General Letter 15.

…

5. I arrived at Gloucester, Mass., on 21 September and found the *Detroit* flying the flag of Rear Admiral A. L. Willard, US Navy, and the *Shawmut*.[4]

The usual visits having been exchanged with the Rear Admiral I then received the calls of Rear Admiral L. R. de Steigneur, commanding the Boston Navy Yard and Major General Brewster commanding the

[1]Mr Vuckin: not identified.

[2]*Constance*: 1915, 3750t, 29k, 4×6in, 2×3in, 8×21in tt.

Curlew: 1917, 4200t, 29k, 5×6in, 2×3in, 8×21in tt. Many 'C' class cruisers were converted 1935–9 to AA ships, with 8–10×4in.

[3]Still VAdm Fergusson.

[4]RAdm A. L. Willard, US Navy (1870–1935): USNA 1891; Capt 1917; Cdt, Washington NY & Supt, N Gun Factory 1915–18; *New Mexico* 1919–21; ND 1921–4; RA 1924; NWC; LC Div 3, Scouting F 1925; Cdr, LC Divs 1926–7; Cdt, Washington NY & Supt, Gun Factory 1927–30; VA & Cdr, Scouting F 1930–2; Cdt, 5th N Dist & Norfolk, Va 1932–4; ret 1934.

Detroit: 1922, 7050t, 34k, 10×6in, 8×3in, 6×21in.

Shawmut: probably a minelayer.

Military District. On the following day I proceeded to Boston by motor car and returned these calls, afterwards calling on the Governor of Massachusetts.[1]

I received the warmest welcome possible from all these officials, indeed this was the case as regards everyone we met during our stay in Gloucester Harbour. The week passed in a succession of entertainments of all sorts, both to Officers and Men.

Every effort was made by Rear Admiral Willard and Captain Kautz of the *Detroit* to make matters easy for us. The motorboats of the ship were placed at our disposal, the men had a standing invitation to witness the cinema on board the *Detroit* each evening, and they were also entertained at a dance on shore given by the *Detroit* and the City of Gloucester which Rear Admiral Willard attended personally.[2]

A much more friendly spirit obtained between the ships' companies than has been my experience heretofore.

I consider a large portion of the credit for the undoubted success of the visit to be due to Captain F. L. Tottenham, Naval Attaché.[3]

161. *The Ambassador to Argentina to the First Sea Lord*[4]

Buenos Aires,
1 August 1927

At this moment we are making an effort to recapture lost ground in South American markets. I am convinced that it is in this year that we must strike. Being a naval people it does not redound to our prestige not to be able to show the white ensign permanently on the coast, for that ensign is the symbol of all our greatness. We now have one Naval Attaché for the whole of South America, whereas the US have a naval mission at Rio, besides Naval Attachés at Buenos Aires, Santiago [Chile] and elsewhere. This will never do. We cannot take a back seat in naval matters. Cost what

[1]RAdm L. R. de Steigneur, US Navy (1867–1947): USNA 1889; Capt *Arkansas* 1918–20, GF; Cdt, Norfolk NY, Va 1920–1; RA & Cdr, F Train, Atl F 1921–3; Cdt, 1st N Dist & Boston NY 1923–5; Bat Div 4 1925–6; Actg VA & Cdr, Bat Divs, Bat F 1926–7; Adm & CinC, Bat F 1927–8; Cdt, 3rd N Dist & New York NY 1928–31; ret 1931.

Maj Gen Brewster, US Army: unknown.

Govr, Mass: unknown.

[2]Capt Kautz, US Navy (1873–1927): USNA 1899; Capt 1921; *Detroit* 1925; *Wyoming* 1925–7; NA, Berlin 1927.

[3]Capt F. L. Tottenham (1880–1967): ent RN 1895; Turkey 1909–11; Capt 1918; Germany 1918–20; *Delhi* 1920–2; NA, Washington, 1922–5; *Excellent* 1926–7; *Rodney* 1928–9; RA 1930; 3CS, 1932–3; VA 1935; C in C, Af 1935–8; Adm 1939; ret 1940.

[4]Sir M. Robertson (b. 1877): FO 1898; Rio, Washington, The Hague; H Cmnr, Rhineland 1920; Agt, Tangier 1921; Amb Argentina Sept 1925–Feb 1930.

it may we must have a cruiser here. I am convinced in my own mind that had we had one last year, or, at least, a Naval Attaché permanently on the spot instead of having to wander around from post to post the Argentine order for cruisers would have come to us and not gone to Italy.[1] Even as regards Brazil, the British-built battleships were overhauled (most unsatisfactorily) in US Navy Yards. It is humiliating.[2]

162. *Report of Proceedings, North America and West Indies Station: Captain J. A. G. Troup to Commander-in-Chief*[3]

Cairo,[4]
Sydney, NS,
15 August 1927

…

2. The welcome extended to our ships by the residents ashore was impressive in its warmth. …

…

8. The breakdown [in the Geneva naval limitation talks] was not considered as likely to have the slightest effect on the amity existing between the two nations and Mr Wickersham in his speech referred to our two nations counting cruisers only for the Policing of the World.[5]

…

13. … A profound respect for Britain was evident on all sides, and regret – and even shame – that the USA did not enter war earlier was freely expressed.

…

15. The evasion of the provision of the Volstead Act is an unfailing topic of conversation; the supply of liquor is somewhat accidental, depending largely on fog at sea to facilitate bootlegging.[6]

[1]Argentinian cruisers built in Italy: *Almirante Brown, Veinticinco de Mayo*: 1929–31, 6800t, 32k, 6×7.5in, 12×3.9in, 6×21in tt.

[2]Brazilian battleships built in UK: *Minas Gerais, Sao Paulo*:1908–10, 19,200t.

[3]Capt J. A. G. Troup (1883–1975): S Af War 1897–1900; Boxer Rising 1900; Mr of F 1920–2; Capt 1922; Capt, Navig Sch 1928–30; *Revenge* 1930–2; Dir, Tac Sch 1933–5; RA 1935; DNI 1935–9; VA 1938; ret 1939; FOIC, Glasgow 1940–4.

[4]*Cairo*: 1918, 4,190t, 29k, 5×6in, 2×3in, 8×21in tt; converted to AA cruiser 1939.

[5]G. W. Wickersham (1858–1936): Repub; Attorney Gen under Taft, 1909–13; Chm, Natnl Cmn on Law Observance & Enforcement 1929–31; internationalist.

[6]Prohibition forbade the importation of liquor into the USA and was circumvented by fast motor boats bringing it in from the Caribbean and South America and slipping their illicit cargoes ashore under cover of fog.

163. *North America and West Indies Station: The Commander-in-Chief's General Letter No.5*[1]

Calcutta,
Bermuda,
25 October 1927

...

39. I have very seldom listened to a Speech with as much pleasure as the one he [Mr Curtis Wilbur, Secretary of the Navy] made, the chief note of it being that our two Nations and Navies should ever stand together, and laying stress on how much they prized their English descent.

...

43. [The Ambassador's speech at the National Press Club] was received with great and warm applause by reason of the point he made in pointing out that nothing said or done at the Geneva Conference had had the slightest effect on the friendliness of our reception,...[2]

...

47. On my last day I went to the Naval Training Establishment at Annapolis. Everything seems to be done for Mind and Body there, and whether the Boys go to Sea or not – and the larger proportion do not – it would be hard to imagine any Establishment which, by its systems, could produce finer, better brought up Officers or Citizens.

[1]Adm Sir Walter Cowan (1871–1956): ent RN 1884; Af expdns; Omdurman 1898; S Af War 1901; destroyer spist; Capt 1906; *Gloucester* 1910; F Capt *Princess Royal* 1915; Jutland 1916; Cdre, 1 LCS 1917; RA 1918; Baltic 1919; BCS 1921; VA 1923; FO Scotland 1925; C in C, NAWI 1926–8; Adm 1928; ret 1931; Cdo, W Desert 1941; captured1942; repat 1943.

[2]Sir Esmé Howard.

164. *Rear Admiral J. M. Reeves, US Navy, to the CNO*[1]

San Diego,
California,
6 December 1928

Views on the subject of Department of National Defense and a Unified Air Service

…

16. I have recently had occasion to discuss at great length this matter with Vice Admiral Fuller of the Royal Navy during his recent visit to San Diego.[2] During his previous duty in command of the battle cruiser forces of the British Fleet, at which time he had command of some aircraft carriers, Vice Admiral Fuller gained wide experience in the employment of aircraft with the fleet. In his discussion of the matter he showed a better grasp of fundamentals and knowledge of these matters than any other officer in my experience. He was very outspoken in his condemnation of the British system, and equally outspoken in his praise of our system. Insofar as our operations were concerned, he spoke with equal knowledge, because he had the opportunity to see Aircraft Squadrons, Battle Fleet, in operation at their base.

17. From the strategic point of view it can then be said that a separate air department is not only unsound in theory, since it deprives the Army and the Navy of control over the source of supply of aeronautical personnel and material, but is also unsound in practice, as indicated by actual experience in the British Fleet, contrasted with actual experience in our fleet. It may be said with entire confidence that strategically our present organization gives our fleet a definite margin of superiority over the British Fleet. The abandonment of our present organization in favour of the British organization would deprive us of a vital advantage.

…

46. … British aviation, in the separate department, is certainly not further advanced than American aviation. An examination of the performance records of aircraft shows a surprising number of performance

[1]Adm Joseph M. Reeves, US Navy (1872–1948): USNA 1894; Capt *Oregon* 1915–16; *Maine*, Atl F 1917–19; NA, Rome 1919–21; Capt, Mare I NY, S Francisco 1922–3; *North Dakota* 1922–3; NWC 1923–5; air observer 1925; Cdr, Air Sqdns, Bat F, 1925–29 & 1930–1; Gen Bd 1929–30; Adm 1933; CinC, US F 1934–6; Chm, Gen Bd 1936; ret 1936.

CNO: Adm Charles F. Hughes, US Navy.

[2]VAdm Sir Cyril T. M. Fuller (1874–1942): ent RN 1887; Capt 1910; SNO, W Af 1914–16; *Repulse* 1916–17; DP 1917–20; head, UK Secn, P Conf 1919–20; RA 1921; CoS, Atl F 1920–2; ACNS 1922–3; 3SL & Cntrlr 1923–5; BCS 1925–7; VA 1926; CinC, AWI 1928–30; 2SL 1930–2; Adm 1930; ret 1935.

records held by our Navy in service types of airplane. The record of Great Britain, for instance, is singularly uninteresting in the matter of aeronautical records of any kind, and particularly those held by service type airplanes. If aeronautical advancement is dependent upon the form of the organization, then the separate air department appears to be inferior to our present organization.

165. *North American and West Indies Station: Reports of Proceedings, 1930*

Despatch,
San Francisco,
8 September 1930

…

4. *Despatch* together with HMCS *Vancouver*, which had been placed under my orders, sailed [from Esquimalt] at 0600 on 4 August for Seattle in order to attend the annual 'Navy Week' to which these vessels and also *Dauntless* had been invited by the Governor of Washington. …[1]

…

6. Admiral Pratt being present in his flagship the USS *Texas*, I proceeded at once to call upon him …

…

8. The principal event was the 5th International Naval Ball at the Olympic Hotel at which some 3000 people were present. All the whole building was given up to the guests, but owing to the 18th Amendment there was no general spread or buffet in the main reception rooms. Instead private suites and bedrooms on every floor were given over to individual parties at which refreshments were served until early in the morning and the Volstead Act avoided. In consequence during the night it is probable that more liquor was consumed than is ever the case at a similar function in a less teetotal country.

…

10. … The attitude of the Flag Officers … was exceedingly friendly, but by tacit consent the subject of the London Naval Treaty was avoided in conversation. …

[1]*Despatch, Dauntless*: 1918–22, 4,850t, 29k, 6×6in, 3×4in, 12×21in tt.

HMCS *Vancouver*: 'S' class destroyer, *Toreador* (RCN 1928): 1918, 1,087t, 34k, 3×4in, 4×21in tt.

VAdm H. S. Haggard (1874–1960): ent RN 1888; Capt 1913; *Ajax* 1919–21; DTSD 1921–3; FO Submarines 1925–7; 4SL 1928–30; CinC, AWI 1930–2; ret 1932.

Govr, Wash: unknown.

166. *Minute by Director of Naval Intelligence*[1]

25 November 1930

Invitation to US Squadron to visit England, 1930–1934

… Among American Naval Officers there seem to be two currents of opinion: those who know and like the British Navy and British Naval Personnel, and those who do not know us and regard us with suspicion and even hostility. Generally speaking, I think it is true that where American Naval Officers have come into contact with our Navy, either in the War or elsewhere, they have tended to become pro-British, and the hostile element which sometimes betrays itself in speeches and writings generally comes from those who have not been much in contact with us. This is borne out by reports from British men-of-war who have been in contact with units of the US Fleet.

The conclusion would appear to be that the more we see of the American Fleet the better our relations will be. In this case, if we extend an invitation to the American Fleet to visit this country and they accept it, we shall improve relations at practically no cost, for the actual entertainment allowance, however liberal, is practically negligible in comparison with normal costs of running a fleet.

… the knowledge of American Naval Officers and ships acquired by our personnel cannot but be beneficial.

167. *Report of Proceedings of Captain H. E. C. Blagrove*[2]

Norfolk,
11 August 1933

…

22. *Indianapolis* had twice been under orders to proceed directly to the West coast and twice had been cancelled; on the last occasion, I am told, by direct order from the President about two weeks before, in order that she should meet *Norfolk* at Bar Harbor.[3] She is marvellously fitted out,

[1]RA C. V. Usborne.

[2]Capt H. E. C. Blagrove: Capt 1927; *Curacoa* 1931; *Sussex* 1934; *Warspite*; *Norfolk* 1937; RA, Jan 1939; d. Oct 1939.

[3]*Norfolk*: 1930, 9925t, 32.5k, 8×8in, 8×4in, 8×21in tt.

RAdm John M. Smeallie, US Navy (1886–1947): USNA 1905; cdr, Destroyer Div 39, 1926–9; ND 1929–32; Capt *Indianapolis* 1932–5; ONO 1935–6; NWC 1936–7; CoS, Scouting Force 1937–9; RA 1938; Cdt, 16th N Dist & Cavite, Philippines 1939–40; ret 1942.

Indianapolis: 1932, 10258t, 32.5k, 9×8in, 8×5in, Took A-bomb to Okinawa, 1945; torpedoed on return voyage.

partly because she is quite new and partly because she is designed to hoist the C-in-C's flag when he desires to tranship from a battleship to a fast cruiser.

Her printing office is the size of *Norfolk's* gun room and contains a complete linotype installation. Her sickbay, operating theatre, dispensary and dental room are as elaborate and efficient as anything that could be found in a modern city. The same may be said of her galleys, bakery, plate-washing and potato peeling machinery, or of less essential items such as the barber's shop and ice-cream bar.

Needless to say, these things convey the impression of being far in advance of similar fittings in our own ships, but no doubt they can only be done by considerably increased expenditure.

23. I am glad to say that a real *entente* was established between *Indianapolis* and the British ships [including *Danae*].[1] … Our officers and men did all in their power to improve friendly relations and were conspicuously successful. Captain Smeallie [US Navy] went out of his way to show us every courtesy. He invited me one day to walk round divisions and inspect his men and their ship; …

… I infer that General Drills are not often practised in the US Navy. …

168. *Vice Admiral Sir Matthew Best to Chatfield*[2]

York,[3]
7 November 1935

…

Mr Swanson, Secretary of the Navy, made a very friendly and outspoken speech at a lunch he gave the day after we arrived. His direct references to common language, common ancestors and the need for a clear understanding and co-operation between the two countries surprised his own people as well as the members of our own Embassy.

I have spent quite a considerable time with Admiral Standley, and he appeared to me to be communicative. …

… he struck me as being straightforward and not talking for effect. …

[1]*Danae*: 1918, 4850t, 29k, 5×6in, 3×4in, 12×21in tt; *Conrad*, Polish N, 1944.

[2]VAdm Sir Matthew Best (1878–1940): Jutland; Capt, *Nelson* 1927; CoS, Atl F 1927–9; RA 1928; 2CS 1929–31; VA, Malta, 1931–4; VA 1932; CinC, AWI, 1934–7; Adm 1938; ret 1939. On a visit to Washington, DC.

[3]*York*: 1930, 8250t, 32k, 6×8in, 4×4in, 6×21in tt.

Standley gave me the impression that he accepted the justice of our claim for 70 cruisers.

...

The political attitude is simple to explain. The public opinion cry is – at all costs keep out of everything European. I do not think this is necessarily the President's attitude, but he is bowing to public opinion.

...

Mr Swanson is a sick man and is a figurehead. He has had two strokes and is inclined to be ga-ga. Colonel Roosevelt, the Assistant Naval Secretary, is the working unit; shrewd, pro-British and a gentleman. But he gives nothing away. The Ambassador says he is a capable man.[1]

169. *C-in-C, North America and West Indies Station, to the Secretary of the Admiralty*[2]

30 July 1936

Report on visit of Apollo *to San Diego*[3]

...

4. During my visit I came in contact with all the more senior officers, who were open in their discussion of various problems of the US Navy. In matters of detail and technical development, however, all ranks were reticent.

5. In particular I was most impressed with the degree to which the US Navy, from the most senior officers downwards, is imbued with a practical knowledge of flying matters; there is little doubt that in this subject they are going ahead fast. Not only are their numbers large, but their equipment is of the most up-to-date type and their organization works smoothly.

...

12. The US regard the Hawaiian Islands as the key to their Pacific strategy and it is thought that they will use these flying boats for patrol along the supply route to Honolulu, and for extended coastal reconnaissance. They are manned entirely by naval officers and ratings.[4]

[1]Col Henry L. Roosevelt (1879–1936): Asst Sec N 1933–6.
Sir Ronald Lindsay (1877–1945): several postings; Amb to Turkey 1925–6; Amb to Germany 1926–8; Pmnt U Sec, FO 1928–30; Amb to US 1930–9.

[2]VAdm Best.

[3]*Apollo*: 1936, 7,000t, 32.5k, 8×6in, 4×4in, 8×21in tt; transferred to RAN 1938 as *Hobart*.

[4]Probably Consolidated Catalina (PBY-5): amphibian/flying boat, 1935, 2×1,200hp, 179mph, 3100m, 8 crew, 5mg, 2,000lb bombs. The US Navy ordered 60 in 1936. Later served with several air forces.

170. *Vice Admiral Sir Matthew Best to Chatfield*

6 October 1936

…

I met the American Fleet at San Pedro during a week-end, when they were in from exercises, and had an interesting two-hour talk with Admiral Hepburn, a pleasant open-faced officer who reflects his feelings in his face. He is quiet and dislikes public lunches and other similar functions which fall to his lot. He freely discussed matters in connection with his service

… He thinks that the age of their Flag Officers is too high. He hopes that Admiral Leahy will relieve Admiral Standley at Washington, and considers he is most suitable for the appointment.[1]

He thought that the 5in gun in their service was more efficient than our 4in gun, and spoke highly of the accuracy and results of their 5in AA fire.

He deprecates the absence of the pom-pom in his service, and said that at present they banked on a large number of Lewis and machine gun types for defence against low-flying aircraft.

He was hoping for an early reorganisation of the Naval Air Arm in our service, as he would not feel that the system in his own service would be secure until that had come about. The Washington politicians intermittently tried to use our system as a lever for a similar re-adoption in the American Navy.

He confessed to not being clear in his mind as to the best use to put the [US Navy's] FAA to in fleet work. He said it was difficult to express his meaning, but stated that his mental picture of the situation was not clear, …

171. *Vice Admiral Sir Sydney Meyrick to Chatfield*[2]

4 April 1937

…

Admiral Leahy the CNO was most forthcoming, and genuinely, I think, pro-British. If it wasn't for Congress I think he would be a happy man, but he told me he had an awful lot of questions to answer there.

[1]Adm William D. Leahy.

[2]Adm Sir Sidney J. Meyrick (1879–1973): ent RN 1893; GF 1916–18; Capt 1919; *Courageous* 1920–1; 6DF 1921–2; *Revenge* 1922–3; DTSD 1926–7; *Nelson* 1927–9; Capt, RNC 1929–32; RA 1932; NS to FL 1932–4; 2CS 1934–6; VA 1936; CinC, AWI 1937–40; Adm 1940; ret 1942.

He was also sorry about the bigger battleship and said he would like to see the limit at about 25,000 tons. There was a general feeling amongst all the Admirals that ours was a common cause with theirs in the Pacific – but not so in Europe, though even [so] some felt they might be with us 'before the end'.

172. *Commanding Officer, HMS Wellington, to Rear Admiral Commanding, New Zealand Division, and Admiralty*[1]

26 May 1937

Wellington arrived Canton Island 26 May and found US minesweeper *Avocet* base ship for American Eclipse expedition anchored in the only permanent berth practicable for *Wellington.*[2] As Canton Island is British territory *Avocet* was requested to shift berth, [but] did not do so stating the engines were being overhauled.

We anchored in temporary berth. On calling on Captain Hellweg, US Navy, Commander of expedition he admitted having been informed officially at Honolulu that the Phoenix Islands had been incorporated in the Gilbert and Ellice group, but that the State Department [at] Washington did not admit British jurisdiction over Canton and Enderby Islands.[3]

Utmost cordiality exists and suitable berths for both ships are being amicably [sought].

...

[1]CO: Cdr G. N. Loriston-Clarke: Cdr 1936; *Victory*, RN Barracks, Sept 1939; *Southdown* 1941; Actg Capt 1942; *Canton* 1943; *Drake* 1944; *Sparrowhawk* (Hatston) Oct 1944.

Wellington: sloop, 1934, 990t, 16,5k, 2×4.7in, 1×3in.

Cdre/RAdm, New Zealand Sqdn: Capt Hon E. R. Drummond: Capt 1926; CoS, CinC Portsmouth 1930–2; 'D' cruisers 1932–5; Cdre, NZ Sqdn 1935.

[2]*Avocet*: seaplane tender, 1918, 840t, 12k, 2×3in.

[3]Capt Hellweg, US Navy (b. 1879): USNA 1900; *Columbia* 1920; Cdr, Destroyer Sqdn 14, Scouting F 1924–6; *Oklahoma* 1928–30; Supt, N Observatory, Washington, DC, 1930–46; ret 1935.

173. *Rear Admiral Commanding, New Zealand Division, to Admiralty and High Commissioner, Western Pacific, Wellington*[1]

13 June 1937

Wellington informs me that recent comprehensive exploration of Canton Island indicates great possibilities for development as [an] aircraft base for all types of machines.

This [is] equally well known to the USA officers' and scientists' party and possibly accounts for their refusal to recognise the claim of British Sovereignty *vide Wellington's* 2201/26 [May] [above]. As *Wellington* left Canton [Island] before US minesweeper *Avocet*, I shall visit Phoenix Group in *Achilles* when on passage from Honolulu to Suva early in August.[2]

174. *Commodore Hon E. R. Drummond to Secretary of the Admiralty*[3]

29 June 1937

… the following signal was received from the High Commissioner, Western Pacific, on 9 June:

Telegram from *Wellington*:

'I learn from ship named that USS *Avocet* remaining Canton Island after departure *Wellington*. I am uneasy as to American intention and consider it important to know of anything untoward happening. Would it be possible for *Achilles* to call Phoenix Islands on voyage from Christmas Island to Nukunono early in August [? 1937]'

I [the High Commissioner] intend to visit the Phoenix Group in *Achilles* accordingly during the first week in August.

2. It appears that sudden decision by the American Government to send an expedition to Canton Island might possibly have been the result of an unfavourable report from the experimental flight to New Zealand on the intermediate bases [at] Kingman Reef and Pago Pago. Both these bases seem unsuitable for the heavy flying boats which Pan American Airlines intend to use.

[1]H Cmnr, W Pac: Sir Arthur F. Richards (1885–1978): Col Ofc 1908; Malaya 1915–29; Govr, N Borneo 1930; Govr, The Gambia 1933; Govr, Fiji, & H Cmnr, W Pac, 1936; Govr, Jamaica 1938.

[2]*Achilles, Leander*: 1933, 7,000t, 32.5k, 8×6in, 4×4in, 8×21in tt; part of NZ Sqdn.

[3]Sec of Admy: Sir Archibald Carter (1887–1958). India Office 1909–36; Sec Admy 1936–40; Govt bodies 1940–7; Pmnt U SSt, India 1947.

This conclusion is borne out by para. 17 of the CO, *Wellington's*, report where it is clearly indicated that the expedition originated not from the International Eclipse Expedition, who considered it a waste of money to go to Canton Island, but from the National Geographic Society, who said that an expedition was being sent to Canton Island under the auspices of the US Navy.

…

4. The question of alternative bases had therefore to be considered by the American Government. Their eyes would turn naturally to the Phoenix Group for the following reasons:

(a) The Group is situated approximately half-way between Honolulu and New Zealand.

(b) The flight between Honolulu and New Zealand could easily be done in two stages using Canton Island as an intermediate base: each stage can be approximately 1800 miles as compared with the 2419 miles between America and Honolulu.

(c) Reasonable landing facilities for stores, etc., exist at Canton Island and the construction of a small pier would make these facilities very good. Anchorage is not good but practicable.

(d) Canton Island could be made a suitable base for heavy flying boats, and possibly for land machines.

(e) Ownership by the US appears to them to be possible: it is clear to them that they do not intend at present to recognise British Sovereignty over Gilbert and Ellice Islands and they may be considering possession of these by occupation.

…

175. *Admiralty to Commodore, New Zealand Division*

21 July 1937

General policy of HM Government is to establish sovereignty over islands likely to form useful links in air routes. Phoenix Group have recently been incorporated in Gilbert and Ellice Islands by Order in Council and steps have been taken to protest at Washington against visit of *Avocet* without prior notification and to communicate a copy of the Order in Council to US Government.

176. *Admiralty to Commanding Officer, HMS Leander*[1]

29 July 1937

It has been suggested that Henderson, Oeno and Ducie Islands in the Pitcairn Group will provide landing facilities for flying boats and landplanes. Request you will take any necessary steps on passage to New Zealand to reaffirm British title to these islands. A report should be forwarded on their possibilities as a future base for aircraft.

Commanding Officer, HMS Leander, *to Admiralty and Commodore, New Zealand Division*

6 August 1937

Air survey and brief and sea ground survey of Ducie[,] Henderson and Oeno Islands has been carried out and British title reaffirmed.

177. *Memorandum by Naval Intelligence Department*

31 December 1937

... Report on USA: Aircraft Bombing and Torpedo Attacks

19. AP bomb salvoes are ballistically and tactically inferior to Naval AP projectiles.
20. The 'very near miss' or explosion close to the hull of a heavy delay fuze demolition bomb salvo is ballistically equivalent to a torpedo or mine. It is superior to Naval AP projectiles, but inferior tactically.
21. A deck salvo of heavy demolition bombs is ballistically and tactically inferior to a Naval AP salvo.

A deck salvo of heavy fuze demolition bombs is ballistically superior to one of heavy demolition bombs.

22. Effect on ships of a heavy salvo of heavy AP bombs on deck, or of a 'near miss' by salvo of heavy delay fuze demolition bombs.
(a) Battleships: not immune but ship remains afloat and capable of further action.
(b) Carriers: Ship and aircraft out of action. Ship not sunk.
(c) Cruiser: out of action but not sunk.

[1]Capt. J.W. Rivett-Carnac (1891–1970): Capt June 1934; Cdre Cmdg NZ Sqdn, Nov 1936, & Capt, *Leander*; DTSD March 1940; *Rodney* July 1941; RA July 1943; FO Br Assault Force, BPF Nov 1944; Actg VA (Q), BPF, *Beaconsfield* March 1945–7; ret 1947.

(d) Destroyers, Submarines, auxiliary craft: sunk.
23. Employment of bombs.
(a) Horizontal High Altitude Bombing.
Most powerful means of attack. Used against battleships.
(b) Dive Bombing.
(i) Limited weight, single bomb, low impact speed. No substitute for horizontal high altitude bombing. Compares unfavourably with progress of horizontal low altitude high speed bombing.
(ii) Useful against all ships.
...
(d) Horizontal Low Altitude High Speed Bombing.
See dive bombing. Under trial. Compares favourably with dive bombing. Used against all ships.
24. *Defence.*
All types of the above forms of defence [fighters, anti-aircraft fire, manoeuvring, smokescreens, searchlights, formation, construction] are sufficient but are not a positive defence against damage by bombing of units or fleet. Improvements are in progress.
25. *Bombing in general.*
(a) Does not decide naval battle. Requires repeated hits and attacks, incompatible with low loading and reloading capacity and facilities.
(b) Does not substitute [for] or compete with naval gunnery, technology, ballistics, strategically or tactically, and needs improvement in all these phases.
(c) More trials are needed for further decision.
26. Naval aviation bombing should acquire decisive importance by improving impact speed and accuracy. Developments considered for experiment are –
(a) Propelled bomb, to increase AP impact speed and internal damage.
(b) Self-directed bomb, to increase accuracy.

Staff conclusions on use of torpedo-carrying aircraft.

27. (a) Effect.
Ballistically inferior to large torpedo from destroyer and submarine, and to mine.
Tactically: ditto.
On ship: battleship, carrier, cruiser not sunk.
Destroyers, submarines, auxiliaries: sunk.
On Fleet: indirect harassing. Crippling, sinking of destroyers, submarines, auxiliaries.

(b) Accuracy.
Insufficient conclusively. Improving technically, tactically, by training. Inferior to accuracy of torpedoing by destroyers and submarines.
(c) Employment.
Tactical harassing. Is not a substitute for bombing.
…
(e) Defence.
As for other aircraft, plus barrage fire and use of searchlights by destroyers during low altitude zone of the approach. Sufficient to limit damage. Improving.
28. Torpedoing in general.
(a) Does not decide naval battle.
Does not substitute for or compete with bombing.
Requires repeated attacks and hits, incompatible with loading and reloading facilities.
Does not substitute for torpedoes fired by destroyers and submarines.
(b) Not yet definitely adopted for aircraft and requires improvement both technically and strategically. Would acquire decisive importance by improvements in range and accuracy.
(c) An improvement under consideration is the development of a form of combined glider and motor air torpedo to be launched at long range and controlled by wireless or some self-directing device.

178. *Memorandum by Naval Intelligence Department*

14 May 1938

Foreign development of the torpedo as an air weapon

USA:

Torpedo attacks are carried out against capital ships and cruisers, both at sea and in harbour. Attacks are carried out in conjunction with high-bombing and dive-bombing. Torpedo attacks are also carried out at night. It is believed that more attention is being paid to the development of the torpedo as a weapon owing to the difficulty of reducing the speed of dive in modern bombers.
…

179. *Reports by Captain Lord Louis Mountbatten to the Staff Intelligence Officer, Kingston, Jamaica*[1]

18 February 1938

Reports on USS Philadelphia *[and]* Fanning

Whilst on half pay at Kingston, Jamaica, I visited USS *Fanning* on 31 January 1938, at the invitation of the CO, Lt Cdr E. H. Geiselman, US Navy.[2]

2. I made a point of asking to be shown nothing confidential, particularly since *Fanning* was only completed last October. In consequence I was not able to make a detailed tour of inspection.

3. All main armament guns are HA/LA, semi-automatic with power ramming. The foremost two guns are in turret mountings.

4. Although 12 torpedo tubes are carried in three quadruple mountings not more than eight can be discharged simultaneously as only the foremost mounting is on the centre line.

…

6. … The Bridge is completely covered. The CO, who served afloat in destroyers during the war (and may presumably be regarded as an experienced destroyer officer) stated that few changes in design had contributed more to the fighting efficiency of destroyers than enclosed bridges. He claimed that in bad weather conditions and at high speeds all bridge personnel could carry on their functions as efficiently as was possible only at slow speed in good weather conditions with open bridges. In fact he claimed that enclosed bridges for destroyers are as essential as enclosed cockpits for aircraft.

…

… I visited USS *Philadelphia* on 31 January 1938, at the invitation of of the CO, Captain Jules James, US Navy.[3]

[1]Capt Lord Louis Mountbatten (1900–79): ent RN 1913; son of AoF Prince Louis of Battenberg, FSL 1914; *Lion* 1916; Capt 1937; Capt (D) 5DF & *Kelly* 1939–41; *Illustrious* June 1941; A/Cdre, Comb Ops, Oct 1941; VA & Chief, Comb Ops, April 1942; A/Adm & Sup Allied Cdr, SE Asia, Oct 1943; Viceroy, Gov-Gen & Earl, India,1947–8; RA, 1CS 1948; VA 1949; 4SL 1950; CinC, Med 1952; Adm & SACMED 1953; FSL 1954; AoF 1956; Chief of Defence Staff 1959–65; assassinated in Ireland 1979.

Staff Intelligence Officer, Jamaica: not known.

[2]*Fanning*: 1937, 1488t, 36.5k, 5×5in, 12×21in tt.

Lt-Cdr Ellis H. Geiselman, US Navy (1895–1970): USNA 1917; *Fanning* 1937–8; Exec Ofcr *Arizona* (sunk Pearl Harbor 7 Dec 1941; Capt *Detroit* Pac, 1942–3; ONO 1943–7.

[3]*Philadelphia*: 1938; other details below.

Capt Jules James, US Navy (b. 1885): USNA 1908; Capt 1936; NA staff 1934–7; *Philadelphia* 1937–9; NI 1939–41; RA & cdr, Bermuda 1941–3; Cdt, 6th N Dist & Charleston NY, SC 1943–5; Cdr, US N Forces, N Af Waters & Med 1945–6; ret 1946.

2. The Captain offered to show me any part of the ship which interested me. I stated that I had recently served in the Naval Aviation Department of the Admiralty and was therefore most interested in the aircraft equipment of the *Philadelphia* but that I particularly did not wish to be shown anything of a confidential nature. The Captain stated that he was not normally allowed to show his hangar to visitors but that he would show it to me if I undertook not to tell anyone of my visit who could be likely to inform Washington. This undertaking I readily gave since it precluded the possibility of the US Naval Authorities asking for any reciprocal information.
3. The Captain then introduced me to his FAA officers and led me aft. As has been announced in the press, *Philadelphia* has been given a special square stern to provide sufficient space to construct a huge hangar right aft, below the level of the upper deck. This stern is less square than that of the *Adventure* but not so rounded as that of a destroyer.[1]
...
8. I then went down into the Hangar which occupies the full width of the ship and extends from abaft the after gun barbette to the actual stern. It appears to be at least two decks deep and has one main support in the centre.
...
15. The peacetime complement of aircraft is four.
16. The senior pilot stated that the war complement of aircraft had still to be settled and depended on the experience of *Philadelphia*. He thought the ultimate complement would be 12 aircraft, of which half would be IE and half IR. ...
17. He stated that *Philadelphia* was a compromise. The Bureau of Aeronautics wanted a cruiser-carrier to carry 12 aircraft and have a flight deck. The Naval Staff said this would be a bad cruiser and a bad carrier and refused to agree. The Bureau of Aeronautics then proposed a genuine cruiser to carry six IE and six IR catapult aircraft. The US Naval Constructors then objected that so large a hangar would weaken the ship and be a potential source of danger in action. It appears that the naval staff having won the battle of the Cruiser-Carrier sided with the Bureau of Aeronautics against the Constructors over the *Philadelphia*. Both the Captain and the Senior Pilot agreed that she was a success and disproved the gloomy forecast of the constructors.
18. Asked on how many days they expect to be able to operate their aircraft the Captain replied 'At least one day'. By landing in the slip and

[1]*Adventure*: cruiser-minelayer, 1927, 6740t, 28k, 4×4.7in, 280 mines; stern converted to cruiser style.

using a Heine Canvas he thought on most occasions he would be able to recover his aircraft, but that as he would carry 100% reserves they could afford to risk aircraft in a way which no other catapult ship could. Asked if they would not have preferred two Cruisers without aircraft and one Carrier to carry 18 IE in place of the 18 in three *Philadelphias*, the Captain replied 'No' and the Senior Pilot 'Yes'.

19. Both officers agreed that the large after deck of *Philadelphia* could easily be converted for gyro-planes to land on as soon as this type of plane was sufficiently developed.

Note by Captain Reginald Portal, for Director of Aviation Material:[1]

25 April 1938

The great defect in the aircraft arrangement in the *Philadelphia* is that there is, apparently, no means of loading the aircraft to the catapult without using the crane. This arrangement, if combined with one fixed athwartship catapult and landing arrangements would be excellent for operating aircraft, but the desirability of constructing a ship with such a large compartment as the hangar appears to be very doubtful.

2. The track arrangement in the hangar is most ingenious. Stowing space for more than three IE aircraft appears to be very tight, and it does not seem that aircraft of FAA size (i.e., folded width 18ft) could be accommodated.

3. It appears to DAM that a better 'cruiser-carrier' could be built combining three systems, *viz.*:

(1) Our D. IV. H. catapult equipment.

(2) The *Gotland* (Swedish) system of each aircraft on its own independent transporting catapult's structure.[2]

(3) The *Philadelphia* hangar and lift arrangement.

Note by Captain Victor Danckwerts, Director of Plans:

3 May 1938

…

2. It is considered that the use of the after part of the ship for the stowage of aircraft is worth serious consideration in our cruiser designs now. Apart from any considerations in regard to the operation of existing aircraft,

[1] RAdm R. H. Portal (1894–1983): RNAS 1914–18; *York* 1939–41; *Royal Sovereign* 1941–2; ACNS (Air) 1943–4; FO, N Air Stas, Australia 1945; JCS, Australia 1946–7; FO (Air) Home 1947–51; Adm & ret 1951.

[2] *Gotland*: aircraft-cruiser, 1935, 4,700t, 28k, 6x6in, 4x3in, 6x21in tt, 6 aircraft; converted to AA cruiser 1943–4.

such an arrangement will, presumably, be required as soon as the autogyro type of aircraft is sufficiently developed, which must surely occur, if not in the immediate future, at least within the next 25 years. Cruisers designed now will still be in service 25 years hence.

Note by Captain D. A. Budgen, Director of Training and Development:[1]

n.d., May 1938

…

2. Regarding the totally enclosed bridge in *Fanning*, and the remarks of her CO, it is not considered that such an arrangement would find favour in our service. Our latest types of destroyer bridge, as fitted in 'H', 'I' and 'Tribals', has been evolved from many years' experience and, so far as is known, returns only one marked shortcoming, *viz.*: that the personnel stationed at the after end of the upper bridge are insufficiently protected from wind and weather.

3. … the divergence of the views expressed by the Captain and Senior Pilot … are of particular interest in connection with the need for small carriers for trade protection duties, working with cruisers, which DTD has frequently stressed.

4. It is incontestable that carrier-borne aircraft can be effectively operated over a far greater range of weather conditions, and – in reliefs – over longer periods than cruiser-borne catapult aircraft. Moreover, the fighting efficiency of a cruiser is inevitably compromised to some extent, both structurally and tactically by the requirement that she shall carry and operate aircraft.

5. It is, therefore, considered that, to obtain fullest value from the air on trade routes – as elsewhere – the solution lies in units of one carrier and several cruisers rather than relying on that doubtful starter and still more doubtful finisher the cruiser-borne catapult aircraft.

Note by Dr S. V. Goodall, Director of Naval Construction:[2]

3 June 1938

Such a large compartment at the after end of the ship, near the waterline, with a watertight cocoon of doubtful efficiency, involves the acceptance of risk in action or heavy weather to which the US Navy constructors were entirely justified in objecting.

[1]Capt D. A. Budgen: Capt 1930; *Defiance*, Devonport Torpedo Sch 1936; DTD 1938; D Loc Dfc Sept 1939; Capt & Cdre, *Afrikander I* March 1940; RA ret, Sea Tpt Div 1942.

[2]Sir Sidney V. Goodall (1883–1965): RN Engnrg C; RNC, Greenwich; Dir N Cnstrn 1936–44; Asst Cntrlr, Warship Prodn 1942–5.

	Southampton	*Philadelphia*
Standard displacement	9100 tons	10,000 tons
Shaft Horse Power	75,000	95,000
Main armament	12×6in	15×6in
	(4 triple turrets)	(5 triple turrets)
HA and minor armament	8×4in (4 twins)	8×5in
	2×4-barrel pom-poms	1×1in
	2×0.5in	10×0.5in
Torpedo armament	2 triple 21in tubes	0
Aircraft	3 Walrus[1]	12 Scout-Observation Curtis.[2]
Complement	743	681 (?868 wartime) [Admiralty estimate].

[1]Supermarine Vickers Walrus: spotter/reconnaissance/rescue seaplane, 1933, 1×775hp, 135mph, 600m, 4 crew, 2mg, depth charges.

[2]Curtis Scout/Observation floatplane: 1 engine, *c.*190mph.

PART VI

EDGING TOWARDS AN ALLIANCE
1937–1939

British readers, accustomed to discussions about the coming of war between 1937 and 1939, and to accounts of the great Anglo-American operations after December 1941, might be surprised that the majority of documents in this Part concern Anglo-American co-operation before the Second World War and in the Far East. This is because the first test of the inter-war peace came in China in 1931 and the democracies were faced subsequently with an aggressive autocracy, especially after the 'incident' at the Marco Polo Bridge near Beijing in July 1937, which was followed by a full-scale war between China and Japan. Though part of the cause was Japanese aggrandisement, the forces of Nippon were responding also to burgeoning Chinese nationalism; moreover, there was little love lost between the Western powers and the government of Chiang Kai-Shek.[1] The Western powers, with long-established (if small-scale) trading operations and a considerable missionary presence in China, had a common interest in protecting their merchants, missionaries, ships and commercial enterprises from the savage and, at times, indiscriminate warfare between China and Japan. There was a sub-text to their endeavours, as some elements in the Japanese hierarchy were intent on driving them out of China. In that drive the British were 'kicked and cuffed incessantly' as the Japanese sensed that one Empire was on the way down as its own Empire rose, with the battleground being a third ancient Empire [208]. The British, in fact, blew hot and cold in their struggle with Japan, alternating between apparent appeasement and stout assertion of their historic position. That was because the topsy-turvy situation in Europe affected their power to defend themselves in the Far East – and they could not rely on American help if it came to shooting. The American Admiral on the spot, Harry E. Yarnell, Commander-in-Chief of the Asiatic Fleet, who was strongly pro-British, did his best to support his British friends and got on well with the successive British Commanders-in-Chief of the China Station, Admirals Sir Charles Little

[1]Marco Polo Bridge: Following a small-scale encounter between Japanese and Chinese troops on 7 July 1937, a full-scale (albeit undeclared) war erupted between the two powers.

Chiang Kai Shek (1887–1975): Natnst Pres of China, 1924–49.

and Sir Percy Noble.[1] He was seconded by the Chief of Naval Operations, Admiral William D. Leahy, also pro-British, who hankered after a definite arrangement for joint action. Yarnell, Little and Noble exchanged information, engaged in joint protests and made contingency plans to safeguard civilians [180–85, 187–9, 191, 192, 194, 197–9, 202, 203, 206–8]. An especially notable example of close co-operation was the *Panay* incident of December 1937, when officers and men of all ranks of both navies assisted one another in the aftermath of a Japanese air attack on the American gunboat, which was sunk and suffered casualties; other British and American vessels were also bombed [191–3, 195, 198].[2]

Anglo-American concerns went far wider than the broad canyons of Chinese rivers. There was much discussion about how each would react to Japanese aggression against their insular possessions in the Pacific, such as Hong Kong, Singapore and the Philippines [181, 185, 189, 192, 194, 199]. There was talk, also, on the sensitive subject of the exchange of technical information [204]. As the war clouds gathered, official America grew increasingly jittery about the Atlantic, too. The Americans were concerned to protect their eastern seaboard in a likely European war but even more pressing was the fate of the West Indies, sitting astride the approach to the Panama Canal. American and British officials pondered the possibility that a hostile power might acquire these possessions; linked to that frightening prospect was the proposal that certain territories be handed over to the United States in settlement of the outstanding debt from the First World War. In the event, the dollar sign disappeared in favour of a benevolent American neutrality involving 'hemispheric defence' in which the Americans would require bases in certain British colonies [209, 213–15]. Here lies the origin of the 'Destroyers-for-Bases' deal of 1940.[3]

Even before the dark days of the early Churchill premiership, Britain was in dire straits, a threadbare imperium seeking to protect a world-wide seaborne trade and scattered colonies and dominions. Britain was

[1]Adm Sir Percy Noble (1880–1955): ent RN 1894; sig spist; GF 1914–18; Capt 1918; *Calliope, Calcutta* 1919; *Barham* 1922; *Ganges, St Vincent* (trng) 1925–7; DOD 1928–9; RA 1929; D N Eqpt 1931; 2CS 1932; VA & 4SL 1935; CinC, China 1937–40; Adm 1939; W Apps 1941; head, BAD Oct 1942–June 1944; ret 1945.

[2]USS *Panay*: river gunboat, 1927, 450t, 15k, 2×3in. The bombing and sinking of the *Panay* and three oil barges, the strafing of survivors, and attacks on other American and British ships can hardly have been accidental, since the ships were clearly marked as neutrals. The incident, moreover, was the culmination of months of violent harassment of Western warships and merchantmen by the Japanese. Tokyo and local Japanese flag officers moved quickly to offer apologies and compensation, thus defusing further America's already damp response.

[3]The Destroyers-for-Bases deal of Sept 1940 was a decidedly unneutral act by the USA but one which gave a major boost to US defence capability in the W Atlantic. Since the (over-age) destroyers proved of little value, the Americans got the better of the deal – but Churchill rightly regarded it as a first step to the much-coveted Anglo-American alliance.

concerned, too, to preserve the balance of power in Europe and its traditional dominance of the Mediterranean, a position dating back to Nelson. As Chatfield, the First Sea Lord, recognised, the Royal Navy did not have the strength to fight three enemies simultaneously – Germany, Italy and Japan [186, 188, 201, 210]. In the Pacific and Far East, it was certain that Britain would need American aid to defend its position against Japanese aggression. It was equally certain that, in the aftermath of the Washington Treaties of 1922, it would require a firm partnership between the USA and Britain to deter or subdue Japan; neither navy could do it alone. There would have to be a substantial British fleet based on the new naval base at Singapore, with the bulk of the US Navy at Pearl Harbor, to effect a two-front or pincer grip on Japan [180, 181, 185, 189, 194, 199].

The great handicap to further, more concrete British-American joint action was America's determinedly neutral stance, first enacted in 1935, extended in 1936 and made permanent in 1937. The President and many of his officials were dismayed by the Neutrality Act and its later revisions and sought means to circumvent it. Franklin D. Roosevelt castigated its proponents, arguing that it limited the Commander-in-Chief's power to defend neighbouring countries like Canada and thus indirectly the United States itself. In a bid to sustain America's longstanding role as China's moral guardian and to deter Japanese aggression, he refused to implement the Act in the (undeclared) Sino-Japanese conflict, with the added bonus that by doing so he helped China more than Japan [180, 205]. Despite an analysis showing that in an Anglo-German war, Britain would probably gain from the Act, its crucial defect from the British point of view was that in a crisis likely to lead to war, as Chatfield expressed it, 'the Americans will stand aside' [186, 205].

The United States was, however, deeply divided. While the majority of Congress, the press and the public were determined never to get involved in war again, especially in Europe, President Roosevelt, his State Department, and a few other close associates like Admiral Leahy, were aware that in the mid-twentieth century it was not possible for America to 'stand aside' from world crises. Roosevelt himself resolved to wait on events and use them to educate the American people in their responsibilities – and their responses; it was a slow process and, as the reaction to the Quarantine Speech (October 1937) or the near-success of the Ludlow Amendment (January 1938) showed, one fraught with setbacks.[1] Roosevelt

[1]Quarantine Speech: in the heartland of 'isolationism', Chicago, 5 Oct 1937. It was a stirring condemnation of aggression but proposed almost no action, though provoking a strong press, public and political reaction against it.

Ludlow Amendment: An attempt by Representative Louis Ludlow (Dem, Ind) to amend the Constitution so that the USA could not declare war without a favourable referendum vote. It came to a House vote on 10 Jan 1938, with the FDR administration managing to exert just enough pressure to defeat it by 21 votes (209 to 188).

did what little he could in the face of straitjacket legislation and lurking public and political furore to identify the USA with Britain and France.[1] The US Navy, under Leahy's pragmatic leadership, and with the blessing of a President who was an old friend of Leahy and effectively his own Secretary of the Navy, took steps to bring about an agreement with the Royal Navy. At first Leahy held exploratory talks with the British Naval Attaché in Washington but found them fruitless [189, 190].[2] He then sent the US Navy's Director of Plans, Captain Ingersoll, to London to confer with his opposite number at the Admiralty.[3] Because of America's commitment to neutrality, there could be little more than the exchange of information and certain tentative communications arrangements. Within those constraints, the Ingersoll–Phillips exchanges were remarkably frank, airing the joint use of waters and ports, a joint demand that Japan reveal her building plans, and spelling out each navy's available strength for Pacific operations, their other commitments and their states of readiness. The Americans had envisaged relatively low-key talks, under cover of extreme secrecy but, while the British respected the Americans' nervous desire to keep the discussions confidential, they invested the talks with far more meaning. Within a couple of days of his arrival, Ingersoll met the Foreign Secretary (Anthony Eden) and after that Chatfield, the Deputy Chief of Naval Staff (Admiral Sir William James) and finally the First Lord, Duff Cooper, and the Minister for the Co-ordination of Defence, Sir Thomas Inskip, along with other naval officers and Foreign Office officials.[4]

[1]A typical gesture by FDR, about all he could do, was to invite King George VI, Queen Elizabeth and the Canadian PM, Mackenzie King, over from Canada to Washington and (informally) Hyde Park, NY (FDR's home), in the summer of 1939, thus indicating his solidarity with the democracies.

[2]Capt Frederick C. Bradley (1888–1951): ent RN 1904; Capt 1930; *Australia*, *Canberra* 1931–4; NA, Washington, 1935–8; *Edinburgh* 1939; RA, ret 1941; CSO, Greenock, 1942; NA, Lisbon 1944–6.

[3]Adm Royall E. Ingersoll, US Navy (b. 1881): USNA 1905; CNO staff 1917–18; ONI; NWC; Capt, *Augusta, San Francisco*; chief, WPD 1935–8; RA & CruDiv 6 1938; Asst CNO 1940; VA & CinC, Atl F 1 Jan 1941–15 Nov 1944; cdr, W Sea Frontier 1944–5.

VAdm Sir Tom S. V. Phillips: ent RN 1903; Dardanelles, Far E 1914–18; NSC 1919; UK N Rep, LN 1919–22; Capt 1927; Capt (D), 6DF 1928–30; Asst DPD 1930–2; *Hawkins* 1932–5; DP 1935–8; Cdre (D), HF 1938–9; RA & VCNS 1939; Actg VA 1940; CinC, EF 1941; d on *Prince of Wales* 10 Dec 1941.

[4]Anthony Eden (1897–1977): Brig-Maj 1914–18; Con MP, Warwick & Leamington 1922–57; M for League Affairs, then FS 1935–8; SSt Doms 1939; SSt War 1940; FS Dec 1940–5, 1951–5; PM 1955–7; Earl of Avon.

DCNS: VAdm Sir William James (1881–1973): Dep Dir, NSC 1923–5, & Dir 1925–7; N Asst to FSL 1928; CoS, Atl F 1929, & MF 1930; Cdr, BCS 1932–4; DCNS 1935–8; CinC, Portsmouth 1939–42; chief, N info 1943–4; Con MP, Portsmouth N 1943–5.

A. Duff Cooper (1890–1954): FO; W Frt 1917–18; MP 1924–9, 1931–44. SSt War 1936; FL 1937–8; M of Info 1941; Res Minr Far E 1941; Amb to France 1944–7.

Sir Thomas Inskip (1876–1947): Solr-Gen 1922–3, 1924–8, 1931–2; Attny-Gen 1928–9, 1932–6; Minr for Co-ord Defence 1936–9; Doms Sec 1939–40; Ld Chllr 1939–40; Ld Chf J 1940–6; Viscount Caldecote 1939.

As Ingersoll realised, the British were desperate for a firm commitment to their side [200, 201]. Ingersoll's meetings were in January 1938 but by June 1939 the situation in the world had become much more grave and again Leahy was keen to explore an agreement, at least for a possible wartime partnership. The result was a visit, equally secret, by an officer from the Admiralty Planning staff, Commander Hampton, to Leahy in Washington; two conversations were held, no more conclusive than Ingersoll's had been, but on a broader canvas, with the Americans now interested in the Atlantic dimension as well as the Pacific. As with the Ingersoll mission, that of Commander Hampton in June 1939 kept alive the possibility of an Anglo-American naval condominium first sketched out in 1919 [211, 212].[1] In the heat of war, naval conversations became altogether more precise, as in the 'ABC' conversations of 1941 – but the story of that belongs in the next volume.

[1]Cdr T. C Hampton: Cdr June 1936; PD May 1937; *Eagle* May 1939; Capt *Carlisle* 1941; killed off Crete 22 May 1941.

180. *Eden to Sir Robert Lindsay*[1]

The Foreign Office,
London,
18 January 1937

American Neutrality

… Mr Bingham told me that he was hopeful that it would shortly be possible to modify the present legislation of the US in order to give the President some discretionary power. The recent legislation had been passed through Congress at the end of an exhausting session. It had not then satisfied the President. He had even given an example to some of the Opposition leaders, who had come to see him. 'Imagine,' he said, 'the Japanese landing at Vancouver and look at the position in which you are putting the President of the US if he cannot discriminate between Canada and Japan!'

2. I replied that I was most interested and encouraged to hear what the Ambassador had told me. As he would recall, I had more than once pointed out to him that the present neutrality legislation in the US really favoured a potential aggressor, as it meant that a victim of aggression, who was, in the nature of things, less likely to be prepared, would have his chief source of foreign support cut off from him. I said that the Ambassador would no doubt have observed with how much gratification the German press had underlined the present American neutrality legislation.

3. Mr Bingham replied that he fully agreed with my view, and that he much hoped that some modification would shortly be forthcoming.

181. *Admiral Harry E. Yarnell, US Navy to Admiral William D. Leahy, US Navy*

25 March 1937

…

Whether England would stand for Japanese occupation of the [Philippine] islands I don't know. I am inclined to believe she would not if the situation in Europe was not too serious. There has been a notable stiffening on the part of Great Britain in the Far East in the past year. She is hurrying along with her Singapore base and is strengthening the defenses of Hong Kong. …

[1]Sir Robert Lindsay (1877–1945): FO 1898; Egypt Govr 1913–19; Wash 1919–20; Amb Turkey, Germany; Amb US 1930–39.

182. *Report of Meeting at Tsingtao with the Mayor*

6 August 1937

…

The suggestion was made by Admiral Yarnell to the US and British Consuls and was concurred in by Admiral Little that it might be well if the American and British Ambassadors represent to their respective countries the desirability of requiring Japan to give notice of her intention to bombard defenceless cities in accordance with the recognised rules of war.

183. *Captain A. C. Bennett, US Navy, to Yarnell*[1]

Tsingtao,
16 August 1937

…

… Today at 1430 we conferred with the British again to perfect plans of cooperation in the event of concentration or evacuation. We believe that the chances of evacuation are quite remote and even temporary concentration of nationals is a remote contingency. However, we are proceeding with details as far as we can foresee them. The British DD *Dainty* and *Decoy* are here and Commander Dick of *Dainty* is working closely with me.[2]

184. *Yarnell, Little and Vice Admiral Le Bigot, French Navy, to Vice Admiral K. Hasegawa, Imperial Japanese Navy*[3]

Shanghai,
22 August 1937

…

On 20 August several shell fell in the water in the immediate vicinity of the *Augusta*. One fell on the deck of the *Augusta* killing one man and

[1]Capt Andrew C. Bennett, US Navy: CO, Sub Sqdn 5, *Canopus,* 1937; RA & CO, Advanced Group, Amphibious Force, Atl F 1942; NOIC, Oran, Nov 1942.

Canopus: submarine tender, 1919, 7750t, 13k, 2×5in, 4×3in.

[2]*Dainty, Decoy*: 1932, 1375t, 36k, 4×4.7in, 1×3in, 8×21in tt.

Cdr Dick:Cdr 1933; Capt June 1940; BAD 1942; Cdre & CoS to CinC Med 1943; *Belfast* 1944–5; RA 1949; ret 1953; later at NATO HQ.

[3]VAdm Le Bigot was the local FO of the French N; VAdm K. Hasegawa led the 6th F from the coast defence ship *Idzumo*.

wounding 18 others. Three large shell passed over the *Lamotte-Picquet* and *Sacramento* striking a Chinese Customs vessel and a building in the French Concession.[1] The danger to which the neutral vessels are placed by this gunfire of the opposing forces in their immediate vicinity is apparent. The neutral men-of-war must remain in this vicinity to have access to their sectors in the perimeter of the Settlement and to protect their nationals. They cannot be withdrawn.

In order to reduce the danger to neutral vessels at the naval buoys, it is strongly urged that Japanese men-of-war be kept below Hongkow creek at all times in order that as great an interval as possible be kept between the vessels under your command and those of the neutral powers. …

185. *Leahy: Diary*

Washington,
24 August 1937

…

Fighting between the Japanese landing forces and Chinese troops within the city limits of Shanghai has been prosecuted vigorously for nearly two weeks with no decisive result. The consensus of opinion here is that Japan will eventually succeed … [in] defeating the troops of China and that destruction of property in the city will cost many millions of dollars. Many of the American civilians resident in Shanghai have already been evacuated by the C-in-C, Asiatic Fleet, Admiral Yarnell. The American defense forces at present consisting of one regiment of marines will be reinforced by another regiment from San Diego, California, that should reach Shanghai via the transport *Chaumont* about 30 September.[2]

If it were possible to obtain an equitable agreement with Great Britain to share the effort and the expense, this appears to be a wonderful opportunity to force Japan to observe Treaty agreements, and to depart from the mainland of Asia, which would ensure Western trade supremacy in the Orient for another century. The cost of accomplishing this purpose at a later date will be enormously increased, and it does still appear inevitable that a major war between the Occident and the Orient must be faced at some time either now or in the future.

[1]*Lamotte-Picquet*: 1926, 7250t, 33k, 8×6.1in, 4×3in, 12×21.7in tt.
Sacramento: gunboat, 1914, 1140t.
Augusta: 1931, 9006t, 32.5k, 9×8in, 4×5in, 6×21in tt. Flagship of the Asiatic Fleet.
[2]*Chaumont*: 1921, 7555t, 20k.

186. *Chatfield to Admiral Sir Roger Backhouse*[1]

8 October 1937

…

I am concerned about the Far East situation and where we may find ourselves dragged by the sentimentalists. I am afraid that Roosevelt's speech will do more harm than good. It encourages the anti-Japanese enthusiasts – yet you may be quite sure if it ever comes to any trouble in the Far East the Americans will stand aside.[2] We have got quite enough troubles on our hands in Europe to make it most undesirable to send the Fleet out to the Far East as the sanctions against Italy meant sending the Fleet out to the Mediterranean. I have, however, warned the Foreign Office of the danger and I hope that wise counsels will prevail.

187. *Admiral Sir Lewis Bayly to Yarnell*[3]

London,
17 October 1937

… you have found yourself in what is probably the most responsible position there is at present; and what is more defying your politicians by the good old rule of keeping the flag flying. I was delighted when I read of your refusal to run away. … I don't know Little, but I am told that he is a very able man, and I have no doubt that you will be, as a US sailor described Sims and me, like two kittens in a basket, …

[1]AoF Sir Roger Backhouse (1878–1939): ent RN 1892; gun spist; Harwich force 1914–16; F Capt, *Lion*, 1916–18; DNO 1920; *Malaya* 1923; IDC 1926; RA, 3BS, Atl F 1928–32; VA 1929; 1BS & 2nd i/c, Med F; Adm 1934; CinC, Home F 1935–8; FSL 1938–39; AoF July 1939.

[2]The Quarantine speech, made by FDR in Chicago, 5 Oct 1937.

[3]Adm Sir Lewis Bayly (1857–1938): ent RN 1871; NA, Washington 1900–2; Home F destroyers 1907–8; RA & Pres, NWC 1908–11; capital ship sqdns 1912–14; VA & CinC, Channel F Dec 1914–15; Pres, N Staff Coll, Greenwich 1915; CinC, Coast of Ireland, July 1915–March 1919; Adm 1917; ret 1919. On his relationship with Sims, see M. A. Simpson, 'Adm W. S. Sims, US Navy, & Adm Sir Lewis Bayly, RN: An Unlikely Friendship and Anglo-American Cooperation, 1917–1919', *Naval War College Review*, vol XLI, no. 2, spring 1988, pp. 66–80.

188. *Yarnell to Bayly*

Shanghai,
28 November 1937

...

One of the few pleasant features of the Shanghai 'incident' has been my association with Admiral Little. He is a fine officer, of rare good judgment, and delightful personality. We have worked closely together – 'like two kittens in a basket'. There is about the British naval officer an aura of solidity and reliability which is a great comfort to those who are associated with them in times of stress.

I am delighted that on completion of the present rearmament program the British Navy will assume its proper role in the defense of the Empire. The safety of the Empire means too much in the maintenance of Anglo-Saxon ideals of liberty and good government to be jeopardised.

189. *Leahy: Diary*

Washington,
28 November 1937

At noon had an hour's conference with the Secretary of State in his office during which the international situation, both in Europe and Asia, was thoroughly discussed and a decision was reached that I should endeavor to have a completely informal unofficial talk with the British Naval Attaché on the possibility of a naval demonstration in Asian waters by European Powers.[1]

190. *Leahy: Diary*

Washington,
29 November 1937

At 5.0 [p.m.] met Captain Bradley, the British Naval Attaché, at the apartment of Rear Admiral Holmes, and after a very informal discussion with him on international affairs concluded that he is not in possession of

[1]Sec of State: Cordell Hull.

any information as to the prospects of a naval demonstration in China by the interested European Nations.[1]

191. *Leahy: Diary*

Washington,
12 December 1937

During supper I received telephone information from the United Press, and later from the Commander of the Yangtze Patrol, that the USS *Panay* in the Yangtze River near Nanking was sunk today by a bombing attack with an unknown loss of life.

192. *Leahy: Diary*

Washington,
13 December 1937

Despatch information is received that three Standard Oil barges of approximately 1100 gross tons with refugees on board were sunk at the same time as the *Panay*. The Japanese Government and the Admiral at Shanghai admit that the bombing was done by naval planes. Both expressed their regrets and promised steps to prevent further attacks.

Several British merchant ships and two British gunboats were also attacked yesterday and damaged but not sunk. Personal contact with the Department of State is convincing that which can be done by the English language to protect Americans has already been done. It is, in my opinion, time now to get the Fleet ready for sea, to make an agreement with the British Navy for joint action, and to inform the Japanese that we expect to protect our Nationals.

[1]RAdm Ralston S. Holmes, US Navy (b. 1882): USNA 1903; Capt 1925; RA 1936; ret 1943; CO, *Mayflower* [Pres. yacht] 1920–2; 2nded to Brazil N 1923; destroyers 1925; NWC 1927–8; NA, Rome 1928–30; *Cincinnati* 1930–1; CoS, Cruisers, Scout Force 1931–2; USNA 1932–5; CoS, Battle Force 1935–7; DNI 1937–9; destroyers 1939–40; Gen Bd 1940–1; Cdt, 11 N Dist & San Diego NB 1941–2.

193. *HMS Bee to HMS Folkestone*[1]

[Yangtze River,]
13 December 1937

Have informed senior Japanese military officer at Wuhu that I intend to proceed down river at noon today Monday to investigate safety of USS Gunboat *Panay* which may have been damaged by an attack. I can get no reply from her by wireless.

194. *Leahy: Diary*

17 December 1937

At 1100 conferred with the President in his study at the White House regarding the Oriental situation, as to the practicability of sending a division of light cruisers on a visit to Singapore in January or February [1938], and as to the possibility of future staff conversations with the British Navy.

195. *Yarnell to Captain J. G. L. Dundas*[2]

[Shanghai,]
17 December 1937

I will appreciate it if you will send the following message from me to Admiral Little:

'I wish to express to you and the officers and men concerned the deep appreciation of myself and the personnel under my command for the prompt and courageous assistance rendered to the personnel of the USS *Panay*. The British naval officers with unselfish disregard for their own personal safety proceeded immediately to the scene of the bombing and in the face of threatened force and armed opposition rendered all possible aid until all Americans were out of danger.

The initiative and courageous action of Rear Admiral Holt and Captain O'Donnell, and the officers and men of HMS *Bee*, the fine cooperation of Vice Admiral Crabbe, Captain Dundas, and the welcome assistance of Lieut-Commander Barlow and the officers and men of HMS *Ladybird*

[1]*Bee*: river gunboat, 1915, 645t, 2×6in, 1×3in.
Folkestone: 1930, 1045t, 16.5k, 2×4in.

[2]Capt J. G. L. Dundas (1893–1952): Capt 1935; Asst DP 1938; *Victory* 1940; *Nigeria* 1941; Cdre, *Nile* 1942; RA & ACNS 1944–5; *President* 1945; VA ret 1948.

exemplify those high standards which are the proud tradition of the Royal Navy.'[1]

196. *Leahy: Diary*

22 December 1937

I decided to send Captain Ingersoll to London on the French SS *Normandie*, sailing from New York on the 26 [December], to discuss the requirements of the London Treaty of 1936 in regard to measurements of tonnage and caliber of guns.[2]

197. *Yarnell to Leahy*

[China,]
22 December 1937

...

All of the actions since present affair began toward the British indicate that they [the Japanese] intend to drive them out. While this policy is not so apparent towards Americans, they [the Japanese] are undoubtedly just as anxious to get us out as they are the British.

...

With reference to our own policy, it is my firm conviction that we should stick with England and France in all our dealings in the Far East. It is inconceivable to me that we as a nation are going to give up our rights of trading or living in China and confine our activities to our own continental limits. As for pulling chestnuts out of the fire, England stands to pull just as many out for us as we do for her. If these three countries stand together they can dominate the situation in the Far East. If they do not, they will be defeated singly and in detail.

[1]RAdm Reginald V. Holt (1884–1957): Capt 1925; Capt-in-Charge, Bermuda 1928–30; CoS, Nore 1931–3; *Shropshire* 1933–4; Capt, *Britannia* 1934–6; RA 1936; SNO Yangtze 1937–9; VA 1939; ret 1940.

Capt G. E. M. O'Donnell: Capt Nov 1937; NA, Athens Sept 1939; NA, Ankara 1940; *Enterprise* 1942; *Valiant* 1944; Damage Contr Bd, *President* 1945.

VAdm Lewis G. E. Crabbe (1882–1951): Eur 1914–19; King's Hbr Mr, Rosyth, 1927–9; SNO, Persian Gulf, 1930–3; RA & SNO, Yangtze, 1935–7; FOIC, Liverpool, 1939–40; Cdre, RNR, 1941–5.

Lt-Cdr H. D. Barlow: Lt-Cdr 1935; *Ladybird* Aug 1937; Sqdn Recreation Ofcr, *Resolution* July 1938; *Pembroke* [Chatham] April 1940; *Dido* 1942; *Seaborn* N Air Trng Sta 1944–5.

Ladybird: river gunboat, 1916, 625t, 14k, 2x6in, 1x3in.

[2]*Normandie*: CGT, 1935, 83,243t, 30k; destroyed by fire, NY hbr, 1942.

Discussion of the London Naval Treaty of 1936 was a cover.

198. *Little to Yarnell*

[China,]
25 December 1937

… It is curious the *Panay, Ladybird* affair happening immediately I had left and I am glad that in that incident our ships were able to co-operate together as they have invariably done since I have been here and that is one of the features of my sojourn in the Far East which is the pleasantest and which will always be a most happy memory for me. It has been so natural and you, Sir, have gone out of your way to do everything that is possible in any difficulty that I have been in, to help me.

199. *Leahy: Diary*

10 January 1938

At 1400 I conferred in the White House with the President, the Secretary of State, [and] the Under Secretary of State on the Oriental situation.[1] It appears that the British Government contemplates directing its fleet to complete preparations short of mobilization, in which case we may dock ships of the US Fleet to clean bottoms and then advance the date of our Fleet Problem and send the Fleet to Honolulu.

This seems to be contingent upon action by Great Britain.

It was decided to withhold public announcement of a planned visit by three cruisers to Singapore until information of British probable action is received.

200. *Memorandum for the Chief of Naval Operations*

Washington,
January 1938

Record of Conversations between Captain Ingersoll, US Navy, and the Naval Staff at the Admiralty

31 December 1937.

Arrived Southampton, fine passage, averaged 30.03 knots. Customs authorities had instructions to facilitate my entry. Met at London discreetly

[1]U Sec State: Sumner Welles (1892–1961): SD; Tokyo 1915–17; Buenos Aires 1919–20; L Am Div, SD 1920–5; Asst SSt 1933; U Sec 1937–43. An FDR confidante.

by Willson and Harrill.[1] Willson informed me that the Chargé, Mr Johnson, wished to see me as soon as he could.

31 December [Friday], 3.00 p.m. – Conference [in] Mr Johnson's office.
Present: Mr Johnson, Captains Ingersoll and Willson.

Mr Johnson stated that he had been informed that I was *en route* but that the exact purpose of my trip was not known. I informed him of the purpose – that is to obtain naval information on which to plan and base discussions, if necessary, for future action. I also informed him that if it was necessary for the Department [of the Navy] to give any reason for my absence, it was stated that I was seeking information regarding interpretation of the 1936 [London Naval] Treaty. I also told him that I desired Captain Willson to accompany me in my conversations with the British for three reasons:

(a) So that there might be some continuity after my departure,
(b) So that there might be a check on what transpired at the conversations, and
(c) Better opportunity to remember and record conversations.

Mr Johnson informed [me] that Mr Eden wished to see me at 11.00 a.m. the next day.

1 January [Saturday] 1938. 11.00 a.m. Conference at the Foreign Office.
Present: US – Mr Johnson, Captain Ingersoll.
UK – Mr Eden, Sir A. Cadogan.[2]

Conversation opened with routine pleasantries. Mr Eden then said that while he knew Captain Ingersoll was coming to London, he did not know the exact purpose, and asked me what had been said in the conversations between the President, Mr Hull, and the ambassador. I told him that I did not know, except that apparently as a result of these conversations, the President had directed Admiral Leahy to send me to London to obtain naval information on which to plan and base decisions, if necessary, as to future action. I explained my status (re-treaty) and Mr Eden remarked that was plausible. He inquired about the dispatch of cruisers to Sydney and

[1]Capt Russell Willson, US Navy: NA, London 1937–9; RA & Supt, USNA 1941–2; CoS to CNO March 1942; Pac F Aug 1942; DCinC Nov 1942; ret Dec 1942; JCS staff, Nov 1942–5.

Cdr William K. Harill, US Navy (b. 1891): USNA 1914; N Sea Barrage 1918; pilot; avtn svc 1921–35; Asst NA (Air), London 1937–8; Capt *Ranger* 1941; Pac F air replcmts 1942–4; FO (Air), W Coast 1944.

[2]Sir Alexander Cadogan (1884–1968): Amb to China 1935; DU Sec, FO 1936–7; Pmnt U Sec 1938–46; Pmnt Reprv, UN 1946–50.

possibly Singapore, and I informed him that the decision to send them to Sydney had been made after I left Washington and that I knew nothing about it, except what I had read in the radio news on the *Normandie*. I got the impression that Mr Eden was more interested right now in immediate gestures to impress the Japanese than he was in future long-range planning. I suggested to him that I thought the best method to expedite matters was to get in touch at once with the Admiralty and Mr Eden agreed. He said that he thought that the FO part of the business was over. Sir A. Cadogan then made an appointment for me to see Vice Admiral James, DCNS.

1 January [Saturday], 12.00 noon. Conversations at Admiralty.
Present: US – Captain Ingersoll.
UK – Vice Admiral James.

Captain Ingersoll presented his compliments and stated he was coming at the suggestion of the Foreign Secretary. Captain Ingersoll explained very briefly the purpose of his trip and his status. Admiral James made an appointment for me to see Admiral Chatfield, Chief of the Naval Staff, on Monday at 11.30 a.m. Admiral James brought up the question of the visit of the three cruisers to Singapore and Captain Ingersoll gave him the same reply that he made to Mr Eden.

3 January [Monday], 11.30 a.m. Conversation at Admiralty.
Present: US – Captains Ingersoll, Willson.
UK – Admirals Chatfield, James.

Admiral Chatfield opened the conversation with very cordial greetings and stated he had been informed of the gist of the conversation with Mr Eden on the 1st. He stated that he had, of course, no instructions from his Government, and Captain Ingersoll stated that he likewise had none, except to seek naval information that would be helpful in making future plans and decisions. There then followed a rather general discussion of the whole situation, both Eastern and European, and its bearing on naval matters of the two services.

I told Admiral Chatfield that I had jotted down various topics that I thought would be profitable to discuss and he said that I should go right ahead with the discussion with Captain Phillips, in charge of the War Plans Division. This I will commence at 3.30 p.m., 3 January [Monday].

During the course of the conversation the following information regarding the British situation developed.

(a) There has been political pressure to have the British forces in the Far East reinforced by 'driblets'. The Admiralty has apparently resisted and does not want to send a force unless it alone can cope with the Japanese fleet.

(b) He stated that the Admiralty has been getting this force prepared, with the necessary train, for some time, and that it would be ready 15 January to start, if required by the 'Government'.

(c) He stated that he would want to mobilize 10 days before this force started, in order to have the ships in reserve ready to cope with any European situation, particularly as regards Germany.

(d) He stated that the eastern entrance to the Mediterranean would be held by occupying Egypt, probably with troops from India. That Malta and Cyprus would probably have to be abandoned.

(e) He stated that France would take care of the western Mediterranean.

(f) He stated that the political movements should keep step with the naval situation, but that it might, because of circumstances, be difficult to accomplish. He also said that the political and naval steps of the two nations [US and UK] should be kept in step, and that circumstances – particularly new 'incidents' affecting one nation primarily, might also make this most difficult.

Captain Ingersoll outlined in general the steps that had been taken so far by the US, that is –

(a) That certain security measures had been taken by the Fleet.

(b) That measures that could be taken without causing concern, such as docking, filling up crews of certain units, etc., would be taken.

He stated that the Navy could not be mobilized, reserves called in nor merchant ships take over, unless a National emergency were declared by the President.

He stated that our first step would probably be to take a position of readiness covering our West Coast and the Hawaiian islands and that an advance of the whole Fleet beyond this position was not desirable until the Fleet was ready to move on and not return.

Following this discussion Admirals Chatfield and James brought up the subject of capital ship construction by the Japanese. I believe they consider that some sort of joint action by the US, Great Britain and France should be taken to ascertain from the Japanese what size ships they are building and what size guns are contemplated for them. I believe they are ready to throw over all quantitative limitations if Japan will not give any definite information or indicate that they are building ships which are exceeding [the] limitations of [the] 1936 Treaty.

In addition to the information given above, Admiral Chatfield indicated –

(g) He is not apprehensive of German submarines but is apprehensive of British trade routes in the Atlantic, fearing that the Germans will use the three 'pocket' battleships and the two 27,000 ton new ships, which will be ready in May, as raiders.[1]

(h) He broached the subject of coordination and stated that as a principle he believed that [as] the two fleets would be widely separated at first and probably for some time, there could not be unity of command in a tactical and strategic sense and that strategic cooperation was all that was possible.

(i) He stated that it was desirable to arrange early the means of communication and the exchange of intelligence between the two fleets whenever it became necessary.

(j) He stated that Singapore would not be completed for 18 months but he was doing everything to expedite [it]. He stated there were two docks ready, but that Singapore was not prepared to handle large repairs of ships damaged in action. It could support the force contemplated to be based there in other respects.

3 January [Monday], 3.30 p.m. Conversation at Admiralty.
Present: US – Captains Ingersoll, Willson.
UK – Captains Phillips, Creasy, Commander Hampton (all War Plans Division).[2]

Captain Phillips stated that he had not been present at the meeting in the forenoon, but that Admiral Chatfield had told him something about it. Captain Ingersoll again went over the points he had discussed in the morning. A general discussion was then held of all aspects of the situation and a meeting was arranged for 3.30 p.m., 5 January, to discuss details.

In the course of the discussion at Admiralty, 3.30 p.m., 3 January, the following points came up:

(a) The force which the British are getting ready to send to the Far East, if necessary, is as follows:

[1] 'Pocket battleships': *Admiral Scheer, Admiral Graf von Spee, Lűtzow* (ex-*Deutschland*): 1933–6, 11700t, 28k, 6×11In, 8×5.9in, 6×5.1in, 6×21in tt.

Battlecruisers: *Scharnhorst, Gneisenau*: 1938–9, 34841t, 32k, 9×11in, 12×5.9in, 14×5.1in.

[2] AoF Sir George Creasy (1895–1972): ent RN 1908; t spist; N Sea 1914–18; Tac Sch; Capt 1935; Asst DP 1936–8; 1DF 1938–40; Dunkirk; Pers Asst to FSL; DASD 1940–2; *Duke of York* 1942; RA 1943; CoS to ANCXF 1943–4; FO (Submarines) 1944–5; FO (Air), Far E 1947; VA 1948; 5SL & DCNS, VCNS 1949–51; Adm 1951; CinC, Home F 1952; CinC, Portsmouth 1954; AoF 1955.

Battleships	9	
Battlecruisers (*Hood*)	1	
Aircraft Carriers	2	
Cruisers (heavy and light)	15	(including 2 with destroyers and those of Cape and East Indies stations)
Destroyers	54	
Submarines	10	

The foregoing does not include two CA's and 3 CL's of the Australian and New Zealand navies which they definitely assume will be available.

Summary of Forces available in Far East:

	To send	*China*	*Australia & NZ*	*Total*	*No. 'needed' on WHL memo.*
BB	9	–	–	9	7
BC	1	–	–	1	–
CV	2	2	–	4	3
CA/L	15	5	5	25	35
DD	54	9	5	68	30

(b) The British consider it is essential to get the means of communication between the two fleets arranged as soon as possible and distributed so that no delays will result if concerted action is required. The following, as a result of discussions, seemed necessary.

(1) Calls.
(2) Code, of high security, for Admirals.
(3) Code, of less security, for all ships.
(4) Contact code (they call it a 'repeating' code).
(5) Radio and signal procedure.
(6) Recognition signals.
(7) Schedules and frequencies of shore stations.

During 4 January [Tuesday], the Admiralty Communications Experts will look into what they have available for issue and will let us know on Wednesday [5 January] what can be done. No decisions have been made but we discussed the desirability of a British communications expert going to Washington. I suggested that US Communications Office ascertain what we can do to provide facilities from reserve stocks or otherwise. More on this subject will be sent after discussion on 5 January [Wednesday].

(c) A discussion was held on the subject of a distant blockade or quarantine. No definite understanding was reached, but from the discussion it is believed that the British are prepared to cover the line from Singapore, via Southern Philippines at least as far east as New Hebrides and that the US could cover to the Eastward via Fiji, Samoa, Hawaii and US. They assumed that we would close the Panama Canal, and cover the west coast of South America to any Japanese vessel that might slip by the long lines in the eastern Pacific. We will get more definite information on 5 January [Wednesday].

(d) One interesting point was the British interest in Manila. They are apprehensive of their ability to hold Hong Kong against an attack from the land side. They consider Manila superior to Hong Kong as an operating base in the China Sea and consider it reasonably safe, and much safer than Hong Kong, from air attacks from Formosa. Just as the meeting broke up they enquired about the repair facilities at Cavite and Olongapo, which we told them we would give them on Wednesday [5 January]. Captain Ingersoll told them that we could probably hold the entrance to Manila [for] a few weeks but could not prevent a landing in force or prevent capture by a major attack with the present garrison. The British do not believe the Japanese would attempt to take the Philippines while occupied in China and believed they are safe if the British Fleet were at Singapore and the US Fleet at Hawaii or to the westward thereof.

(e) The British believe that even if no war with Japan results because of future 'incidents' or other reasons, that a demonstration by the two fleets in the Pacific, the British at Singapore and the US at Hawaii or further west, will be necessary in order to bring about peace terms between Japan and China that will continue for the other nations of the world the principle of the 'open door' in China. In other words, if there are no further 'incidents' the real test will come when peace terms are under discussion.

(f) The British do not expect any help from the French in the Far East, except possibly the use of French ports, such as Camranh Bay in Indo-China, or French Islands in the Pacific.

(g) The British believe the Dutch will be 'benevolent' provided they are assured that 'they will not be let down' if the Japanese should attempt to take any of their East Indies possessions.

(h) The British are not counting on any aid from Russia. They believe she might possibly act independently against Japan if conditions were favorable to her.

(i) The British Navy is concerned about their troops and ships in North China. They want to get them out. They said they would move them out if the fleet started for Singapore, possibly at the same time or just before.

(j) The UK cannot definitely commit the Dominions in any action in concert with the UK, as the Dominions like to maintain their independent dominion status. They feel sure that Canada, Australia and New Zealand will cooperate with them against Japan and that there would be no question that Australian and New Zealand ports could be used by the US, such as the Admiralty Islands (south of the Carolines), which are an Australian mandate.

(k) Captain Ingersoll mentioned in a casual way when speaking of taking a position of readiness that the US might want to station seaplanes at Christmas or Fanning Islands in lieu of Palmyra or Kingman Reef. The remark did not bring forth any comment.

(l) The British said that they thought the US might want to use the southern detour, via Samoa, Fiji and Torres Straits, for moving forces to the Far East, instead of using the more direct and perhaps less safe route through the Japanese mandated islands. From this we assume that there would be no question of availability to use British Territorial Waters. Captain Ingersoll stated that the choice of routes, if we moved westward, would probably be made after reconnaissance of the mandated areas.

The British inquired how many ships the US would be able to mobilize in the Pacific and about when they would be ready. Captain Ingersoll stated that the vessels of the fleet in commission in the Pacific could move as far as Hawaii as soon as they were fuelled and filled up with stores. If they were fully manned and docked it would require 12 to 15 days. It would probably require at least a month to assemble the necessary train to permit them to move beyond Hawaii. He said again that we could not mobilize and place in commission vessels out of commission, fill up the vessels in the Atlantic with full crews, and take over merchant ships unless the President declared an emergency. The British said that it was their opinion that if any concerted action was taken that the British Fleet and the US Fleet should arrive at Singapore and Hawaii respectively, at approximately the same date.

(m) Exchange of information by informal agreement is now taking place between the British DNI and Washington regarding Japanese naval construction and the Mandated Islands. The

British believe this should be extended now to include movements and location of Japanese naval units.

(n) I mentioned to Captain Phillips the desirability of having an Assistant British [Naval] Attaché in Washington with knowledge of British war plans. I will take this up with Admiral Chatfield later.

5 January [Wednesday], 3.30 p.m. Conversation at the Admiralty.
Present: US – Captains Ingersoll, Willson.
UK – Rear Admiral Troup (DNI), Captains Phillips, Creasy, Commander Hampton (War Plans Division), Captain Glover (Signals).[1]

At the meeting there was a general discussion of the codes, ciphers, calls and signal procedure necessary if joint operations were undertaken. Discussion was also held as to the Communications Liaison Officers that would be required at various places.

...

A discussion was also held as to the Communications Liaison necessary. The British consider that it would be necessary, in order to get communications flowing freely at the outset, ... to have a US Communications Officer and one enlisted radio operator at each of the following British stations which are named in order of importance:

(1) British Flagship in Far Eastern waters.
(2) Singapore.
(3) Hong Kong.

Captain Ingersoll stated that the quickest way to get this communications personnel placed would be to have them ordered from the Asiatic fleet or from the Radio Station at Cavite. It was similarly considered necessary that there should be a British Communications Officer and a radio rating at the following places:

(1) Flagship, US Fleet.
(2) Flagship, US Asiatic Fleet.
(3) Communications Office, Washington.

The latter assignment might later be changed to the West Coast or Pearl Harbor.

Further discussion was held on a distant blockade or 'quarantine':

(a) We agreed that we might assume that all ports and waters in the jurisdiction of both nations would be available for the use of the vessels of both nations.

[1]Capt P. F. Glover: Capt June 1936; DSD June 1937; Cdre, *Lanka* 1941; *Dragon* 1942; *Saker* [BAD] 1943.

(b) The British stated they were prepared to stop all Japanese traffic crossing a line roughly from Singapore through the Dutch East Indies, New Guinea, New Hebrides, and around to the east of Australia and New Zealand. This they feel they can do because the greater part of this line is a land barrier with comparatively few narrow passages through it. They did not believe it was practicable to assign any definite line in the mid-Pacific to be held by the US, such as the line New Hebrides, Hawaiian Islands, US, because of the great distances involved. They considered that the US could prevent all west bound trade to Japan by controlling by embargo or ships, the entire Pacific Coast from Alaska to Cape Horn. They stated that [the] problem would be very much simpler if the President could influence South American Republics to cooperate in the quarantine by non-intercourse, embargoes, boycotts, or similar measures.

In discussing the question of assistance to Japan by Germany and Italy and in discussing the possibility of 'pirate submarines' appearing in the Atlantic, the British stated that they were certain that they could hold the Strait of Gibraltar in such a manner that the passage of submarines through the Strait of Gibraltar would be very hazardous.

The British inquired further about the facilities at Cavite and Olongapo and were informed by us that Cavite could maintain submarines and that Olongapo could repair and dock all classes of ships up to and including heavy cruisers and that while the dock at Olongapo had sufficient capacity to lift a heavy cruiser the controlling factor was the length of the ship. They inquired particularly if there were mines and nets at Manila and we informed them that there were mines and minelaying vessels but no nets.

The British said that they contemplated feeding their Fleet in the Far East from Australia.

In discussing again the force that they will send to the Far East it appears that we misunderstood the number of capital ships which they will send to the Far East or else they have changed their mind since the previous meeting. They now state that the number of capital ships will be eight and one battlecruiser. This apparently may be subject to a change when the German battlecruisers are completed, that is, they might retain the *Hood* in home waters and substitute a battleship for her.

As regards sending a War Plans officer of the Admiralty to Washington and also sending a War Plans officer from Washington to London, it seems that with the knowledge which the British War Plans Division now has of US War Plans, this is not necessary at the present time. As the coordination of the fleets' activities develops it will probably be necessary to enlarge the Naval Communications facilities in London and to further consider the question of exchanging 'War Plans' officers.

7 January [Friday], 4.30 p.m. Meeting at the Admiralty.
Present: US – Captain Willson.
UK – Captain Glover.

The technical problem of providing a joint Radio Call List was discussed and necessary preliminary information concerning US requirements was supplied by Captain Willson – the discussion to be continued at [the] next meeting.

Captain Willson furnished Captain Glover a list of Unit Commanders and shore authorities as a basis for incorporating in the addendum to the British call lists. The list of ships in alphabetical order was to be furnished [on] Monday [10 January] and the whole checked over on receipt of [the] US Naval Call List from Paris.

10 January [Monday], 3.30 p.m. Meeting at the Admiralty.
Present: US – Captains Ingersoll, Willson.
UK – Rear Admiral Troup, Captains Phillips, Creasy, Commander Hampton (War Plans), Captain Glover (DSD).

This … memorandum … will be submitted to Lord Chatfield, CNS, for approval in so far as it concerns information regarding the British Navy and views. Captain Ingersoll stated he could not definitely commit the Navy Department, but he believed that the statements he had made would be approved by Admiral Leahy, CNO, or by higher authority if necessary.

A further discussion was held on the details for communication facilities between the two fleets.

The discussion regarding secure war calls developed that the best and quickest way to get the calls ready would be the following:

(a) The US Fleet would use its own secure war calls for communications within the US Fleet.
(b) The British Fleet would use its own secure war calls for communication within the British Fleet. We understand new secure calls will be prepared immediately for this purpose.
(c) The Admiralty will prepare an addendum to the present British secure war calls giving secure war calls for vessels of the US Navy and shore stations. These and the present British secure war calls would be used for communication between the two fleets.
(d) Captain Willson was requested to cable to Washington whether

secure calls of a particular nature would interfere with US secure calls.

Captain Willson agreed to furnish the British DNI the number of copies of code and other communication publications required by the US Navy and their distribution.

12 January [Wednesday], 3.00 p.m. Meeting at the Admiralty.
Present: US – Captains Ingersoll, Willson.
UK – Captains Phillips, Creasy, Commander Hampton (War Plans Division).

...

Captain Ingersoll again inquired about the relative desirability of Christmas and Fanning Islands for seaplane operations and was informed that there was about a mile take off at Fanning Island. Christmas Island lagoon has been surveyed but the chart not yet made. The British stated there were many coral heads in the Christmas Island lagoon. The coral heads in Fanning Island lagoon would have to be marked by beacons before use by airplanes.

... radio calls in the form 'letter figure letter figure' would not conflict with all US radio calls.

13 January [Thursday], 1.15 p.m.

The First Lord of the Admiralty, Rt Hon A. Duff Cooper, gave a lunch at the Admiralty House to which Captains Ingersoll and Willson were invited. The following British officials were present:

Rt Hon Sir Thomas Inskip, Minister for the Coordination of Defense; Admiral Chatfield, CNS; Sir Alexander Cadogan, Foreign Office; Vice Admiral James, DCNS; Captain Phillips, War Plans Division.

The conversation at the luncheon was entirely social and had no bearing on the purpose of Captain Ingersoll's trip. However, the fact that luncheon was given and the make up of the British members of the party may be an indication of the importance which the British attach to the 'conversations'.

13 January [Thursday], 2.30 p.m. Conversation at the Admiralty: First Sea Lord's Office.
Present: US – Captains Ingersoll, Willson.
UK – Admiral Chatfield, Captain Phillips.

At the luncheon Admiral Chatfield expressed a wish to see Captain Ingersoll after lunch. Admiral Chatfield asked Captain Ingersoll to convey to Admiral Leahy his appreciation for sending an officer from his office to consider the way and means of cooperation between the two navies, should it ever become necessary. He stated the conversations had been most helpful to them in obtaining a better understanding of what the mutual problem would be if it developed.

He stated that had not gone beyond the potential of moving the two fleets towards the Far East in connection with whatever political and economic moves might be made. He stated that if such parallel action did not bring forth results that further parallel action might be necessary. He did not think that need be discussed at the present time.

He then took up the question of what action could be taken by the signatories of the 1936 Naval Treaty to force Japan to give an answer regarding whether or not she was building vessels whose characteristics exceeded those of the Treaty. He stated that the CID had been studying the recent note from the Chargé d'Affaires of the American Embassy [in London] on the subject of Japanese naval construction.

He stated that, while the American note had only referred to the possibility that Japan was exceeding the Treaty limits in the tonnage of capital ships, he considered that, should it be ascertained that Japan was exceeding tonnage limitations or refused to give any satisfaction, that the signatories should use an escape clause to exceed the existing limits for battleships and also (which he considered equally important) that signatories should use an escape clause to exceed the existing limits for cruisers, both tonnage and guns.

He said that it should be put up squarely to Japan that if she does not keep within tonnage limits that the two nations are going to outbuild her in numbers and quality, and that she will be held responsible for the unlimited race in armaments.

Captain Ingersoll then stated that he would convey Admiral Chatfield's views to Admiral Leahy. He informed Admiral Chatfield that he was sailing on the 18th January [Tuesday] and took his leave.

13 January [Thursday], 4.0 p.m. The Admiralty: Captain Phillips's Office.
Present: US – Captains Ingersoll, Willson.
UK – Captain Phillips, Commander Hampton.
[This was signing of agreed record and leave taking.]

14 January [Friday], 1.30 p.m. White's Club, London.
Present: US – Mr Johnson, Captain Ingersoll.
UK – Sir A. Cadogan.

After luncheon a brief conversation took place in which Sir Alexander Cadogan expressed the pleasure of the Foreign Office that the conversations had produced satisfactory understanding between the two navies and then the conversation turned to the possible necessity of the signatories to the London Treaty of 1936 invoking an escape clause in order to meet Japanese construction beyond Treaty limits. Sir Alexander Cadogan referred to the fact that the UK had unilateral limitation treaties with Germany and Russia but stated that if it were found that the Japanese were exceeding the limits of the 1936 Treaty that it would be necessary to notify both Germany and Russia that UK would find it necessary to invoke the escape clause in order to build ships that could meet the new Japanese capital ships. Captain Ingersoll told Sir Alexander Cadogan briefly what Admiral Chatfield had told him at the Admiralty the day before in regard to the Admiralty's views on the subject of the 1936 Treaty.

14 January [Friday], 3.0 p.m. Memorandum of a Conversation at the Admiralty: DNI's Office.

There was a general discussion of the details concerning the communication facilities agreed upon in previous conversations between Captains Ingersoll and Willson and Admiralty Officials.

201. *Record of Conversations: Agreed between Captain T. S. V. Phillips, RN, and Captain R. E. Ingersoll, US Navy*

11 January 1938

1. *Composition, state of readiness and initial movement of Fleets.*

US Fleet:

2. The US Navy view is that no gesture should be made unless the Fleet now in commission is brought up to 100% full complement and prepared in all respects for war. The ability to bring the Fleet up to full complement depends on the issue by the President of a Declaration of National Emergency.

3. The present state of the US Fleet in commission as regards personnel is as follows:

Submarines and aircraft on the Pacific Coast: 100%

Advanced Force, consisting of two Squadrons of heavy Cruisers and two Squadrons of Destroyers and one Carrier is now being completed, as far as is practicable, to full complement.

Capital Ships, Cruisers, Destroyers and Auxiliaries on the Pacific Coast, other than Advanced Force: 85%

Atlantic Coast – three Battleships, *Wyoming*, and one Squadron of Destroyers are used as a training squadron with about 50% complement.[1]

4. It is the intention of the US Navy Department to send first to Honolulu the Advanced Force, together with about 15 submarines. These could leave at any time. There are already about 75 patrol planes and about 20 submarines at Honolulu.

5. There are six submarines and 36 aircraft in the Panama Canal Zone.

6. It is understood that all available capital ships would probably be sent to Honolulu. Allowing for two or three ships refitting and three on the Atlantic Coast, nine or ten capital ships could be ready to sail in 10–15 days after the Declaration of National Emergency.

7. Subsequently the Navy Department visualize a gradual advance across the Pacific after air reconnaissance, making use of Japanese Mandated Islands as necessary, and finally establishing themselves at Truk or some other position in the same general area.

8. They do not at present envisage proceeding immediately to Manila or any other Philippine port.

9. A Fleet Supply Train with about one month's supplies could sail about 20 days, and transports, tankers and auxiliary vessels about 30 days, after the Declaration of National Emergency.

10. The US Navy Department intends also to have two submarines and a small number of aircraft and a seaplane tender to operate from a base at Unalaska.

British Fleet

11. The Admiralty policy is to send to the Far East a force which is sufficient to engage the Japanese Fleet under normal tactical and strategical conditions. In general, this Fleet would proceed to the Far East as a single tactical unit.

12. The force which it is at present intended should form the Far Eastern Fleet is as follows (some of these ships are already in Far Eastern waters):

Battleships	8	
Battlecruisers	1	
Aircraft Carriers	3	
8in Cruisers	8	
6in Cruisers	11	(including 2 attached to Destroyer Flotillas)
Cruiser Minelayer	1	

[1] *Wyoming*: 1911, 26000t, trng ship 1931–46. The three old battleships were usually *Texas*, *New York*, *Arkansas*.

Destroyer Flotillas	7 [54 ships]
Submarines	25

Together with the necessary Depot and Repair Ships and certain minor war vessels.

Two 8in cruisers and one 6in cruiser from Australia and two 6in cruisers from New Zealand are in addition to the above and all come, probably, under the orders of the Admiralty.

13. The exact composition of the Far Eastern Fleet is subject to modification with the passage of time: for instance, at a later date, it may be desirable to send nine battleships to the Far East and to retain both battlecruisers in Home Waters.[1] The above figures, however, serve as a general guide to British strength in Far Eastern waters.

14. It is understood that the ships of the Home and Mediterranean Fleets would be ready to sail for the Far East at 10–14 days' notice if mobilization was ordered after 15 January 1938.

15. The British Fleet would proceed initially to Singapore. This base will not be fully completed for 18 months. The dry docks there are ready but Singapore is not prepared at the present time to handle large repairs of ships damaged in action. It can support, mainly by commercial facilities, in other respects the force contemplated to be based there.

General Policy

16. Both parties agree that, in principle political movements should keep in step with the Naval situation, but it is realised that this may be difficult to accomplish. Both parties also agree that the political and Naval measures of each nation should be kept in step with those of the other nation. To this end it is agreed that it is desirable that the arrival of the British Fleet at Singapore and the US Fleet at Honolulu should, as far as possible, be synchronised. Nevertheless, it is recognised that circumstances, and in particular any incident affecting one nation rather than both, may make it difficult to carry out the above policy.

17. It is assumed that all waters of the British Commonwealth, including the Dominions, will be available for the use of US Naval Forces and that all waters of the US, including the Philippines, will be available for the use of the British Naval Forces.

18. It is understood that the Government of the UK cannot commit the Governments of the Dominions of the British Commonwealth to any action in concert with the UK. The Admiralty feels sure, however, that Canada, Australia and New Zealand would co-operate with the UK against Japan in the circumstances under consideration.

[1] *Renown*, *Repulse*.

19. The Admiralty is not at the present time anticipating any direct aid from the French or the Dutch in the Far East, but they consider that it is possible that the latter might adopt a benevolent attitude of neutrality. The Admiralty are not counting on any aid from Russia.

20. In the event of Germany proving hostile a most serious problem would arise. The Admiralty is not as seriously apprehensive of submarines as they believe they can successfully deal with them. They are, however, seriously apprehensive of British trade routes in the Atlantic, should the Germans use their three Pocket Battleships and the two new 27,000 ton ships as commerce raiders.

21. An even more dangerous situation would arise should hostilities with Italy supervene after the greater part of the British Fleet had proceeded to the Far East. It would be necessary for the Admiralty to rely entirely on the alternative route to the East via the Cape of Good Hope. In these circumstances the main problem in the Mediterranean would be to hold the Suez Canal and Egypt. The Admiralty would have to depend on the French Navy to hold the Western Mediterranean and some of her naval forces would have to be based on Gibraltar to secure the Western entrance. They would themselves, however, keep anti-submarine forces at Gibraltar. In this connection the Admiralty is of the opinion that the Strait of Gibraltar can be made hazardous for the passage of enemy submarines.

22. In the event of such a general European war it would almost certainly be necessary to effect a considerable reduction in British strength in the Far East. With the reduction of British strength in the Far East under these conditions the possible necessity of direct tactical co-operation between the US and British Fleets would require further consideration.

Policy with regard to Forces now in the Far East.

US Forces

23. It is understood that the US Navy Department would like the US garrisons now in North China to be withdrawn and that in emergency the US Asiatic Fleet would withdraw from North Chinese waters.

British Forces

24. The Admiralty is also concerned regarding the British garrisons in North China. Should parliamentary action in regard to the movement of the two Main Fleets be decided upon, consideration would have to be given to the accurate timing of the withdrawal of the British troops in North China to Hong Kong, and the major units of the British China Fleet would also have to withdraw to that place or to Singapore.

Arrangements for Inter-communication between British and US Fleets

25. It is agreed that since the two fleets will be widely separated at first and probably for some time there could not be unity of command in a tactical or strategical sense in the near future. It is, however, agreed that strategic co-operation will be necessary and that such co-operation will require common communication facilities.

26. The following arrangements have been agreed upon to this end:

(a) The Admiralty will distribute to all ships of the British Fleet, and arrange to deposit at the British Embassy, Washington, at Gibraltar and in the Far East for issue to ships of the US Navy, the necessary copies of the following books:

(1) A suitable Code.
(2) Re-cyphering Tables for use with the Code by the Higher Command.
(3) Re-cyphering Tables for use with the Code by the other Flag Officers.
(4) Re-cyphering Tables for use with the Code by all ships.
(5) A Key Memorandum containing special recognition signals for use by both Fleets.
(6) A book of War W/T Call Signs for both Fleets.

(b) A copy of the British Naval W/T organisation will be issued by the Admiralty with the books to be distributed to the US Fleet.

(c) The US Navy Department will make available the necessary copies of their Pacific and Asiatic Fleet W/T organisation for distribution to the British Fleet. These will be deposited as soon as practicable with the US Embassy in London, on board the Flagship of the US Squadron in the Mediterranean, and on board the Flagship of the US Asiatic Fleet.

(d) Commercial W/T procedure will be used for inter-communication.

(e) The Admiralty will propose frequencies for inter-communication if and when the occasion arises.

(f) Direct inter-communication by W/T between individual ships of the two Fleets will not normally be necessary until tactical co-operation is envisaged.

27. The inter-communication procedure outlined above will be subject to adjustment between the C's-in-C of the two Main Fleets.

Interchange of Communication Personnel

28. To facilitate inter-communication between the two Fleets it is agreed that the following interchange of personnel with experience in W/T would be desirable.

(a) One Officer and one rating from the US Asiatic Fleet to be lent temporarily to Hong Kong and Singapore W/T Stations.
(b) One Officer, if and when available, and one CPO Telegraphist to be lent temporarily from the British China Fleet to the US Asiatic Fleet Flagship.
(c) One Officer and one rating to be lent temporarily from the British and US Navies to the US and British Main Fleets respectively.
(d) One British Officer to be appointed for duty with the US Navy initially at Washington. One Officer from the US Navy to be attached to the staff of the US Naval Attaché in London and to be available for communication duties.

General Liaison

29. Both parties agree that no further measures for general liaison purposes are necessary at the present time.
30. Should, however, parliamentary action be decided upon by the two Governments, it would be necessary to appoint a British Officer with knowledge of war plans to Washington and a US Officer with similar knowledge for duty in London.

Strategical Policy

31. Should the Governments decide that a distant blockade is to be established, the British Naval Forces will be responsible for the stopping of Japanese trade on a line running, roughly, from Singapore through the Dutch East Indies past New Guinea and New Hebrides, and thence round to the Eastward of Australia and New Zealand.
32. The US Navy will be responsible for operations against Japanese trade throughout the West Coast of North and South America, including the Panama Canal and the passage round Cape Horn.
33. The US Navy will also assume responsibility for the general Naval defence of the West Coast of Canada.
34. In these circumstances it is agreed that no hard and fast line of demarcation between the areas in which the two Fleets will operate need be laid down at this stage.

202. *Leahy to Yarnell*

14 January 1938

…

You have received despatch information that four cruisers are en route to Sydney to take part in an annual celebration to be conducted in Australia, and that three of the light cruisers, under the command of Townsend, are going to stop at Singapore en route home in order to be present at the formal opening of the docks at that British naval base.[1] It is intended that these ships will return to join the Fleet upon the completion of their visit to Australia and at Singapore. The *Louisville* will make short visits to Melbourne, Adelaide, Hobart and Auckland. …[2]

203. *Yarnell to Little*

USS *Isabel,*[3]
Shanghai,
15 January 1938

… To me also it has been a most pleasant experience to be associated with you during the past 15 months and especially during the recent hostilities in Shanghai. …

…

There will be difficulties about sending our ships up the Yangtse, as the Japanese now claim that such movements will interfere with their military operations. At first they were inclined to deny the use of the river altogether but owing to strong representations being made by Great Britain and the US to the Tokyo government, they have now modified their reason for not allowing passage through the bar to that of interfering with their operations. …

[1]RAdm Julius C. Townsend, US Navy (1881–1939): Capt, Philadelphia NY 1929; *Texas* 1931; ONO 1933; RA, Cru Div 2.

[2]*Louisville*: 1931, 9006t, 32.5k, 9×8in, 4×5in, 6×21in tt. The other light cruisers are unspecified.

[3]*Isabel*: patrol yacht, 1917, 710t, 17k.

204. *Extract from the Minutes of the Board of Admiralty*

12 May 1938

Exchange of Technical Information with the US Navy

3547. The Board considered a memorandum on a proposal to exchange technical information with the US Navy.

The proposal had originated in a suggestion by the American Naval Attaché that an exchange of information might take place between us on the subject of Boom Defence and Damage Control in Action.[1] The Admiralty technical departments, while favouring the exchange of technical information in principle, believed that on these particular questions we had much more information to give than to gain, and accordingly opposed the exchange. Other departments, however, pointed out that on general grounds we had much to gain from co-operation with the US Navy, and that on the assumption that war between our two countries was out of the question, we had nothing to lose by helping them with information, provided that their discretion and security arrangements could be trusted.

The First Lord suspected that the scepticism which Admiralty departments had shown as to the value of any information which the American Navy had to give might be exaggerated.[2] He accordingly directed that a list of subjects on which we believed that we had something to learn from the Americans should be prepared.

The Board had before them a list of such subjects, prepared by the technical departments concerned. There were about 70 on which we should be ready to give reciprocal information, and about 20 on which we could not offer any information of the same kind in return.

The following questions were considered by the Board –

(a) Were we, on political and general grounds, to attempt to exchange technical information with the US Navy, even in cases where our technical departments believed we had more to give than we were likely to get?

If the answer to (a) was affirmative: (b) were we to attempt to exchange information on which we had no reciprocal information to give? (c) Were we to agree to the exchange of information on (i) Damage Control, (ii) Boom Defence, the subjects originally mentioned by the US Naval Attaché? The technical departments suggested that (i) should be declined and that if (ii) was to be discussed at all, discussion should be

[1]US NA: Capt Willson.
[2]FL: Duff Cooper.

limited to Anti-submarine booms and standard type gates. (d) How was the exchange to be carried out? It had been suggested that it should take place gradually so that we might be continually aware whether we were obtaining an adequate *quid pro quo.* DSR had proposed that all the information treated should pass through a single technical officer, who would be responsible for consulting the technical department concerned and for controlling the rate of exchange. DNI and DNE, however, considered the present system satisfactory. Under this arrangement the exchange of information would take place verbally between the Naval Attaché and the DNI or his representative, or in writing, or by interviews between the Naval Attaché and an appropriate technical officer. DSR had further proposed that a clear distinction should be made between gear in the experimental stage and gear which had been or become or was becoming a part of normal equipment. Information regarding the former should be exchanged only after very special consideration.

In the discussion of the Board, it was generally agreed that the US should be treated exceptionally. No public decision to agree upon a comprehensive exchange of information was possible, owing to the appearance of an alliance between the two countries which would thereby be created, and the political difficulties which would arise in America. It was, however, agreed that if the US Naval Authorities asked for information on any subject we should where possible give it, demanding as a *quid pro quo* information which we ourselves desired, possibly on some different subject. There are certain matters which are kept as secret as possible, even in the Royal Navy itself, and we clearly could not give the US information which was withheld from the Fleet. Where, however, we decided that information might properly be given, it was agreed that we should be as frank as possible.

As regards the two specific questions of Damage Control and Boom Defence, the Board agreed that information might be given, it being left to the Controller and ACNS to decide the *quid pro quo.*

205. *Memorandum Submitted by the Foreign Office in Consultation with the Admiralty and the Industrial Intelligence Centre to the Committee of Imperial Defence*

7 September 1938

…

2. Before examining the effect of this legislation [the US Neutrality Acts, 1935, 1936 and especially the permanent one of 1937] it is worth noticing that there is an appreciable prospect that it would not be applied

or would only be very partly applied in a major war; alternatively, that its application would break down. … The recent failure to apply the Act to the Sino-Japanese case also indicates a reluctance to do so where its operation would clearly favour an aggressor.

…

6. It is, however, necessary to note that insofar as the neutrality legislation does operate to lessen the possibility of the US being compelled by the pressure of public opinion to enter the war (and that it does this to some extent at least cannot be denied), it operates to the disadvantage of this country, since it is possible to conceive of circumstances in which the US might enter a war on the side of this country, and very difficult to conceive of any in which it would actually enter a war against us on the side of Germany. On the other hand insofar as the neutrality legislation may diminish the likelihood of friction between us and the US arising out of our exercise of sea power, it should be to our advantage.

…

9. The practical effects of the application of the above provisions would seem to be as follows –

(1) *War material*

Germany is unlikely to be counting to any extent on obtaining arms, ammunition and implements of war from the US, partly because her own potential output is so large and partly because our command of the seas would in any case render it difficult for her to obtain delivery. To this extent, therefore, the mandatory provisions of the Act would impose little or no further disability on Germany.

(2) *Other goods or raw materials essential to war*

The 'cash and carry' section of the Act, if applied, should increase Germany's difficulty in obtaining essential supplies from the US.[1] In the first place US vessels would not be available for the carriage of such supplies, so there would be greater competition (in which we, owing to our greater financial strength, should hope to have the advantage) for cargo space in other neutral tonnage. In the second place, Germany's foreign exchange position would make it difficult for her to comply with the provision that goods of the class under consideration must have passed out of US ownership before export to a belligerent. This difficulty would of course be intensified if we were able, as a retaliatory measure or by some other means, to attack German exports and so render it impossible for her to establish credits abroad.

[1] 'Cash and Carry': Any country in a war zone wishing to purchase supplies from the US had to do so by paying cash and transporting the goods in their own ships.

10. … if our command of the sea were less complete or less effective, the neutrality legislation would constitute an important reinforcement to it, while in any case its application must assist us by tending to cut off German supplies at the source instead of leaving them to be cut off *en route* by us. …

(1) *Contraband Control*

… The application of the 'cash and carry' section would not only tend to reduce the amount of goods on the contraband list exported from the USA to or for Germany but would also reduce very considerably the chance of friction between ourselves and the US by decreasing the number of US ships and the amount of US exports with which our contraband control would be obliged to interfere. …

…

(3) *Navicerts*[1]

The application of the Act in its entirety should facilitate the working of the navicert system by reducing the number of applications from US shippers in respect of articles covered by the 'cash and carry' provisions, and so decreasing to some extent the amount of irritation caused by the rejection of such applications.

…

12. The foregoing paragraphs show that the integral application of the Act would be likely to be of some assistance to us from the point of view of economic warfare against Germany.

(a) by reinforcing the measures which we are likely to take to bring economic pressure to bear upon Germany and

(b) by diminishing the possibility of these leading to friction between ourselves and the USA. On the other hand it seems clear that these advantages would be outweighed by the fact that, if the Act were applied, either integrally or partly, we should be entirely precluded from obtaining munitions of war from the US, while obstacles might be placed in the way of our obtaining other commodities owing to the operation of the 'cash and carry' clause.

[1] 'Navicerts': Certification from British consuls and port controls that cargoes carried by neutral ships were not destined for Germany, either directly or indirectly.

206. *Commander Ralph Edwards, RN, to Yarnell*[1]

23 November 1938

Yangtse C-in-C has just telegraphed to say that unless any unforeseen circumstance prevents him he now expects to arrive in Shanghai on 5 or 6 December.

He has asked me to tell you that he is looking forward to meeting you and discussing the problems on which our interests appear to be identical. This of course with particular reference to our main problem in the reopening of the Yangtse and the movement of warships thereon.

[PS] I understand he doesn't want this published to the world.

207. *Yarnell to Admiral Sir Percy Noble*

USS *Isabel*,
Shanghai,
28 December 1938

...

The next three or four months are apt to be very interesting ones for us out here. If Europe goes to war, Japan will undoubtedly take over the Concessions and perhaps serve notice to all whites to leave China. However, it may not be as easy as she thinks. We are living in interesting times.

208. *Yarnell to Leahy*

10 January 1939

...

Our British friends have been kicked and cuffed incessantly and the astonishing feature is the amount of it they have taken with no effective reaction. Hong Kong is cut off entirely and never a protest from the British Government. There is a probability that Great Britain will arrive at a 'dirty peace' with Japan. That is, some agreement under which British interests in the Far East would receive some promise of protection from the Japanese in return for British approval of Japanese action in China. This is very possible under the Chamberlain regime. If the British are stupid enough the Japanese will permit them to do business in the Far East, once

[1]Adm Sir Ralph Edwards (1901–63): ent RN 1914; Eur 1914–18; Capt 1939; *Gambia*, RNZN 1939; CoS, Eastern F 1942–4; RA & ACNS 1948–50; FO 2 i/c, Med F 1951–2; VA 1952; 3SL & Cntrlr 1953–4; Adm 1955; CinC Med & cdr, Allied N Forces 1957.

a stranglehold has been secured in China, the Empire is in a bad way. Its safety calls for greater vision than has been shown so far.

209. *The Ambassador to the United States to the Foreign Secretary*[1]

5 April 1939

The Cession of British Possessions in the West Indies to the USA in settlement of War Debt

...

4. There is one factor which might in the future become of importance in the question of War Debts. Americans are disposed to think that war in Europe is imminent and that in it the British Empire may be destroyed. What in that case would happen to those islands and territories which in British hands have given rise to no uneasiness but which transferred to an aggressive Power might constitute a serious menace to the security of the Panama Canal? I cannot say that there has been any serious discussion about these strategic points in the Atlantic or Caribbean Sea, but it seems to be in the air that US does not feel quite so safe today as it used to only a short while ago, and it seems more possible now than it has been in the past that a transfer of some of them in connection with the war debt may become the subject of thought in responsible circles.

210. *Foreign Office to the Ambassador to the United States [draft]*

8 June 1939

As Your Excellency is aware, HMG have recently had under consideration the question of the naval dispositions in a war involving operations not only in Europe but also in the Far East. The principles upon which HMG have for many years based their naval strategy is that the safety of the UK and the safety of Singapore are vital to the security of the Empire; and it has therefore always been their firm intention, in the event of hostilities or a threat of hostility with Japan, and irrespective of the situation in home waters, to send a fleet to Far Eastern waters sufficient for the protection of Singapore. This policy was, however, determined at a time when it could reasonably be hoped that Italy would be neutral, and when it would

[1]Amb: Sir R. Lindsay.
FS: Edward Wood, Lord Halifax (1881–1959): Pres Bd Ed 1922–4; MAg 1924–5; Viceroy of India 1926–31; Visct 1934; SSt for War 1935; LPS 1935–7; LPC 1937–8; FS 1938–40; Amb to US 1941–6; Earl 1944.

therefore have been possible to despatch an adequate fleet to the Far East without losing the necessary margin of superiority in home waters.

2. It is now necessary for HMG to take into account the fact that, in any war between this country and Germany, Italy would in all probability range herself with Germany. It is useless to disguise the fact that the present and future naval strength of this country is not sufficient, and indeed is not designed, to engage three naval powers simultaneously and HMG have therefore been obliged to reconsider the naval dispositions which they would make if they found themselves at war with Germany and Italy and if Japan entered the war, or appeared likely to do so, on the side of the Axis Powers. The conclusion they have reached is that they would, in such circumstances, be obliged to maintain in home waters and in the Mediterranean a sufficient force to give them a margin of superiority over the joint fleets of Italy and Germany and so enable them to give adequate protection to their allies and support to the victim of any possible aggression. At the same time the importance of protecting Singapore and the Pacific Dominions is such that they cannot contemplate a complete reversal of their earlier intention to despatch a fleet to Far Eastern waters; and they have accordingly decided that, in the circumstances envisaged, they would still endeavour to despatch such a fleet to the Far East, although its size, and the moment at which it could be despatched, are matters which would have to be decided in the light of the general strategical situation at the time.

3. In the circumstances described above, the attitude and naval dispositions of the US would obviously be of cardinal importance. Although this factor is at present too uncertain to justify HMG in basing their own plans upon any estimate of it, and although they would not feel entitled to ask the US Government for information as to their probable attitude in hypothetical circumstances, they consider, nonetheless, that there would be some advantage in informing the US confidentially of the difficult naval situation in which they would find themselves if faced by a hostile combination consisting of Germany, Italy and Japan. Such a communication might conceivably elicit a useful statement of the intentions of the US Government, and it would, moreover, be consistent with the frank exchange of views which have recently taken place on problems of common interest to the two Governments.

4. I accordingly request that, if you see no objection, Your Excellency will make a formal communication to the US Government on the lines of the preceding paragraphs of this despatch. Its confidential character should, of course, be emphasised, and I am prepared to leave it to your discretion whether to make it verbally or in writing, and whether to address it personally to the President or to the competent authority at the State Department.

211. *Commander T. C. Hampton, RN, to the Director of Plans*

27 June 1939

Report of Proceedings 26 May–26 June 1939
Appendix I: Report of Meeting held on 12 June 1939

At the outset of this meeting the US representatives were given a full account of the factors outlined in Paper No. SAC 16 [not reproduced] leading up to the conclusion that, in the event of Japan intervening when we are engaged in war with Germany and Italy, it is not at present possible to state at what stage a fleet would be sent to the Far East, nor to enumerate precisely the number of capital ships that could be spared for this purpose.

2. In putting forward the foregoing appreciation it was pointed out that the strategical situation envisaged in this document differs materially from the situation under discussion when Captain (now Admiral) Ingersoll, US Navy, visited the Admiralty in January 1938.

3. Admiral Leahy expressed his interest in this appreciation but confined his remarks to the situation that would arise if Great Britain and France warred with Germany and Italy and the US remained neutral. He said that in the event of war in Europe he thought that it was the present intention of the President that the US Fleet should be moved to Hawaii as a deterrent to Japan. He expressed the opinion that the Japanese would be unlikely to embark on large scale operations against Australia or New Zealand while the US Fleet based on Hawaii was in a position to interrupt their lines of communication. He agreed, however, that the US Fleet at Hawaii was not in a position to conduct naval operations in the vicinity of Japan. As far as the US Navy is concerned there were no marked changes from the position set out in the agreed record of conversations [with Captain Ingersoll in 1938].[1]

4. As regards the Atlantic, it was the intention of the US Government to establish air patrols for the protection of neutral shipping in the Caribbean Sea and in the approaches to the Panama Canal, and also on the East Coast of South America. These patrols would operate from shore bases and the necessary arrangements had been made with certain South American countries. There would also be a patrol of four long-range 8in cruisers between the East Coast of South America and the USA. It was possible that information obtained by these patrols might be passed to British naval forces in the Atlantic via the Navy Department

[1]See Docs. 200–201.

in Washington. The three old battleships would be retained in the Atlantic together with certain patrol craft.

5. Admiral Leahy was evidently reluctant to commit himself to a statement of naval plans in the event of the USA becoming allied to us, and it was thought best to refrain from pressing him too closely on this point at this stage. He was also most unwilling to put anything in writing in the form of a record of these meetings. I am satisfied that this attitude was due to the fear of compromising security and to the difficulty of evading questions if he appeared before Congress for interrogation. In this connection it is important to appreciate the very real difficulties with which the US naval officer is faced when being cross-examined by politicians on subjects on which it is not possible, in the public interest, to disclose the exact situation. For example, Admiral Ghormley said that he had never read the agreed record of conversations prepared in January 1938 until the day before my visit 'in case he was interrogated on the subject by Congress'.[1]

6. In the circumstances I agreed that no written record of these discussions should be prepared, being of the opinion that Admiral Leahy was likely to be more forthcoming verbally than he would be if asked to commit these views to paper.

7. The question of the distribution of signal books and ciphers was broached at this meeting, but it was evident that neither Admiral Leahy nor Admiral Ghormley was fully aware of the arrangements made in this connection, and Admiral Ghormley undertook to investigate the position.

(The results of the above meeting were discussed with the Naval Attaché on 13 June and it was felt another attempt should be made to invite Admiral Leahy to discuss the question of co-operation in war.[2] Accordingly, a further interview was requested on the grounds that there were one or two points arising out of the first meeting which required further discussion.)

Report of Meeting held on 14 June 1939

The arrangement for distribution of [signal] books to the US Fleet was discussed and the US representatives expressed themselves as satisfied that the present arrangements would enable all US units to co-operate with British units throughout the world in case of necessity. Some further

[1]VAdm Robert Ghormley, US Navy (b. 1883): USNA 1906; Gen Bd 1927; *Nevada* 1935–6; staff appts; DWPD 1938–9; Asst CNO 1939–40; Spl N Obsvr, London, 1940–2; CinC, S Pac Area 1942.

[2]NA: Capt C.A. Curzon-Howe (b. 1894): ent RN 1907; Falklands, Dardanelles, Jutland; Capt 1935; *Dundee* 1937–8; NA, Washington, 1938–41.

copies of signal books, codes and ciphers would be required as and when US ships in reserve were brought forward. Certain minor amendments to the table of US W/T organisation might be required but these could be readily promulgated to all concerned if and when the books were distributed. I undertook to recommend that the question of the distribution of these books to enable all units of the British Fleet to co-operate with the US Navy throughout the world should be investigated.

2. Admiral Leahy was invited to put forward his views on the co-operation of the two Fleets in the event of war with Germany, Italy and Japan. In his preliminary remarks the CNO made it clear that this conception went well beyond 'parliamentary action' as he understood the meaning of the phrase and that any expression of opinion that he might give was purely personal and could not be considered as part of a set war plan. Subject to these provisos his views were as follows.

3. Broadly speaking, the US Fleet should control the Pacific and the allies should control European waters, the Mediterranean and the Atlantic. The American naval forces already in the Atlantic would remain there and would co-operate with British naval forces.

4. The US Fleet should move to Singapore in sufficient force to be able to engage and defeat the Japanese Fleet if met with on passage. Admiral Leahy considered that at least 10 capital ships would be required in the Far East. He was strongly opposed to the despatch of small or weak forces to Singapore. In his opinion the question of whether the US Fleet would eventually be despatched depended to a certain extent on the size of the fleet which we could spare to co-operate with them. Public opinion in the US would, he thought, be averse to sending the Fleet to assist us unless we could despatch an 'adequate token force' to co-operate. He could not define in detail what would be considered an 'adequate token force' since it must depend on circumstances at the time, but he was of the opinion that some capital ships would be expected.

5. As regards the passage to Singapore, discussion showed that the US Naval Staff have no detailed plan, although it is understood that this question is now being examined. Admiral Leahy considered that it might take up to 60 days to collect the necessary supply ships and oilers to accompany the Fleet. In these circumstances he was not satisfied with a period before relief of 90 days for Singapore. He suggested that it should be at least 120 days if the relief of the fortress was to depend on the arrival of the US Fleet. At this point he again emphasised his views as to the danger of attempting relief with inferior US forces. Admiral Leahy was informed that in the opinion of the Naval Staff it would be desirable that the British naval forces in the Far East should be under the strategical control of the US C-in-C but that this matter was one for decision by the

Government at the time. Admiral Leahy agreed generally but was evidently unwilling to discuss plans for co-operation in detail.

6. In reply to a question, Admiral Leahy was informed as to the present position with regard to docking and repair facilities at Singapore. It was pointed out that in the event of the US Fleet being based there in war, it would probably be necessary for a number of skilled and semi-skilled personnel, as well as some labourers, to be sent there from the US. 2500 was stated to be the total number required.

7. Enquiry as to the US intentions regarding the Philippine Islands showed that their views correspond with our policy concerning Hong Kong and though they intend to hold the Philippines for as long as possible in war, they realise the difficulty of relieving the Islands and do not expect to be able to base their Fleet there.

8. Turning to the Atlantic, Admiral Leahy was asked as to the practicability of maintaining the air patrols on the East Coast of South America if the USA became a belligerent while the South American countries remained neutral. He replied that arrangements existed whereby the more important countries in South America would declare war simultaneously with the US and the patrols would therefore be maintained.

9. The British convoy arrangements in the Atlantic in the event of a European war were outlined in broad terms and Admiral Leahy expressed the opinion that in the event of the US entering the war, arrangements for co-operation in the organisation of convoys and all other detailed arrangements for mutual support in the Atlantic could readily be co-ordinated at the same time, working on the basis of the arrangements in 1917–18.

10. Enquiry as to the possibility of co-operation in HF/DF elicited the reply that HF/DF is still in the experimental stage. Promising results have been obtained from trials but naval stations are not yet equipped with this apparatus The question of the location of US HF/DF stations and the possibility of co-operation will be further investigated by the [British] Naval Attaché. It was not possible to pursue technical questions of this nature since knowledge of my visit was confined to Admirals Leahy and Ghormley and I was not in consultation with the US technical staff officers.

Conclusions

11. Although I am fully conscious that the results of my visit are in some respects disappointing, I am convinced that Admiral Leahy was warmly appreciative of the action taken in sending a naval officer to Washington to inform him personally of the latest developments in British strategical thought.

12. In assessing the value of these conversations it is necessary to bear in mind the following considerations:

(1) President Roosevelt is probably far ahead of the majority of his people in his championship of the democracies. He also takes a great personal interest in the Navy and its problems. The Presidential election in 1940 may, however, lead to radical changes of policy.

(2) Admiral Leahy is also extremely pro-British and has the entire confidence of the President. He is about to be relieved as CNO by Admiral Stark but this is unlikely to involve any immediate change in naval policy since the latter officer is reputed also to be pro-British.

(3) A leakage concerning my visit would have political repercussions out of all proportion to the importance of the conversations themselves. The number of Americans who can be trusted with secrets of high political significance is apparently strictly limited, hence it was necessary to confine my contacts to the CNO and the Director of Plans, with the result that matters of detail were to some extent precluded from the discussions. In this connection it is of interest that the Naval Attaché in Washington was told by Admiral Leahy to arrange our meetings directly with him and that the US DNI was on no account to be informed of my visit.[1]

(4) It is evident that the US Navy have no detailed plans at present for active co-operation with the British Fleet in war. On the other hand, the broad views as to the conduct of the war at sea as expressed by Admiral Leahy appear to agree fundamentally with those put forward by the DCNS prior to my departure.[2]

13. Finally, I have to report that the discussions took place in an atmosphere of complete mutual confidence and friendliness and I have to acknowledge the extremely courteous manner in which I was received by both Admiral Leahy and Admiral Ghormley.

212. *Minute by Director of Plans*[3]

28 June 1939

Commander Hampton returned from his visit to the USA on Monday, 26 June 1939. …

[1]US DNI, June 1939: VA Walter S. Anderson, US Navy (b. 1881): USNA 1903; Capt & CoS, CinC, US F 1927–9; *West Virginia* 1932–3; NA, London, 1934–7; Cru Div 4, 1937–9; DNI June 1939–40; Bat Div 4, Bat Force 1941–2; Pearl Harbor, 7 Dec 1941; Pres, Bd of Inspn 1942–4; Cdr, Gulf Sea Fr & Cdt 7th N D, Miami; VA 1945.

[2]DCNS June 1939: It seems as if VAdm James resumed office when VAdm Sir Andrew Cunningham was apptd to be CinC, Med F, June 1939, & was succeeded by RAdm T. S. V. Phillips.

[3]DP June 1939: Capt Danckwerts.

Though little positive result was achieved and nothing was committed in writing, it is considered that his visit has been of value in keeping before the US's highest naval authorities, and probably the President, the difficulties facing us at the present time, and in obtaining some information as to the state of thought of the US naval authorities as to their possible actions.

2. I consider that Commander Hampton carried out a delicate and difficult task with great discretion and ability.

3. It is proposed to forward copies of Commander Hampton's report to the following only: Prime Minister, Secretary of State for Foreign Affairs, Minister for Co-ordination of Defence.[1]

213. *S. H. Phillips (Admiralty) to J. Balfour (Foreign Office)*[2]

29 June 1939

Cession of British Possessions in West Indies to USA in settlement of war debt

...

From the purely strategical point of view, we would be averse to surrendering what would appear to be the only islands of first-class value, namely, Trinidad, Jamaica and Bermuda. In addition, although St Lucia is not now regarded as having its old importance as a coaling station, we would be loath, in view of its special naval connections and past history, to see it transferred to the US.[3]

...

... the US Government might consider asking for something very much less than the cession of the whole of the British West Indies, for example, the transfer of British Honduras or the Bahamas, a great part of whose trade is already with the US, in return for the cancellation of the whole of the War Debt, the arrangement being looked at as a political one for removing a possible source of contention between the two countries, rather than a strictly financial transaction.

...

[1]PM: Neville Chamberlain. FS: Lord Halifax. Minr for Co-ord Defence: Sir T. Inskip.

[2]S. H. Phillips: Prin Asst Sec, Admy.

J. Balfour (1894–1983): interned Germany 1914–18; FO 1919; various for postgs; FO 1939; Amb, Argentina 1948–51; Amb, Spain, 1951–4.

[3]St Lucia: a Nelson-era naval base.

... if there is a likelihood of the US attempting to continue an isolationist policy even in the very hypothetical circumstances where the break-up of the British Empire appears not unlikely, no reason is seen why it should be made easier for them to adhere to such an attitude by ceding British West Indies and Western Atlantic bases beforehand. ... it is to be hoped that the US would feel constrained to step into the war to meet what must be a growing threat to themselves. ... it is to be hoped that the US would feel herself compelled by the Monroe Doctrine to intervene to prevent any occupation of them by the enemy, ...

214. *Ambassador to the United States to the Foreign Secretary*

1 July 1939

1. I was called to the White House today most secretly by the President. The Secretary of State, the Under Secretary of State and CNO were present at the discussion which ensued. The following is [the] scheme which the President developed.
2. In case of war in which the US Government would be neutral, it would be his desire that the US Government should establish a patrol over the waters of the Western Atlantic with a view to denying them to warlike operations of the belligerents. This purpose would be publicly declared on the outbreak of war.
3. This is the idea on which Naval manoeuvres of last winter were carried out. Submarines were sent out far into the Atlantic and their task was to make their way undetected to the West Indies. In nearly every case submarines were picked up by aeroplane patrols and the conclusion reached was that the patrol was efficient up to 500 miles from land.
4. So far as his own public is concerned the President would find historical justification for his scheme in the quasi-warlike operations conducted in 1798 by the US naval forces to clear West Indies waters of French and British privateers.[1]
5. The President's scheme would have the result of releasing a number of HM ships from convoy work for other duties nearer home (and as he pointed out it would be theoretically neutral as releasing in a similar manner ships of the enemies of Great Britain).
6. However the experience of the manoeuvres showed that the use of certain bases not the property of the US Government would be requisite to the efficiency of the patrol. There would be some in Brazil and

[1]War of 1798: A dispute over neutral rights between France and the US, leading directly to the creation of the US Navy.

Fernando Noronha was mentioned. Four bases in British territory would be needed, *viz.*, Trinidad, St Lucia, Bermuda and Halifax.

7. In order that the use of these bases during a war by a neutral might continue without too severe a break with ordinary procedures of neutrality, it would be important that agreement in virtue of which facilities should be accorded should be made during time of peace. The use of bases during war would then be represented as merely continuance of the facilities accorded during peace.

8. The nature of that agreement gave place to considerable discussion. One point laid down at the outset and maintained throughout was that it should be revocable at notice.

9. … in response to the request made by US Government orally to me HMG would authorise the Governors of Trinidad, St Lucia and Bermuda to allow the US planes and ships to use the waters of those Colonies and the US Naval Authorities to lease premises, land stores, and in general make use of the ports. Purpose for which these facilities would be requested and accorded would be to enable US Government to carry out to a further stage experiments for the development of Naval patrolling initiated in the manoeuvres last winter. You may therefore if you so choose consider that this request is now hereby made to HMG.

12. I now ask whether HMG are willing to countenance this scheme and whether they will authorize me so as to inform the US Government accordingly.

…

14. I think that a US Navy ship will be sent to Trinidad or Bermuda almost immediately on notification that instructions had been issued by HMG.

15. I pointed out that security would be gravely imperilled as soon as US naval authorities got to work in the ports but this did not seem to worry the President.

215. *Governor of Trinidad to Secretary of State for the Colonies*[1]

1 September 1939

US Naval Officer arrived here on 28 August and on the following day, having selected Murcurapo Pasture as site for seaplane base, asked most urgently that lease should be signed with the least possible delay. … Formalities were completed this morning …

[1]Govr of Trinidad: Sir Aubrey W. Young (1885–19–): Maj, Indian Army 1908–19; FO 1919–21; Asst Sec, Col Ofc 1921–6; Mid E, Gibraltar, Iraq; Govr, Nyasaland 1932; Govr, N Rhodesia 1934; Govr, Trinidad & Tobago 1938.
Col Sec: W. Ormsby-Gore.

DOCUMENTS AND SOURCES

The National Archives (formerly the Public Record Office), Kew, Richmond, Surrey.

Admiralty Papers [ADM]
Foreign Office Papers [FO]

The National Maritime Museum, Greenwich, London.

The Papers of Admiral of the Fleet Lord Chatfield [CHT]

The Churchill Archives Centre, Churchill College, Cambridge.

The Papers of Earl Alexander of Hillsborough [AVAR]
The Papers of Lord Hankey [HNKY]

The National Archives, Washington, DC

General Records of the Navy, Records of the General Board, RG8 [GB]

The Library of Congress, Manuscripts Division, Madison Building, Washington, DC

The Papers of Josephus Daniels [DANIELS]
The Papers of Admiral William Shepherd Benson [BENSON]
The Papers of Rear Admiral Hilary P. Jones [JONES]
The Papers of Fleet Admiral William D. Leahy [LEAHY]
The Papers of Admiral William Sowden Sims [SIMS]
The Papers of Admiral Harry E. Yarnell [YARNELL]

Operational Archives Branch, Naval Historical Center, Navy Yard, Washington, DC

The Papers of Admiral William Veazie Pratt [PRATT]

Franklin D. Roosevelt Presidential Library, Hyde Park, NY

Assistant Secretary of the Navy File [FDR/ASN]
President's Secretary's File, box 142 [FDR/PSF, box 142]

Numbered Document Sources

Part I: The Washington Conference, 1919–1923

1	Future Naval Programme	25 Mar 1919	ADM 167/58
2	Naval Policy	17 July 1919	ADM 167/59
3	Post-War Naval Policy	12 Aug 1919	ADM 116/1774
4	Comparison of British and US Navies	3 Sept 1919	BENSON
5	Naval Policy and Expenditure	24 Oct 1919	ADM 116/1773
6	War against the USA	Oct 1919	ADM 1/8571/295
7	Naval Situation in the Far East	21 Oct 1919	ADM 1/8571/295
8	Size of Fleet	7 Jan 1920	ADM 167/61
9	Political Situation	12 Jan 1920	ADM 116/3124
10	Speech by Josephus Daniels	6 Feb 1920	FDR/ASN
11	Gas Warfare	7 May 1920	ADM 116/1775
12	Building Program for 1922	24 Sept 1920	GB 420-2
13	Naval Construction	14 Dec 1920	ADM 116/1775
14	Admiralty and League of Nations	14 Aug 1920	ADM 1/8592/131a
15	Abolition of S America Squadron	25 Jan 1921	ADM 116/1775
16	Hankey: Diary	30 Jan 1921	HNKY 4/13
17	Naval Estimates 1921–1922	28 Feb 1921	ADM 116/1776
18	Naval Situation of the British Empire in War between Japan and USA	1 June 1921	ADM 1/8948
19	Policy on Limitation of Armaments	5 Oct 1921	ADM 116/3445
20	Reuter's Telegram	16 Nov 1921	ADM 116/3445
21	Hankey to his wife	13 Nov 1921	HNKY 3/39
22	Admiralty on US Proposals	13 Nov 1921	ADM 116/2149
23	Auxiliary Combatant Craft	13 Nov 1921	ADM 116/2149
24	Chatfield to Beatty	15 Nov 1921	ADM 116/2149
25	Further Considerations on US Proposals	17 Nov 1921	ADM 116/2149
26	Notes on US Proposals	18 Nov 1921	ADM 116/2149
27	Hankey to Lloyd George	17 Nov 1921	HNKY 8/22
28	Memorandum by Naval Staff	21 Nov 1921	ADM 116/3445

29	Hankey to Lloyd George	25 Nov 1921	HNKY 8/22
30	Notes on US Treaty Obligations	1 Dec 1921	ADM 116/2149
31	Hankey to Lloyd George	2 Dec 1921	HNKY 8/22
32	Hankey to his wife	10 Dec 1921	HNKY 3/39
33	Washington Naval Treaty	6 Feb 1922	ADM 116/3445
34	Root Resolutions on Submarines	Feb 1922	ADM 1/8622/54
35	Memorandum by Plans Division	5 April 1922	ADM 116/3165
36	Sims to Rear Admiral Andrews	30 Mar 1922	SIMS, box 46
37	British and US Capital Ships	29 Nov 1922	PRATT, box 7
38	Real Value of Naval Treaty	4 May 1923	PRATT, box 2
39	Minute by Alex Hunt	13 Aug 1923	ADM 1/8653/263

Part II: The Geneva Conference, 1922–1927

40	Building Program for 1924	31 May 1922	GB 420-2
41	Defence Sub-Committee, CID	30 Nov 1922	ADM 116/3165
42	Needs of the Navy	2 Nov 1924	GB 420-2
43	Further Limitation of Navies	3 June 1925	GB 438-1
44	Reduction in Armament	15 Jan 1926	JONES, box 4
45	Jones to Pratt	1 Feb 1926	JONES, box 4
46	Pratt to Jones	3 Feb 1926	PRATT, box 2
47	Mercantile Tonnage	30 June 1926	ADM 116/2609
48	Memorandum by Jones	10 Nov 1926	JONES, box 4
49	Memorandum by Jones	7 Jan 1927	PRATT, box 2
50	Pratt to Rear Admiral Coontz	10 Mar 1927	PRATT, box 2
51	Limitation of Armament: Cruisers	17 Mar 1927	ADM 116/3371
52	Further Limitation of Naval Armament	25 April 1927	PRATT, box 8
53	National Policies of Great Britain	21 April 1927	PRATT, box 8
54	Further Limitation of Naval Armament	25 April 1927	PRATT, box 8
55	Further Limitation of Naval Armament	4 May 1927	PRATT, box 8
56	Further Limitation of Naval Armament	13 May 1927	PRATT, box 8
57	Consideration of National Policy	2 June 1927	PRATT, box 8
58	3rd Conference of British Delegation	24 June 1927	ADM 116/2509
59	4th Conference of British Delegation	29 June 1927	ADM 116/2509
60	5th Conference of British Delegation	1 July 1927	ADM 116/2509
61	Statement to Technical Committee	5 July 1927	ADM 116/2509

62	Defended Naval Ports of the USA	n.d. *c*. July 1927	ADM 116/2609
63	Conference of British Delegation	11 July 1927	ADM 116/2609
64	Jones to Secretary of the Navy	21 July 1927	JONES, box 2
65	Hankey: Diary	12 Oct 1927	HNKY 1/8
66	Belligerent Rights at Sea	30 Nov 1927	ADM 116/3620

Part III: The First London Naval Conference, 1927–1930

67	Rear Admiral Schofield to Jones	24 Feb 1928	JONES, box 4
68	US Naval Aircraft	14 Sept 1928	GB 449
69	General Naval Policy	6 Oct 1928	PRATT, box 3
70	Jones to the Secretary of Navy	18 June 1929	JONES, box 4
71	Churchill: Equal Fleets Not Equality	2 July 1929	GB 438-1
72	Auxiliary Surface Combat Vessels	13 July 1929	GB 438-1
73	Dawes to Stimson	18 July 1929	GB 438-1
74	Stimson to Dawes	21 July 1929	GB 438-1
75	Dawes to Stimson	22 July 1929	GB 438-1
76	Stimson to Dawes	23 July 1929	GB 438-1
77	Stimson to Dawes	25 July 1929	GB 438-1
78	Dawes and Gibson to Stimson	29 July 1929	JONES, box 5
79	Notes on Cruiser Situation	1 Aug 1929	ADM 116/3371
80	Dawes to Stimson	1 Aug 1929	GB 438-1
81	Stimson to Dawes	2 Aug 1929	GB 438-1
82	Dawes to Stimson	4 Aug 1929	GB 438-1
83	Dawes to Stimson	9 Aug 1929	GB 438-1
84	Admiralty to FO	26 Aug 1929	ADM 1/8743/112
85	Pratt to Gertlin	27 Aug 1929	PRATT, box 3
86	Stimson to Dawes	28 Aug 1929	GB 438-1
87	Madden to Alexander	5 Sept 1929	ADM 1/8743/112
88	Proposals on Naval Disarmament	11 Sept 1929	GB 438-1
89	General Board to Secretary of Navy	11 Sept 1929	JONES, box 5
90	MacDonald to Alexander	n.d. *c*. Sept 1929	AVAR 5/2/4
91	Conversations between MacDonald and Herbert Hoover	20 Sept 1929	ADM 116/3372
92	Hankey: Diary	7 Oct 1929	HNKY 1/7
93	Hankey: Diary	8 Oct 1929	HNKY 1/7
94	British Naval Bases in W. Hemisphere	8 Oct 1929	GB 438-1
95	Hankey: Diary	17 Oct 1929	HNKY 1/7
96	Capt Ritchie to R. Campbell	28 Nov 1929	ADM 1/8743/112
97	Rear Admiral Moffett to Secretary of Navy	4 Dec 1929	GB 438-1
98	British Delegation: Cruisers	3 Jan 1930	ADM 116/2747

99	Naval Air Strength	3 Jan 1930	GB 438-1
100	Battleships	6 Jan 1930	GB 438-1
101	Alexander: Speech at Sheffield	10 Jan 1930	AVAR 5/2/10
102	The Basis of British Naval Strategy	14 Jan 1930	ADM 116/2746
103	Memorandum by Jones	5 Feb 1930	PRATT, box 9
104	Pratt to Stimson	13 Feb 1930	PRATT, box 9
105	Meeting of British Delegation	9 Feb 1930	ADM 116/2747
106	Comparisons of Battleships	17 Feb 1930	PRATT, box 9
107	Rear Adm Cone to Pratt	22 May 1930	PRATT, box 9
108	8in and 6in Gun Cruisers	15 April 1930	PRATT, box 9
109	Naval Attaché, London, to CNO	n.d. *c.* 1930	PRATT, box 8
110	British Naval Proposal on Carriers	n.d. *c.* 1930	PRATT, box 8
111	London Naval Treaty	22 April 1930	AVAR 5/2/10
112	Jones to Senator H. Johnson	13 June 1930	JONES, box 2
113	Plan for Treaty Navy	30 July 1931	GB 438-1

Part IV: The Second London Naval Conference, 1930–1936

114	Pratt to Secretary of the Navy	12 Oct 1931	PRATT, box 3
115	Cruisers	6 Feb 1932	ADM 1/8762/252
116	General Board to Secretary of the Navy	30 Sept 1932	JONES, box 5
117	Indirect Purpose to Limitation	18 Jan 1933	GB 438-2
118	US Naval Construction 1934	7 Sept 1933	ADM 116/2998
119	Replacement of 8in Cruisers	16 Sept 1933	GB 438-2
120	Conversation of MacDonald and Davis	2 Mar 1934	FDR/PSF, box 142
121	N. H. Davis to Roosevelt	6 Mar 1934	FDR/PSF, box 142
122	Ambassador Bingham to Roosevelt	8 Mar 1934	FDR/PSF, box 142
123	W. Phillips to Roosevelt	21 Mar 1934	FDR/PSF, box 142
124	Memorandum of Conversation	12 April 1934	FDR/PSF, box 142
125	Bingham to Roosevelt	23 April 1934	FDR/PSF, box 142
126	Requirements for 1935 Conference	April 1934	ADM 116/3373
127	Memorandum by Chatfield	April 1934	ADM 1/8802
128	Building Program for 1935	9 May 1934	GB, box 62
129	Chatfield to Warren Fisher	4 June 1934	CHT 3/1
130	Experts' Meeting	21 June 1934	GB 438-2
131	Roosevelt to Davis	26 June 1934	FDR/PSF, box 142
132	Davis to Roosevelt	27 June 1934	FDR/PSF, box 142
133	Memorandum by R. L. Craigie	27 June 1934	ADM 1/8803
134	Discussion with US Representatives	28 June 1934	ADM 1/8803
135	Davis to Roosevelt	28 June 1934	FDR/PSF, box 142

136	Leigh and Little Memorandum	4 July 1934	GB 438-2
137	Leigh and Little Memorandum	13 July 1934	GB 438-2
138	Leigh and Chatfield Memorandum	13 July 1934	GB 438-2
139	Rear Admiral Leigh to Secretary of the Navy	30 July 1934	GB 438-1
140	1936 Conference on Naval Armaments	1 Oct 1934	GB 438-1
141	Summary of Recommendations	1 Oct 1934	GB 438-1
142	Chatfield to Beatty	10 Oct 1934	CHT 4/2
143	Davis to Roosevelt	6 Nov 1934	FDR/PSF, box 142
144	Roosevelt to Davis	9 Nov 1934	FDR/PSF, box 142
145	Davis to Roosevelt	27 Nov 1934	FDR/PSF, box 142
146	Davis to Roosevelt	14 Dec 1934	FDR/PSF, box 142
147	Meeting of UK and US Delegations	17 Dec 1935	ADM 116/3312
148	UK and US Naval Representatives	23 Jan 1936	ADM 116/3312
149	Davis to Roosevelt	20 Dec 1935	FDR/PSF, box 142
150	Davis to Hull	3 Feb 1936	FDR/PSF, box 142
151	Notes from Davis and Eden	24–25 Mar 1936	ADM 116/3922
152	Treaty of London	25 Mar 1936	FO 94/1310
153	Admiral Standley to Hull	27 May 1936	GB 438-1

Part V: The Sailors Meet, 1919–1939

154	Visit of Lord Jellicoe to USA	20 Jan 1920	ADM 1/8580/22
155	Vice Admiral Huse to Daniels	21 Oct 1920	DANIELS, box 545
156	Vice Admiral Mark Kerr to Sims	14 Oct 1921	SIMS, box 47
157	Rear Admiral Andrews to Sims	30 June 1924	SIMS, box 46
158	Rear Admiral Andrews to Sims	28 Aug 1924	SIMS, box 46
159	C-in-C, N. America, to Admiralty	Jan 1925	ADM 116/2295
160	C-in-C, N. America, to Admiralty	Sept 1925	ADM 116/2295
161	Ambassador to Argentina to CNS	1 Aug 1927	ADM 167/76
162	Captain Troup to C-in-C, N. America	15 Aug 1927	ADM 116/2508
163	C-in-C, N. America, to Admiralty	25 Oct 1927	ADM 116/2508
164	Rear Admiral Reeves to CNO	6 Dec 1928	PRATT, box 3
165	C-in-C, N. America, to Admiralty	8 Sept 1930	ADM 116/2758
166	Invitation to US Squadron	25 Nov 1930	ADM 116/3292

167	Captain Blagrove: Report of Proceedings	11 Aug 1933	ADM 116/2974
168	Vice Admiral Best to Chatfield	7 Nov 1935	CHT 4/11
169	C-in-C, America, to Admiralty	30 July 1936	ADM 1/9143
170	Admiral Best to Chatfield	6 Oct 1936	CHT 4/11
171	Admiral Meyrick to Chatfield	4 April 1937	CHT 4/11.
172	CO, *Wellington*, to Rear Admiral, NZ Division	26 May 1937	ADM 116/3570
173	Rear Admiral, NZ Division, to Admiralty	13 June 1937	ADM 116/3570
174	Drummond to Admiralty	29 June 1937	ADM 116/3570
175	Admiralty to Commodore, NZ Division	21 July 1937	ADM 116/3570
176	Admiralty to CO, *Leander*, and reply	29 July 1937	ADM 116/3570
177	USA: Aircraft Bombing and Torpedoes	31 Dec 1937	ADM 1/9072
178	Foreign Development of Torpedo as an Air Weapon	14 May 1938	ADM 1/1649
179	Captain Mountbatten: Reports on USS *Philadelphia* and *Fanning*	18 Feb 1938	ADM 1/9581

Part VI: Edging Towards an Alliance, 1937–1939

180	Eden to Ambassador to the USA	18 Jan 1937	ADM 116/4102
181	Yarnell to Leahy	25 Mar 1937	YARNELL, box 3
182	Report of Meeting at Tsingtao	6 Aug 1937	YARNELL, box 4
183	Captain Bennett to Yarnell	16 Aug 1937	YARNELL, box 4
184	Yarnell, et al., to Hasegawa	22 Aug 1937	YARNELL, box 6
185	Admiral Leahy: Diary	24 Aug 1937	LEAHY
186	Chatfield to Backhouse	8 Oct 1937	CHT 4/1
187	Admiral Bayly to Yarnell	17 Oct 1937	YARNELL, box 4
188	Yarnell to Admiral Bayly	28 Nov 1937	YARNELL, box 4
189	Admiral Leahy: Diary	28 Nov 1937	LEAHY
190	Admiral Leahy: Diary	29 Nov 1937	LEAHY
191	Admiral Leahy: Diary	12 Dec 1937	LEAHY
192	Admiral Leahy: Diary	13 Dec 1937	LEAHY
193	*Bee* to *Folkestone*	13 Dec 1937	YARNELL, box 12
194	Admiral Leahy: Diary	17 Dec 1937	LEAHY
195	Yarnell to Captain Dundas	17 Dec 1937	YARNELL, box 4
196	Admiral Leahy: Diary	22 Dec 1937	LEAHY
197	Yarnell to Leahy	22 Dec 1937	YARNELL, box 3
198	Little to Yarnell	25 Dec 1937	YARNELL, box 4
199	Admiral Leahy: Diary	10 Jan 1938	LEAHY
200	Record of Conversations between Captain Ingersoll and the Admiralty	*c.* 14 Jan 1938	ADM 1/9822

201	Record of Conversations agreed between Captains Ingersoll and Phillips	11 Jan 1938	ADM 116/3922
202	Leahy to Yarnell	14 Jan 1938	YARNELL, box 3
203	Yarnell to Little	15 Jan 1938	YARNELL, box 4
204	Exchange of Technical Information with USA	12 May 1938	ADM 116/4302
205	FO and Admiralty to CID	7 Sept 1938	ADM 116/4102
206	Commander R. Edwards to Yarnell	23 Nov 1938	YARNELL, box 2
207	Yarnell to Noble	28 Dec 1938	YARNELL, box 2
208	Yarnell to Leahy	10 Jan 1939	YARNELL, box 3
209	Ambassador to USA to Foreign Secretary	5 April 1939	ADM 1/9784
210	FO to Ambassador to USA	8 June 1939	ADM 116/3922
211	Commander Hampton: Report	27 June 1939	ADM 116/3922
212	Minute by Director of Plans	28 June 1939	ADM 116/3922
213	Cession of British Possessions in W. Indies to USA	29 June 1939	ADM 1/9784
214	Ambassador to USA to Foreign Secretary	1 July 1939	ADM 116/3922
215	Governor of Trinidad to Colonial Secretary	1 Sept 1939	ADM 116/3922

INDEX

NAVY RECORDS SOCIETY
(FOUNDED 1893)

The Navy Records Society was established for the purpose of printing unpublished manuscripts and rare works of naval interest. Membership of the Society is open to all who are interested in naval history, and any person wishing to become a member should apply to the Hon. Secretary, Robin Brodhurst, Pangbourne College, Pangbourne, Berks, RG8 8LA, United Kingdom. The annual subscription is £30, which entitles the member to receive one free copy of each work issued by the Society in that year, and to buy earlier issues at reduced prices.

A list of works, available to members only, is shown below; very few copies are left of those marked with an asterisk. Volumes out of print are indicated by **OP**. Prices for works in print are available on application to Mrs Annette Gould, 1 Avon Close, Petersfield, Hampshire, GU31 4LG, United Kingdom, to whom all enquiries concerning works in print should be sent. Those marked 'TS', 'SP' and 'A' are published for the Society by Temple Smith, Scolar Press and Ashgate, and are available to non-members from Ashgate Publishing Limited, Wey Court East, Union Road, Farnham, Surrey, GU9 7PT, United Kingdom. Those marked 'A & U' are published by George Allen & Unwin, and are available to non-members only through bookshops.

Vol. 1. *State papers relating to the Defeat of the Spanish Armada, Anno 1588*, Vol. I, ed. Professor J. K. Laughton. TS.

Vol. 2. *State papers relating to the Defeat of the Spanish Armada, Anno 1588*, Vol. II, ed. Professor J. K. Laughton. TS.

Vol. 3. *Letters of Lord Hood, 1781–1783*, ed. D. Hannay. **OP**.

Vol. 4. *Index to James's Naval History*, by C. G. Toogood, ed. by the Hon. T. A. Brassey. **OP**.

Vol. 5. *Life of Captain Stephen Martin, 1666–1740*, ed. Sir Clements R. Markham. **OP**.

Vol. 6. *Journal of Rear Admiral Bartholomew James, 1752–1828*, ed. Professor J. K. Laughton & Cdr. J. Y. F. Sullivan. **OP**.

Vol. 7. *Hollond's Discourses of the Navy, 1638 and 1659*, ed. J. R. Tanner. **OP**.

Vol. 8. *Naval Accounts and Inventories in the Reign of Henry VII*, ed. M. Oppenheim. **OP**.

Vol. 9. *Journal of Sir George Rooke*, ed. O. Browning. **OP**.

Vol. 10. *Letters and Papers relating to the War with France 1512–1513*, ed. M. Alfred Spont. **OP**.

Vol. 11. *Papers relating to the Spanish War 1585–1587*, ed. Julian S. Corbett. TS.

Vol. 12. *Journals and Letters of Admiral of the Fleet Sir Thomas Byam Martin, 1773–1854*, Vol. II (see No. 24), ed. Admiral Sir R. Vesey Hamilton. **OP**.

Vol. 13. *Papers relating to the First Dutch War, 1652–1654*, Vol. I, ed. Dr S. R. Gardiner. **OP**.

Vol. 14. *Papers relating to the Blockade of Brest, 1803–1805*, Vol. I, ed. J. Leyland. **OP**.

Vol. 15. *History of the Russian Fleet during the Reign of Peter the Great, by a Contemporary Englishman*, ed. Admiral Sir Cyprian Bridge. **OP**.

Vol. 16. *Logs of the Great Sea Fights, 1794–1805*, Vol. I, ed. Vice Admiral Sir T. Sturges Jackson. **OP**.

Vol. 17. *Papers relating to the First Dutch War, 1652–1654*, Vol. II, ed. Dr S. R. Gardiner. **OP**.

Vol. 18. *Logs of the Great Sea Fights*, Vol. II, ed. Vice Admiral Sir T. Sturges Jackson.

Vol. 19. *Journals and Letters of Admiral of the Fleet Sir Thomas Byam Martin*, Vol. II (see No. 24), ed. Admiral Sir R. Vesey Hamilton. **OP**.

Vol. 20. *The Naval Miscellany*, Vol. I, ed. Professor J. K. Laughton.

Vol. 21. *Papers relating to the Blockade of Brest, 1803–1805*, Vol. II, ed. J. Leyland. **OP**.

Vol. 22. *The Naval Tracts of Sir William Monson*, Vol. I, ed. M. Oppenheim. **OP**.

Vol. 23. *The Naval Tracts of Sir William Monson*, Vol. II, ed. M. Oppenheim. **OP**.

Vol. 24. *The Journals and Letters of Admiral of the Fleet Sir Thomas Byam Martin*, Vol. I, ed. Admiral Sir R. Vesey Hamilton.

Vol. 25. *Nelson and the Neapolitan Jacobins*, ed. H. C. Gutteridge. **OP**.

Vol. 26. *A Descriptive Catalogue of the Naval MSS in the Pepysian Library*, Vol. I, ed. J. R. Tanner. **OP**.

Vol. 27. *A Descriptive Catalogue of the Naval MSS in the Pepysian Library*, Vol. II, ed. J. R. Tanner. **OP**.

Vol. 28. *The Correspondence of Admiral John Markham, 1801–1807*, ed. Sir Clements R. Markham. **OP**.

Vol. 29. *Fighting Instructions, 1530–1816*, ed. Julian S. Corbett. **OP**.

Vol. 30. *Papers relating to the First Dutch War, 1652–1654*, Vol. III, ed. Dr S. R. Gardiner & C. T. Atkinson. **OP**.

Vol. 31. *The Recollections of Commander James Anthony Gardner, 1775–1814*, ed. Admiral Sir R. Vesey Hamilton & Professor J. K. Laughton.

Vol. 32. *Letters and Papers of Charles, Lord Barham, 1758–1813*, ed. Professor Sir John Laughton.

Vol. 33. *Naval Songs and Ballads*, ed. Professor C. H. Firth. **OP**.

Vol. 34. *Views of the Battles of the Third Dutch War*, ed. by Julian S. Corbett. **OP**.

Vol. 35. *Signals and Instructions, 1776–1794*, ed. Julian S. Corbett. **OP**.

Vol. 36. *A Descriptive Catalogue of the Naval MSS in the Pepysian Library*, Vol. III, ed. J. R. Tanner. **OP**.

Vol. 37. *Papers relating to the First Dutch War, 1652–1654*, Vol. IV, ed. C. T. Atkinson. **OP**.

Vol. 38. *Letters and Papers of Charles, Lord Barham, 1758–1813*, Vol. II, ed. Professor Sir John Laughton. **OP**.

Vol. 39. *Letters and Papers of Charles, Lord Barham, 1758–1813*, Vol. III, ed. Professor Sir John Laughton. **OP**.

Vol. 40. *The Naval Miscellany*, Vol. II, ed. Professor Sir John Laughton.

*Vol. 41. *Papers relating to the First Dutch War, 1652–1654*, Vol. V, ed. C. T. Atkinson.

Vol. 42. *Papers relating to the Loss of Minorca in 1756*, ed. Captain H. W. Richmond, R.N. **OP**.

*Vol. 43. *The Naval Tracts of Sir William Monson*, Vol. III, ed. M. Oppenheim.

Vol. 44. *The Old Scots Navy 1689–1710*, ed. James Grant. **OP**.

Vol. 45. *The Naval Tracts of Sir William Monson*, Vol. IV, ed. M. Oppenheim.

Vol. 46. *The Private Papers of George, 2nd Earl Spencer*, Vol. I, ed. Julian S. Corbett. **OP**.

Vol. 47. *The Naval Tracts of Sir William Monson*, Vol. V, ed. M. Oppenheim.

Vol. 48. *The Private Papers of George, 2nd Earl Spencer*, Vol. II, ed. Julian S. Corbett. **OP**.

Vol. 49. *Documents relating to Law and Custom of the Sea*, Vol. I, ed. R. G. Marsden. **OP**.

*Vol. 50. *Documents relating to Law and Custom of the Sea*, Vol. II, ed. R. G. Marsden.

Vol. 51. *Autobiography of Phineas Pett*, ed. W. G. Perrin. **OP**.

Vol. 52. *The Life of Admiral Sir John Leake*, Vol. I, ed. Geoffrey Callender.

Vol. 53. *The Life of Admiral Sir John Leake*, Vol. II, ed. Geoffrey Callender.

Vol. 54. *The Life and Works of Sir Henry Mainwaring*, Vol. I, ed. G. E. Manwaring.

Vol. 55. *The Letters of Lord St Vincent, 1801–1804*, Vol. I, ed. D. B. Smith. **OP**.

Vol. 56. *The Life and Works of Sir Henry Mainwaring*, Vol. II, ed. G. E. Manwaring & W. G. Perrin. **OP**.

Vol. 57. *A Descriptive Catalogue of the Naval MSS in the Pepysian Library*, Vol. IV, ed. Dr J. R. Tanner. **OP**.

Vol. 58. *The Private Papers of George, 2nd Earl Spencer*, Vol. III, ed. Rear Admiral H. W. Richmond. **OP**.

Vol. 59. *The Private Papers of George, 2nd Earl Spencer*, Vol. IV, ed. Rear Admiral H. W. Richmond. **OP**.

Vol. 60. *Samuel Pepys's Naval Minutes*, ed. Dr J. R. Tanner.

Vol. 61. *The Letters of Lord St Vincent, 1801–1804*, Vol. II, ed. D. B. Smith. **OP**.

Vol. 62. *Letters and Papers of Admiral Viscount Keith*, Vol. I, ed. W. G. Perrin. **OP**.

Vol. 63. *The Naval Miscellany*, Vol. III, ed. W. G. Perrin. **OP**.

Vol. 64. *The Journal of the 1st Earl of Sandwich*, ed. R. C. Anderson. **OP**.

*Vol. 65. *Boteler's Dialogues*, ed. W. G. Perrin.

Vol. 66. *Papers relating to the First Dutch War, 1652–1654*, Vol. VI (with index), ed. C. T. Atkinson.

*Vol. 67. *The Byng Papers*, Vol. I, ed. W. C. B. Tunstall.

*Vol. 68. *The Byng Papers*, Vol. II, ed. W. C. B. Tunstall.

Vol. 69. *The Private Papers of John, Earl of Sandwich*, Vol. I, ed. G. R. Barnes & Lt. Cdr. J. H. Owen, R.N. Corrigenda to *Papers relating to the First Dutch War, 1652–1654, Vols I–VI*, ed. Captain A. C. Dewar, R.N. **OP**.

Vol. 70. *The Byng Papers*, Vol. III, ed. W. C. B. Tunstall.

Vol. 71. *The Private Papers of John, Earl of Sandwich*, Vol. II, ed. G. R. Barnes & Lt. Cdr. J. H. Owen, R.N. **OP**.

Vol. 72. *Piracy in the Levant, 1827–1828*, ed. Lt. Cdr. C. G. Pitcairn Jones, R.N. **OP**.

Vol. 73. *The Tangier Papers of Samuel Pepys*, ed. Edwin Chappell.

Vol. 74. *The Tomlinson Papers*, ed. J. G. Bullocke.

Vol. 75. *The Private Papers of John, Earl of Sandwich*, Vol. III, ed. G. R. Barnes & Cdr. J. H. Owen, R.N. **OP**.

Vol. 76. *The Letters of Robert Blake*, ed. the Rev. J. R. Powell. **OP**.
*Vol. 77. *Letters and Papers of Admiral the Hon. Samuel Barrington*, Vol. I, ed. D. Bonner-Smith.
Vol. 78. *The Private Papers of John, Earl of Sandwich*, Vol. IV, ed. G. R. Barnes & Cdr. J. H. Owen, R.N. **OP**.
*Vol. 79. *The Journals of Sir Thomas Allin, 1660–1678*, Vol. I *1660–1666*, ed. R. C. Anderson.
Vol. 80. *The Journals of Sir Thomas Allin, 1660–1678*, Vol. II *1667–1678*, ed. R. C. Anderson.
Vol. 81. *Letters and Papers of Admiral the Hon. Samuel Barrington*, Vol. II, ed. D. Bonner-Smith. **OP**.
Vol. 82. *Captain Boteler's Recollections, 1808–1830*, ed. D. Bonner-Smith. **OP**.
Vol. 83. *Russian War, 1854. Baltic and Black Sea: Official Correspondence*, ed. D. Bonner-Smith & Captain A. C. Dewar, R.N. **OP**.
Vol. 84. *Russian War, 1855. Baltic: Official Correspondence*, ed. D. Bonner-Smith. **OP**.
Vol. 85. *Russian War, 1855. Black Sea: Official Correspondence*, ed. Captain A.C. Dewar, R.N. **OP**.
Vol. 86. *Journals and Narratives of the Third Dutch War*, ed. R. C. Anderson. **OP**.
Vol. 87. *The Naval Brigades in the Indian Mutiny, 1857–1858*, ed. Cdr. W. B. Rowbotham, R.N. **OP**.
Vol. 88. *Patee Byng's Journal*, ed. J. L. Cranmer-Byng. **OP**.
*Vol. 89. *The Sergison Papers, 1688–1702*, ed. Cdr. R. D. Merriman, R.I.N.
Vol. 90. *The Keith Papers*, Vol. II, ed. Christopher Lloyd. **OP**.
Vol. 91. *Five Naval Journals, 1789–1817*, ed. Rear Admiral H. G. Thursfield. **OP**.
Vol. 92. *The Naval Miscellany*, Vol. IV, ed. Christopher Lloyd. **OP**.
Vol. 93. *Sir William Dillon's Narrative of Professional Adventures, 1790–1839*, Vol. I *1790–1802*, ed. Professor Michael Lewis. **OP**.
Vol. 94. *The Walker Expedition to Quebec, 1711*, ed. Professor Gerald S. Graham. **OP**.
Vol. 95. *The Second China War, 1856–1860*, ed. D. Bonner-Smith & E. W. R. Lumby. **OP**.
Vol. 96. *The Keith Papers, 1803–1815*, Vol. III, ed. Professor Christopher Lloyd.
Vol. 97. *Sir William Dillon's Narrative of Professional Adventures, 1790–1839*, Vol. II *1802–1839*, ed. Professor Michael Lewis. **OP**.
Vol. 98. *The Private Correspondence of Admiral Lord Collingwood*, ed. Professor Edward Hughes. **OP**.

Vol. 99. *The Vernon Papers, 1739–1745*, ed. B. McL. Ranft. **OP**.

Vol. 100. *Nelson's Letters to his Wife and Other Documents*, ed. Lt. Cdr. G. P. B. Naish, R.N.V.R.

Vol. 101. *A Memoir of James Trevenen, 1760–1790*, ed. Professor Christopher Lloyd & R. C. Anderson. **OP**.

Vol. 102. *The Papers of Admiral Sir John Fisher*, Vol. I, ed. Lt. Cdr. P. K. Kemp, R.N. **OP**.

Vol. 103. *Queen Anne's Navy*, ed. Cdr. R. D. Merriman, R.I.N. **OP**.

Vol. 104. *The Navy and South America, 1807–1823*, ed. Professor Gerald S. Graham & Professor R. A. Humphreys.

Vol. 105. *Documents relating to the Civil War, 1642–1648*, ed. The Rev. J. R. Powell & E. K. Timings. **OP**.

Vol. 106. *The Papers of Admiral Sir John Fisher*, Vol. II, ed. Lt. Cdr. P. K. Kemp, R.N. **OP**.

Vol. 107. *The Health of Seamen*, ed. Professor Christopher Lloyd.

Vol. 108. *The Jellicoe Papers*, Vol. I *1893–1916*, ed. A. Temple Patterson.

Vol. 109. *Documents relating to Anson's Voyage round the World, 1740–1744*, ed. Dr Glyndwr Williams. **OP**.

Vol. 110. *The Saumarez Papers: The Baltic, 1808–1812*, ed. A. N. Ryan. **OP**.

Vol. 111. *The Jellicoe Papers*, Vol. II *1916–1925*, ed. Professor A. Temple Patterson.

Vol. 112. *The Rupert and Monck Letterbook, 1666*, ed. The Rev. J. R. Powell & E. K. Timings. **OP** (damaged stock available).

Vol. 113. *Documents relating to the Royal Naval Air Service*, Vol. I (1908–1918), ed. Captain S. W. Roskill, R.N. **OP** (damaged stock available).

*Vol. 114. *The Siege and Capture of Havana, 1762*, ed. Professor David Syrett. **OP** (damaged stock available).

Vol. 115. *Policy and Operations in the Mediterranean, 1912–1914*, ed. E. W. R. Lumby. **OP**.

Vol. 116. *The Jacobean Commissions of Enquiry, 1608 and 1618*, ed. Dr A. P. McGowan.

Vol. 117. *The Keyes Papers*, Vol. I *1914–1918*, ed. Professor Paul Halpern.

Vol. 118. *The Royal Navy and North America: The Warren Papers, 1736–1752*, ed. Dr Julian Gwyn. **OP**.

Vol. 119. *The Manning of the Royal Navy: Selected Public Pamphlets, 1693–1873*, ed. Professor John Bromley.

Vol. 120. *Naval Administration, 1715–1750*, ed. Professor D. A. Baugh.

Vol. 121. *The Keyes Papers*, Vol. II *1919–1938*, ed. Professor Paul Halpern.
Vol. 122. *The Keyes Papers*, Vol. III *1939–1945*, ed. Professor Paul Halpern.
Vol. 123. *The Navy of the Lancastrian Kings: Accounts and Inventories of William Soper, Keeper of the King's Ships, 1422–1427*, ed. Dr Susan Rose.
Vol. 124. *The Pollen Papers: the Privately Circulated Printed Works of Arthur Hungerford Pollen, 1901–1916*, ed. Professor Jon T. Sumida. A. & U.
Vol. 125. *The Naval Miscellany*, Vol. V, ed. Dr N. A. M. Rodger. A & U.
Vol. 126. *The Royal Navy in the Mediterranean, 1915–1918*, ed. Professor Paul Halpern. TS.
Vol. 127. *The Expedition of Sir John Norris and Sir Francis Drake to Spain and Portugal, 1589*, ed. Professor R. B. Wernham. TS.
Vol. 128. *The Beatty Papers*, Vol. I *1902–1918*, ed. Professor B. McL. Ranft. SP.
Vol. 129. *The Hawke Papers: A Selection, 1743–1771*, ed. Dr R. F. Mackay. SP.
Vol. 130. *Anglo-American Naval Relations, 1917–1919*, ed. Michael Simpson. SP.
Vol. 131. *British Naval Documents, 1204–1960*, ed. Professor John B. Hattendorf, Dr Roger Knight, Alan Pearsall, Dr Nicholas Rodger & Professor Geoffrey Till. SP.
Vol. 132. *The Beatty Papers*, Vol. II *1916–1927*, ed. Professor B. McL. Ranft. SP
Vol. 133. *Samuel Pepys and the Second Dutch War*, transcribed by Professor William Matthews & Dr Charles Knighton; ed. Robert Latham. SP.
Vol. 134. *The Somerville Papers*, ed. Michael Simpson, with the assistance of John Somerville. SP.
Vol. 135. *The Royal Navy in the River Plate, 1806–1807*, ed. John D. Grainger. SP.
Vol. 136. *The Collective Naval Defence of the Empire, 1900–1940*, ed. Nicholas Tracy. A.
Vol. 137. *The Defeat of the Enemy Attack on Shipping, 1939–1945*, ed. Eric Grove. A.
Vol. 138. *Shipboard Life and Organisation, 1731–1815*, ed. Brian Lavery. A.
Vol. 139. *The Battle of the Atlantic and Signals Intelligence: U-boat Situations and Trends, 1941–1945*, ed. Professor David Syrett. A.

Vol. 140. *The Cunningham Papers*, Vol. I: *The Mediterranean Fleet, 1939–1942*, ed. Michael Simpson. A.

Vol. 141. *The Channel Fleet and the Blockade of Brest, 1793–1801*, ed. Roger Morriss. A.

Vol. 142. *The Submarine Service, 1900–1918*, ed. Nicholas Lambert. A.

Vol. 143. *Letters and Papers of Professor Sir John Knox Laughton (1830–1915)*, ed. Professor Andrew Lambert. A.

Vol. 144. *The Battle of the Atlantic and Signals Intelligence: U-Boat Tracking Papers 1941–1947*, ed. Professor David Syrett. A.

Vol. 145. *The Maritime Blockade of Germany in the Great War: The Northern Patrol, 1914–1918*, ed. John D. Grainger. A.

Vol. 146. *The Naval Miscellany*, Vol. VI, ed. Michael Duffy. A.

Vol. 147. *The Milne Papers*, Vol. I *1820–1859*, ed. Professor John Beeler. A.

Vol. 148. *The Rodney Papers*, Vol. I *1742–1763*, ed. Professor David Syrett. A.

Vol. 149. *Sea Power and the Control of Trade. Belligerent Rights from the Russian War to the Beira Patrol, 1854–1970*, ed. Nicholas Tracy. A.

Vol. 150. *The Cunningham Papers*, Vol. II: *The Triumph of Allied Sea Power 1942–1946*, ed. Michael Simpson. A.

Vol. 151. *The Rodney Papers*, Vol. II *1763–1780*, ed. Professor David Syrett. A.

Vol. 152. *Naval Intelligence from Germany: The Reports of the British Naval Attachés in Berlin, 1906–1914*, ed. Matthew S. Seligmann. A.

Vol. 153. *The Naval Miscellany*, Vol. VII, ed. Susan Rose. A.

Vol. 154. *The Chatham Dockyard, 1815–1865*, ed. Philip MacDougall. A.

Vol. 155. *Naval Courts Martial, 1793–1815*, ed. John D. Byrn. A.

Occasional Publications:

Vol. 1. *The Commissioned Sea Officers of the Royal Navy, 1660–1815*, ed. Professor David Syrett & Professor R. L. DiNardo. SP.

Vol. 2. *The Anthony Roll of Henry VIII's Navy*, ed. C. S. Knighton and Professor D. M. Loades. A.